The entangled legacies of empire

Manchester University Press

The entangled legacies of empire

Race, finance and inequality

Edited by Paul Robert Gilbert, Clea Bourne,
Max Haiven and Johnna Montgomerie

MANCHESTER UNIVERSITY PRESS

Published by Manchester University Press
Oxford Road, Manchester M13 9PL
www.manchesteruniversitypress.co.uk

British Library Cataloguing-in-Publication Data
A catalogue record for this book is available from the
British Library
ISBN   978 1 5261 6344 8   hardback
First published 2023

The publisher has no responsibility for the persistence or
accuracy of URLs for any external or third-party internet
websites referred to in this book, and does not guarantee
that any content on such websites is, or will remain,
accurate or appropriate.

Typeset
by New Best-set Typesetters Ltd

Aboriginal and Torres Strait Islander readers are advised that Chapter 14 ('Racial capitalism and settler colonization in Australia: Australian debts to Gurindji economies') contains images and names of people who have died.

Contents

Part III: Borders

Part IV: Emergence

Part V: Gestures

Part VI: Play

Figures

Contributors

Syahirah Abdul Rahman is a Senior Lecturer in Business and Management at the Oxford Brookes Business School. She completed her doctoral studies on financial citizenship development as a lens through which to observe the spread of finance in everyday life. She is currently working in the Innovation Caucus with Innovate UK and the Economic and Social Research Council, studying the dynamics of trust, regulation and standards as institutional logics in innovation-led growth and productivity.

Ilias Alami is a political economist and Marie Curie Fellow based at Uppsala University. He is the author of *Money Power and Financial Capital in Emerging Markets*. His research and teaching interests are in the areas of the political economy of money and finance, development and international capital flows, state capitalism and race/class/coloniality.

Gargi Bhattacharyya's books include *Rethinking Racial Capitalism* (Rowman and Littlefield, 2018), *Crisis, Austerity and Everyday Life* (Palgrave Macmillan, 2015) and *Dangerous Brown Men* (Zed, 2008).

Clea Bourne is a Senior Lecturer in the Department of Media, Communications and Cultural Studies at Goldsmiths, University of London. Her research explores how twenty-first-century economies and markets are mediatized through various actors, practices and discourses. Clea is author of *Trust, Power and Public Relations in Financial Markets*, and has published widely in a range of journals, including *New Media and Society* and *American Behavioral Scientist*, as well as various edited collections.

Ashley Cordes (Coquille) is an Assistant Professor of Communication at the University of Utah. Her research lies at the intersection of Indigenous studies, digital media and cultural studies. Her recent research in these areas has been published in journals such as *Cultural Studies ↔ Critical Methodologies, Journal of International and Intercultural Communication* and *Feminist Media Studies*. She serves as Chair of the Culture and Education Committee of the Coquille Nation.

Catherine Comyn a researcher at Economic and Social Research Aotearoa (ESRA) and a PhD student at King's College London. She is the author of *The Financial Colonisation of Aotearoa* (ESRA, 2022). With roots in historical materialism and critical theory, her research concerns finance capital, colonization and their intersections.

Eve Dickson is a Research Fellow at the University College London Social Research Institute. She was a member of the activist group NELMA (North East London Migrant Action), which campaigned to defend the rights of all migrants and ran an accompanying scheme for people with no recourse to public funds (NRPF). She also worked as a policy officer for Project 17, an organization providing advice and support to migrant families with NRPF.

Jacquelene Drinkall is Lecturer in Art at the School of Creative Arts and Media (CAM) Inveresk, University of Tasmania and is affiliated with Saas-Fee Summer Institute of Art through recent collaborations with Warren Neidich. She has exhibited in Riga Triennale (Latvia), Articulate Gallery (Sydney), Sawtooth Gallery (Launceston) and in 2022 is showing at Outerspace ARI (Brisbane) and in a Venice Biennale pop-up exhibition. She holds BA University Medal and MA (Research) in Visual Art, and a PhD in Art History and Theory. Her recent publications are included in *Leonardo Electronic Almanac, The Psychopathologies of Cognitive Capitalism* and Artbrain.org.

Alessandra Ferrini is a London-based artist-filmmaker and Arts and Humanities Research Council/Techne PhD candidate at the University of the Arts London. Experimenting with the expansion and hybridization of the documentary film, her research questions the legacies of Italian colonialism and Fascism. Exhibitions include Manifesta 12 Film Programme and 13 Paralléles du Sud, Sharjah Film Platform, Istanbul Biennal collateral, 2nd Lagos Biennal, Villa Romana.

Paul Robert Gilbert is a Senior Lecturer in International Development at the University of Sussex. His research focuses on environmental violence and extractive industries, for-profit development contractors and critical pedagogies in international development/development studies.

Max Haiven is a writer and teacher and Canada Research Chair in Culture, Media and Social Justice. His most recent books are *Art after Money, Money after Art: Creative Strategies against Financialization* (2018) and *Revenge Capitalism: The Ghosts of Empire, the Demons of Capital, and the Settling of Unpayable Debts* (2020). Haiven is editor of VAGABONDS, a series of short, radical books from Pluto Press. He teaches at Lakehead University, where he co-directs the ReImagining Value Action Lab (RiVAL).

Laura Anne Kalba is an Associate Professor of Art History at the University of Minnesota, Twin Cities. She is the author of *Color in the Age of Impressionism: Commerce, Technology, and Art* (Penn State University Press, 2017), winner of the 2018 Charles Rufus Morey Prize from the College Art Association and 2016–17 Laurence Wylie Prize in French Cultural Studies. Kalba is currently working on a study of how images, objects and places encoded and enacted shifting notions of economic value from the Railway Mania of the 1840s to First World War.

Zenia Kish is Assistant Professor of Media Studies at the University of Tulsa, and earned her PhD in American Studies at New York University. Her work examines the intersections of finance, food, development and digital media studies. She is co-editor of the forthcoming anthology *#FoodInstagram: Identity, Influence, and Negotiation*, and Reviews and Commentaries Editor at the *Journal of Cultural Economy*. Her current book project examines the media cultures of philanthrocapitalism.

Alysse Kushinski is an interdisciplinary media scholar whose work sits at the intersection of critical theory, aesthetics and visual and material culture. She holds a PhD in Communication and Culture from York University, Canada and was most recently a postdoctoral researcher at Artefact Lab in the Department of Communication at the Université de Montréal.

Tracy Lassiter is an Associate Professor of English at the University of New Mexico-Gallup. Her research areas include petrofiction and postcolonial studies, comics/graphic novels, pedagogy and information literacy. She has previously published on extractive practices in *Imaginations* and *Energy in Literature* (ed. Paula Anca Farca, True Heart Press, 2015).

Linsey Ly is a PhD candidate in the Department of Anthropology at the Graduate Center of the City University of New York. Her dissertation, 'Architectures of Absence', examines the accumulation of modern ghost cities in China and their convergence with rare earths mining as a process terraforming the industrial north into a palimpsest of spectral/spectacular landscapes.

Felix Mantz is an Assistant Professor of International Relations at California State University San Marcos. His research interests include coloniality/decoloniality, anti-systemic resistance, critical pedagogies, and radical political ecology. Felix's recent work focuses on the reproduction of and resistance against colonial relations to land and ecologies in Tanzania. He is also researching global food systems and educational models that present alternatives to the Westernized and modern university.

Kathryn Medien is a Lecturer in Sociology at the Open University. Her main research interests include global histories of imperialism and empire, feminist theory and anti-colonial thought.

Johnna Montgomerie is a Professor of International Political Economy at King's College London. Her research addresses debt in the era of financialization and the gendered political economy of monetary and fiscal policy since the 2008 financial crisis.

Oded Nir is a scholar of Israeli culture and critical theory. His first book, *Signatures of Struggle* (SUNY 2018) is a materialist history of Israeli fiction. His essays have been published in *Criticism*, *Prooftexts*, *Rethinking Marxism* and other journals. Oded is the editor of the peer-reviewed quarterly *CLCWeb: Comparative Literature and Culture*.

Holly Eva Katherine Randell-Moon is a Senior Lecturer in the School of Indigenous Australian Studies, Charles Sturt University, Australia. Her research focuses on settler coloniality, cultural geography, digital infrastructure and biopower. With Ryan Tippet, she is co-editor of *Security, Race, Biopower: Essays on Technology and Corporeality* (2016, Palgrave Macmillan). She co-edits the *Somatechnics* journal.

Rachel Rosen is an Associate Professor at the University College London Social Research Institute. Her research focuses on unequal childhoods, stratified social reproduction and families in precarious migranthood. She was a member of NELMA, an activist group that campaigned to defend the rights of all migrants and challenged injustices towards families with NRPF (no recourse to public funds).

Christian Rossipal is a PhD candidate in Cinema Studies at Tisch School of the Arts, New York University. His research and teaching interests include media, migration and coloniality. Christian is a member of the artist-activist collective Noncitizen.

Debbie Samaniego is a PhD candidate in the Department of International Relations at the University of Sussex. She is a Marshall Scholar who completed her MA in International Relations at Queen Mary University of London. Her research focuses on the intersections of migration, indigeneity, resistance and coloniality/decoloniality in the Americas.

Jon Schubert is a political and economic anthropologist working on neo-authoritarian statecraft and the impact of transnational capitalism in Angola and Mozambique. He is the author of *Working the System. A Political Ethnography of the New Angola* (Cornell University Press, 2017) and SNF Eccellenza Professor for urban and political anthropology in the Division of Urban Studies at the University of Basel.

Kehinde Sorinmade studied Health and Social Care at the College of Haringey, Enfield and North East London. She is a support worker aspiring to be a midwife nurse. She was a member of NELMA, a campaigning and support organization that challenged injustices towards families with NRPF (no recourse to public funds).

Ben Stork holds a PhD in Comparative Studies in Discourse and Society and is a contingent faculty member in Seattle University's Film Studies programme. His scholarship and teaching focus on the relation between moving images, politics and aesthetics. His most recent work argues for the political importance of aesthetics in understanding digital videos of police violence.

Maria Dyveke Styve is a Max Weber Fellow at the Department of History and Civilisation at the European University Institute in

Florence, Italy where she is conducting research on the New International Economic Order. Her research interests span the political economy of development and the extractive industries, South African history, dependency theory, decolonial epistemologies, racial capitalism, critical race theory and economic history.

Imre Szeman is inaugural Director of the Institute for Environment, Conservation, and Sustainability and Professor of Human Geography at the University of Toronto Scarborough. He is author (most recently) of *On Petrocultures: Globalization, Culture, and Energy* (2019) and is working on *The Future of the Sun,* a book examining corporate and state control of the transition to renewables.

Acknowledgements

This volume is the outcome of a long process of collaboration, begun in 2017. The first event the editors co-organized was a workshop supported by Goldsmiths' Political Economy Research Centre and Lakehead University's Reimagining Value in Action Lab (Colonial Debts, Imperial Insolvencies, Extractive Nostalgias) in September 2017, which resulted in a forum published by *Discover Society* in 2018. A follow-up two-day workshop was organized at the University of Sussex, supported by Sussex's Centre for Global Economy and Centre for Colonial and Postcolonial Studies and by Lakehead's Reimagining Value in Action Lab (Finance Capital and the Ghosts of Empire) in April 2019. As the idea for this volume developed, we shared them at a panel on Race, Racism and the Empire of Finance as part of the Intersections of Finance and Society conference hosted by City University's Political Economy Research Centre in December 2019.

While by no means an exhaustive list of those who have shaped our thinking and contributed to this collective project, we owe particular thanks to those who have participated in the Goldsmiths event (Sahil Dutta, Justin Leroy, Ann Pettifor, Anita Rupphrecht), the subsequent *Discover Society* forum (Vincent Guermond, Ndongo Samba Sylla, Lisa Tilley and Alexia Yates) and the Sussex workshop (Joel Benjamin, Cathy Bergin, Nick Bernards, Gargi Bhattacharyya, Rebecca Bramall, Nadine King Chambers, Catherine Comyn, John Handel, Femke Herregraven, Jenny Hewitt, Fanny Malinen, Franziska Mueller, the Museum of British Colonialism, K-Sue Park, Sarah-Jane Phelan, Louise Purbrick, Xavier Ribas, Jerome Roos) and who provided feedback on our early work on this volume at City (Ali Bhagat, Erin Lockwood, Rachel Philips and Maria Dyveke Styve).

The influence of those who are listed above – whether in terms of their theoretical orientations, artistic practice, collaborative ethos or all three – runs through the content and organization of this volume. It has been a genuinely collaborative endeavour, and we are grateful to the contributors. A special thanks to the Lakehead University graduate students who worked on this project: Samuel Cousin, Stella Lawson and Nehikhare Patrick Igbinijesu. And a special thanks to Tom Dark at Manchester University Press, for bearing with us through COVID-19 as we sought to ensure that everyone who started out as part of this volume would be included at its end.

Introduction

*Paul Robert Gilbert, Clea Bourne, Max Haiven and
Johnna Montgomerie*

Race, finance and inequality: enduring legacies

We live in a colonial global economy. It is of course true that many
territories which were conquered, annexed and settled during the
expansion of European empires formally gained their independence
during the twentieth century.[1] Settler colonialism, however, clearly
persists in Britain's former 'white dominions' of Canada, Australia and
New Zealand, as well as in Israel/Palestine.[2] As you might imagine,
the colonial world did not disappear overnight for the citizens of
newly independent former colonies. On the level of crude imperial[3]
relations of exploitation and extraction, much appeared to stay the
same. Ghanaian independence leader Kwame Nkrumah (1965) wrote
in his book *Neo-colonialism* that African industrialization had been
frustrated because of the extraction of Africa's mineral resources for
Western benefit. More than half a century later, the Tricontinental
Institute and Third World Network-Africa observed similar patterns
of economic exploitation. Only 1.7% of global returns from Ghana's
gold remain in Ghana's domestic economy, the majority flows out to
shareholders of British, American, Canadian and Australian mining
companies. Many see this as effective neo- or re-colonization of
many African territories, resulting in *de*-industrialization (Tanoh
2019). Sovereign debts incurred by African governments to pursue
development are the basis for a continued source of pressure by
the World Bank to use meagre taxes and royalties from mining
companies to service their sovereign debt, rather than using that
mineral wealth for the kinds of national development envisioned

by independence leaders (see also Styve, Chapter 21 and Schubert, Chapter 11).

The colonial global economy and its effects are not only found in formerly colonized territories. There are intimate connections between the extraction of wealth and production of poverty and inequality in former colonies, and the accumulation of wealth and even the birth of modern welfare states in the former 'metropoles' or parent states of European empires (Bhambra 2020; Hancox 2021). To stick with the example of Nkrumah and Ghana, upon independence, Nkrumah discovered that the Crown Agents, the quasi-governmental office responsible for managing Britain's colonial finances, had been pressured into investing the foreign currency that Ghana (and other colonies) earned from their raw material exports into long-term UK government bonds (Landricina 2020). That is, Britain had borrowed at very favourable rates from Ghana. What little Ghana had earned through its exports (much of which went to the European financiers documented by Nkrumah in his *Neo-colonialism*) ended up financing Britain's post-Second World War reconstruction, rather than development in the colonies, well into the 1970s.[4]

And, as we shall see, the relations of colonialism and coloniality have also come to shape the patterns of economic wealth and poverty, the labour market and the broader political realm in colonizing countries like the UK and the US, where today race and racism continue to drastically shape people's lives and the fate of nations.

The development of Europe at the expense of its colonies and those enslaved by colonizers has been a central concern of the radical Caribbean scholars Walter Rodney and Eric Williams. There have even been attempts to put a monetary value on the wealth stolen and extracted from slave labour in the Caribbean, as well as the trauma caused by enslavement. One estimate in 2005 was of £7.5 trillion or three times the UK's 2005 gross domestic product (GDP) (Beckles 2007). Such monetary reckonings can never fully account for the harm and injustice resulting from the transatlantic slave trade. There is also a risk that critics will focus their energies on quibbling over 'getting the numbers right', at the expense of recognizing and responding to the intergenerational harms and inequalities that can be found at the centre of our colonial global economy. Still, such estimates are a powerful reminder of the scale that genuinely reparative relations between former colonies and former colonizers will require. And, turning back again to the metropole, we can observe through the work of economic historians how central wealth derived from slavery (whether directly through trafficking in enslaved persons, being 'compensated' for the 'loss' of slave property upon abolition, or in profiting from slave labour in the sugar and cotton trades) has been to the establishment of British infrastructure and institutions. In terms of 'public' infrastructure, the payment of compensation to British slave owners coincided with the 1830s railway boom, and on some lines at least 10% of railway investors were slave owners; in the private sphere, two of the biggest audit and consultancy firms in the UK were founded by families (Deloitte and Waterhouse – now part of PWC) who acquired their wealth from slave ownership and investing in slavery (Draper 2014). The metropoles, as much as the former colonies, are inextricably part and parcel of the colonial global economy.

Accounting for, and giving an account of, injustice

This book has been produced during a period in which a resurgent passion for furthering the decolonization of universities, museums and media institutions is not only accompanied by the watering down and appropriation of anti- and decolonial agendas, but met by a 'recolonial' backlash in a number of former metropoles.[5] In Britain, historical narratives which incorporate 'unpalatable elements of the national story' have been seen as morally threatening and challenging to redemptive visions of Empire (Fowler 2020). More subtle attempts to leave colonialism in the past have been made even by critical scholars famed for their opposition to neoliberalism. David Harvey has argued that 'historical draining of wealth from East to West for more than two centuries has, for example, been largely reversed over the last thirty years' (Harvey 2017: 169). Yet, as Utsa and Prabhat Patnaik (2017) argue in response, such a failure to perceive continuity within the colonial global economy seems to stem from an inadequate analysis of colonialism in the first place. The accumulation of wealth by contemporary Chinese and Indian elites is no 'reversal' of what Utsa Patnaik calls the colonial 'drain' of wealth from India. This drain was facilitated by a convoluted method of accounting through which a portion of Indian tax revenue was transferred directly to London as a 'charge' for being colonized, and buyers of Indian exports would deposit gold in London in exchange for some of those diverted tax rupees. The tax rupees would be used to buy agricultural and manufactured goods created by those taxpayers. Indian productivity, exports and economic activity thus enriched London (much of the accumulated gold was used to invest in extractive endeavours elsewhere in the Empire) and created no earnings or accumulated reserves for India. The most conservative estimate of wealth drained from India between 1765 and 1938 was around £9.2 trillion, or ten times the 2015 GDP of the UK (Patnaik 2017).

There is no doubt that such enormous transfers of wealth – or loot[6] – have had significant effects on the structure of metropolitan and former colonial societies; whether through the financing of quasi-public infrastructure, or through the uneven accumulation of wealth.

Financial colonialism persists today, it was never consigned to history, nor 'reversed' by the growth of 'BRICS'[7] economies or development goals being reached in the Global South. Turning to the 'former' French empire, the CFA franc used by fourteen countries of West and Central Africa[8] was established explicitly to facilitate French reconstruction after the Second World War (on resistance to colonial currencies see Cordes, Chapter 5 and Comyn, Chapter 4). Imposed on 'former' French colonies and tied to the French franc (and subsequently euro), it has always been overvalued, making it cheap for French consumers and companies to buy CFA-zone raw materials, expensive for CFA zone countries to import and uncompetitive to sell their goods anywhere bar France (Pigeaud and Sylla 2021). One of the consequences of pegging to the euro (and historic French control of CFA economic policy) has been a lack of lending to producers and consumers in CFA-zone countries. Any prospect of 'development' has been curtailed, and remittances sent by migrant labourers seeking work in the Parisian metropole have in fact been encouraged as a source of 'development'. Yet many such migrants are forced to live in precarity and are met with racialized hostility (Guermond and Sylla 2018).

A central theme explored by contributors to this book is the relationship between migration, racialized hostility and the new forms of financial insecurity and indebtedness to which migrants from former colonies are subjected (see Dickson et al., Chapter 8 and Medien, Chapter 7). Behind new financial 'innovations' which compound the fears, anxieties and vulnerability of migrants in the metropole is the failure to acknowledge the colonial global economy. By consigning colonial 'drains' of wealth to the past, we overlook the continuation of those drains *and* their after-effects in the colonial present. In addition, a perhaps deliberate failure to recognize that metropolitan welfare states have been built through the extraction and exploitation of wealth from the colonies nourishes racialized hostility towards former colonial subjects and the indigenous inhabitants of settler colonies. Colonialism has always operated through the creation and maintenance of racial hierarchies and exclusions. For instance, racialized distinctions determined who could be a 'sport hunter' and who was a 'poacher' subject to vicious penalties, and there were clear racial disparities regarding who was taxed ('natives') or untaxed (settler agriculturalists in much of British Africa). Such hierarchies did not simply fade away with formal independence. They persisted in the metropole, and they persisted in the imaginations and practices of Western investors seeking a return from former colonies, as several chapters in this collection show (see Alami, Chapter 10, and Kalba, Chapter 18). After all, financial practices and financial institutions have been as intimately entangled with racial hierarchy, racism and white supremacy as have colonizing states and their bureaucracies.

Haiti was the first colony of Europe's modern empires to declare its independence. In 1803, Jean-Jacques Dessalines led the Haitian revolution, tore the white portion out of the French flag and declared the Haitian Republic. France had made it clear that their revolution of 1789 did not extend its liberty, equality and brotherhood to Black Haitians. France recognized Haiti's independence in 1825, yet demanded repayment of 150 million francs extended to former planters (to be echoed by Britain's payment of compensation to slave-owners upon abolition a decade later) and a 30-million-franc loan. Opportunities to invest in Haitian government bonds (to 'lend' to Haiti in return for interest and repayment of the original sum) created a flurry of interest among Parisian investors (Yates 2021). Their financial prospects were premised on a punitive debt imposed on Haiti for demanding Black freedom and equality. Almost a century later, in 1915, the first of several US military occupations would take place to defend the interests of an American financial institution which had taken over management of the national debt, revenue collection and a large interest in national railways (Hudson and Pierre 2021).

The financial institution in question, the National City Bank of New York, made no secret of its white supremacist convictions or ambitions. City Bank decorated its Wall Street headquarters with plantation scenes, staffed its social events with waiters and performers in blackface and, along with other Wall Street banks, circulated stories 'casting Black people as economic illiterates whose engagements with modern banking and finance were marked by repeated incomprehension, befuddlement, and vexation' (Hudson 2017: 15). The rogue bankers at the centre of the legal 'innovations' that allowed US banks to open their first branches overseas – culminating in the effective financial recolonization of Haiti during the early twentieth century – likewise made no secret of their white supremacy in their writing, their daily interaction with Black bank staff and their attitude towards Haiti's people and sovereignty. Racial hierarchies and white supremacy shape modern finance in more ways than just the underwriting of colonial endeavours by those financiers. The extractive dimensions of the colonial global economy are bound up in the entanglements of race, empire and finance, which did not disintegrate with the formal end of European colonialism.

In 2001, the South African rand was devalued, in part because traders in currency futures (contracts allowing their holder to purchase a currency at a certain price at a fixed time in the future) were betting against the rand, based in part on the perceived 'risk posed by a Black African government' (Koelble and LiPuma 2006: 621). In a self-fulfilling prophecy, this devaluation of the rand brought economic turbulence to South Africa. Among contemporary mining investors in the City of London, racial hierarchies are invoked to categorize mineral-rich territories from most stable and compliant (or 'Europeanized') to most 'unruly' (Gilbert 2020). Even financiers' experience of place and architecture in global financial centres is experienced in terms of racial hierarchies and white supremacy. Lars Meier (2016) has described how German financiers experience the City of London as the 'real' centre of world finance, and its architecture as a marker of tangible empire. While whiteness is normalized in the London, in Singapore the same group of financiers construct themselves less as arriving at the centre of the financial world, and more as enabling Singapore to prosper through their (white) presence.

Snapshots of the history of our world

The chapters in this book all share a concern with the entanglement of race, empire and finance in the colonial present. And each and every chapter is organized around an image: a photograph, work of art, map, advert or diagram. For some, the central concern is the relationship between hostile borders, race, migration and personal indebtedness. For others, it is the relationship between extractive infrastructure and the transition from European to Chinese investment in Africa. Several chapters are concerned with the settler-colonial settings of contemporary Canada, Australia, New Zealand and the US. Some are historical, some personal and others based on interviews and ethnographic fieldwork.

We have chosen to organize the book around a set of images to facilitate interdisciplinary dialogue and learning. Using images allows us to bring together writers from a range of disciplines (including political economy, cultural studies, economics, anthropology, sociology, history, media studies and the arts) around a shared format. We have drawn together conversations about race, empire and finance occurring in a vast array of widely dispersed disciplinary nooks and crannies. The hyper-specialization of most academic publications, and the differences in disciplinary writing styles, normally prevent such conversations, but the image-driven approach taken here has offered one route towards interdisciplinary engagement.

More importantly, we believe images make the subject matter accessible. Finance, and the language of finance, can be particularly – sometimes deliberately – alienating, and considerable collective sense-making is required for those on the receiving ends of financial crashes and crises (Bourne 2017). Traversing historical and contemporary case studies from across an array of geographical locations can be discombobulating. Spinning each chapter's argument around a specific image helps to make the scope and subject matter less impenetrable. A third reason is because visual media have proven powerful for tracing and untangling the links between empire, race and finance – just as maps, documents and images have been instrumental in presenting colonial territories as investment opportunities and expanding new forms of racialized personal debt.

To take one example, consider the Traces of Nitrate project.[9] Tracing the connections between nineteenth-century nitrate extraction in Chile and investors in the City of London, Xavier Ribas, Louise Purbrick and Ignacio Acosta assembled documents such as a photograph album documenting nitrate production in 1900, designed as publicity material to raise investment in London and Liverpool. The sanitized images, designed to promote share sales, 'give no indication that this was a time of great unrest and violent repression, a memory they do not contain' (Traces of Nitrate 2009). The photograph album in question was sent to Henry Hucks Gibbs, a British banker and politician based in London who planted an *Araucaria araucana*, the national tree of Chile, in his Tyntesfield country estate near Bristol (Traces of Nitrate 2011). The entanglements of finance and empire, of extractivism and the erasure of violence that are revealed in this snapshot from the Traces of Nitrate can become threads for us to trace further.

We might, for example, go on to discover from University College London's Legacies of British Slave-Ownership project that Henry Huck Gibbs, the recipient of the sanitized photograph album from Chile, belonged to a family which was actively involved in the financing of English and Scottish railways in the 1840s and 1860s. His father's cousin George was both at the centre of railway financing and a slave-owner in Jamaica (Draper 2014). We may then encounter the fact that the Gibbs family home at Tyntesfield was among the houses with links to slavery and colonialism discussed in a report by the UK's UK's National Trust (Huxtable et al. 2020: 106). The report became the centre of a hostile campaign orchestrated by the then UK culture secretary and right-wing media, who accused the National Trust of 'changing the past' by writing histories of exploitation, extraction and Black presence back into the British national narrative and thus 'threaten[ing] national virtue' (Fowler 2020: 126). This hostility to the very idea of a history of Black presence in the colonial metropole, as well as a denial of the degree to which metropolitan wealth, infrastructure and indeed aesthetics depend on a history of colonial looting and enslavement, lies behind the deliberate cultivation of a hostile environment for racialized migrants in the UK. This hostile environment frequently forces migrants into greater risk of indebtedness (see Dickson et al., Chapter 8, and Medien, Chapter 7)

Our entanglements

It is this mode of engagement, of picking up threads and traces, making connections between chapters, images and artworks and other stories found outside this book that we hope to encourage in its readers as you unravel for yourselves the entangled legacies of race, empire and finance. A number of contributors to this book deal explicitly with the problems caused by assuming that colonialism or coloniality (i.e., colonial forms of rule and organization) can be consigned to the past (see particularly Styve, Chapter 21, and Samaniego and Mantz, Chapter 20). How are we to make theoretical sense of colonial traces in the present? How do we know they are 'colonial'? Some scholars of colonialism have cautioned that the language of colonial 'legacies' suggests too easy a connection, too straightforward a continuity between forms of racism, extraction and control in the past, and those found today (Stoler 2016). The contributors to this volume seek precisely to unpick *what* colonial legacies might look like in the present, tracing out from particular images, encounters and events to find sometimes surprising and contradictory relations between former colonizers and the formerly colonized (see Ferrini, Chapter 13, and Abdul Rahman, Chapter 6).

It is for this reason that we have titled this book *Entangled Legacies*. Here, over twenty-five contributors have sought to trace how imperialism, colonialism and capitalism have been woven together throughout the history of the last 500 years. The word 'legacy' calls to mind something inherited, for good or for ill, or a past that is still active in and transforming the present: wealth left by a deceased relative, or a debt owed for a past harm. The term 'entanglement' asks us to recognize that the patterns of economics and histories we will be exploring are dense and complex. The European empires that dominated the world until the post-Second World War era of decolonization were globe spanning. Driven by a combination of central planning and disorganized entrepreneurialism, they shaped global supply chains and migrant labour forces well before the advent of networked computing or the shipping container. We, each and every one of us, are the products of that history. More likely than not, it moved our ancestors from their traditional homes or transformed their way of life, enriching some while immiserating or enslaving others. To speak of entangled legacies, then, is to ask us to dwell with this complexity and pay close attention to both the specifics and the generality. Further, it asks us to understand the complexities and injustices of our own day and age in light of what came before.

Here 'legacies' articulates the ways in which 'pastness' inserts itself into the present, through physical infrastructure, state institutions or financial bonds. We embrace the etymological roots of 'legacy' as that which denotes both an inheritance and a body of persons appointed on a particular mission. We all share a concern with understanding what the colonial past – and enduring colonialism in the present – means for our collective futures. As the chapters in this collection demonstrate, tracing out the legacies of empire means grappling with entanglements of finance, race and inequality. Equally, by considering the legacies of empire to be 'entangled', we emphasize the degree to which indigenous communities and historically marginalized groups in the Global North and the Global South have been caught up in relations of exchange and oppression with colonizing agents for hundreds of years, shaping the experiences, self-understandings and attitudes to history of those in the colonies and the metropole alike. As Michelle Murphy (2018: 121) notes, 'No single being on this planet escapes entanglements with capitalism, colonialism and racism.' Thinking in terms of 'entangled legacies' encourages us to think about the different ways in which empire, race and finance come to be bound up with each other across time and space; it invites us to consider parallels between forms of entanglement in seemingly disparate social and geographical settings; and it also offers a way to think about encounters with colonialism that do not necessarily end in totalizing forms of annihilation or assimilation. We hope that this book might act as a guide towards generating solidarities and tracing out fault lines around which the entangled legacies of empire can be unravelled, or remade.

How to read this book

This collection is organized into eight parts: 'Blowouts', 'Circulations', 'Borders', 'Emergence', 'Gestures', 'Play', 'Control' and 'Imaginaries'. Each part focuses on two or three authors and their respective modes of seeing, such as images and other visual resources. Each chapter highlights ways of engaging with the topic, with 'Works cited' and 'Further resources' sections outlining academic texts, audio and video recordings or blogs on the topic. The dialogue between each voice is drawn out by the editors in a short overview section.

In Part I, 'Blowouts', Szeman (Chapter 1), Lassiter (Chapter 2) and Kushinski (Chapter 3) concern themselves with what lies behind banal images of oil extraction sites 'working properly'. What can we learn from the very *ordinariness* of the images of oil wells and oil derricks that populate settler-colonial landscapes in North America? And when images of leaky infrastructures and oil spills are broadcast to us, what are we really seeing? Is this *transparency*, or do live-streamed images of oil spills disguise more than they reveal?

The images considered by the three chapters in Part II, 'Circulations' are of paper money, coins and a tin can – though it is these *objects themselves*, rather than the pictorial representation of them, which are the authors' real concern. Comyn (Chapter 4), a Ngāti Ranginui/Pākehā writer and researcher, focuses on a banknote issued by Te Peeke Aotearoa, or the Bank of New Zealand. Te Peeke Aotearoa is understood here as an institution that sought to reassert Māori control over credit creation, given the extensive indebtedness to which Māori were subjected through Native Lands Acts titling procedures. Cordes (Chapter 5), chair of the Coquille Nation Culture and Education Committee, then considers 1853 and 1854 US dollars to highlight another dimension of 'financial colonization': the appropriation of Indigenous motifs on 1854 dollar coins, attempting to fold Indigeneity into American settler identity even as Indigenous currency was counterfeited and devalued in an effort by settlers to force sale of their lands. Abdul Rahman (Chapter 6) takes us away from the ongoing settler-colonial economies of Aotearoa/New Zealand and North America to consider the social life of a Milo tin in Malaysia. We move from collective practices of Milo consumption that nourish national sentiment, to the derogatory designation of Malaysian-made cars as 'milo tin cars', to the sale of Malaysia's flagship car company to a Chinese firm. As in Schubert's Chapter 11 on successive Portuguese and Chinese investment in Angolan infrastructure, in Abdul Rahman's Chapter 6 we also find sedimented imperial legacies: the financial – rather than physical – trade of tin on the London Metal Exchange is still of significance to the UK economy, decades after British colonists brutally extracted Malaysian tin to trade for Chinese tea, leaving behind a legacy of racial capitalism that has shaped the automobile labour market in Malaysia today.

In Part III, 'Borders', Dickson, Rosen and Sorinmade (Chapter 8), Medien (Chapter 7) and Rossipal (Chapter 9), turn to the UK and the US to examine racist border regimes which rely upon a refusal to acknowledge colonial citizenship and mobility. The images examined by Dickson et al. and Medien are images of *documents and letters*, powerful artefacts of bureaucracy that produce state authority as much as they reflect it. But, as much as they produce state authority, these documents and letters also induce fear and shame in their recipients who grapple with indebtedness as they try to navigate the outsourced companies which manage the UK's hostile border regime. For Rossipal (Chapter 9), the central image is an advertisement for a firm that engineers indebtedness by inserting itself into the US's predatory, racist border regime. What draws these chapters together is their concern with the way the racialized politics of migration simultaneously produce indebtedness, financial surveillance and 'borders in every street' (Keenan 2018).

The chapters in Part IV, 'Emergence', by Alami (Chapter 10), Schubert (Chapter 11) and Ly (Chapter 12), turn to speculative investment in South Africa, Angola and China. Drawing on a diversity of visual forms – a magazine cover, a photograph from the author's own fieldwork and a satellite image – the authors in Part IV share a concern with the way colonial pasts shape contemporary landscapes of investment, in sometimes unpredictable ways. Angola's rail infrastructure, Schubert (Chapter 11) argues, carries the traces of the extractive orientation of Portuguese colonial rule, even as Chinese 'upgrading' of the railways speaks to a change in patterns of extraction and trade. Ly (Chapter 12) shows that Chinese investment in Inner Mongolia's rare earth-rich frontier zone is the latest in a long line of speculative attempts to bring the Mongolian landscape into the (Han) Chinese future, and equally implicated in attempts made by Euro-American extractive industry corporations to 'green' themselves through investment in rare earth-dependent renewable energy systems. Alami (Chapter 10) emphasizes the racist imaginaries through which investors calculate the 'risk' of investing in Black-ruled South Africa. In all three cases, imaginaries inflected by the colonial past directly influence investment decisions and extractive landscapes in the present. The photographs considered by Ferrini (Chapter 13), Randell-Moon (Chapter 14) and Kish (Chapter 15) in Part V, 'Gestures', all concern moments of (possible) repair and reconciliation. In each case, the authors take us *behind the lens* to consider the framing, authorship and afterlives of the images. Ferrini's (Chapter 13) image of Italy's Berlusconi meeting Libya's Gaddafi is an opportunity to unpick Libya and Italy's complex relationship in the (post)-colonial present. While Libya has sought apologies and reparations from its Italian colonizers, and Italian leaders have been less than forthcoming, a new 'Treaty of Friendship' simultaneously cements Italy's foothold in Libya's oilfields, while also allowing opportunities for Libyan elites to profit from Italian state oil firms. Randell-Moon (Chapter 14) explores in parallel Mervyn Bishop's photograph of the Australian Prime Minister returning land to Gurindji Elder Vincent Lingiari, and the biography of Murri photographer Bishop, to tell a story of long-standing Aboriginal mobility and relations with Country in spite of decades of racial capitalism and settler-colonial exploitation of land and labour. Kish's (Chapter 15) chosen image is from the front cover of 'impact investor' Jacqueline Novogratz's biography, which takes as its starting point Novogratz's discovery of 'her' old sweatshirt worn by a child in Rwanda. Novogratz has spun this personal story of 'connectedness' into a highly personal model of humanitarian investment through her Acumen fund – even as this model denies the historical legacies and contemporary forms of 'connection' entanglement that integrate us into an uneven colonial global economy.[10]

In Part VI, 'Play', the chapters by Nir (Chapter 16) and by Stork (Chapter 17) explore the saturation of childhood by the logics of debt. Whatever we may imagine that the time of childhood *should* be, Part VI highlights the degree to which the time of childhood cannot escape the temporal experience of financialization (Haiven 2012). Nir takes us to an underground playground in Sderot, in Israel/Palestine. In Israel, ballooning household debt and a constant attentiveness on financial markets through which Israelis must plan for their future

and retirement sits alongside a welfare state that provides for poor
Israelis settling in occupied territories. Here, conflict is endless, life
can be planned only by constantly focusing on the financial future
and childhood play is stripped of its embeddedness in a specific time
or place, retreating to the subsurface. Stork (Chapter 17) turns to
the US, where student indebtedness has become a precondition for
social participation (Montgomerie 2013) and a college education is
treated as a 'hedge' against uncertain job market outcomes. Black
students in particular are exposed to widespread predatory lending
– overlapping with the predatory lending that forms part of the
'carceral state' discussed by Rossipal (Chapter 9). Black participation
in higher education, where racial hierarchy is vociferously manifest,
is increasingly reliant on students becoming a 'financialized person'
who provides a 'return' to the philanthropic investors that fund their
future (see also Kish, Chapter 15, on Novogratz).

Part VII, 'Control', draws together considerations of seemingly
futuristic financial infrastructures (data centres) and nineteenth-century
stock exchanges through a consideration of *architecture and archi-*
tectural plans. Drinkall (Chapter 19) considers windowless data
centres as key nodes in the expansion not just of financial transactions
but of financial surveillance as we are reconstituted as credit scores
by algorithms that track our consumer behaviour and indebtedness,
and so determine our 'life chances' (Fourcade and Healy 2013). As
Medien (Chapter 7) shows in her chapter, such algorithmic credit
scores can have enormous consequences for migrants and their
financial precarity. Kalba (Chapter 18) takes us back to the 1850s
and floor plans for the redesigned London Stock Exchange, where
opacity was just as important to traders who preferred not to be
subjected to the eyes of the prying public. This insulated traders
from seeming embedded in, or responsible for, broader financial
relations – including investment in the colonies, during a time when
30% of Britain's wealth was invested overseas. Kalba invites us to
consider the maps which were the primary visual device used by
stock exchange members to envision colonial territories as blank
canvases, ripe for investment opportunity. It is perhaps only *independ-*
ence that has made these former colonies now appear 'risky', rather
than merely inviting, as Alami (Chapter 10) suggests.

In Part VIII, 'Imaginaries', the closing part of the volume shifts
to focus on artworks which both represent and challenge the extractive
forms of finance that characterize the colonial global economy.

Samaniego and Mantz (Chapter 20), Styve (Chapter 21) and Bhattacharyya (Chapter 22) all share a concern with disrupting the notion that colonialism can be consigned to 'the past' in artworks produced by collectives, artists and, in Bhattacharyya's case, the author herself. The form of the artworks challenges any linear narrative of modernization or universal capitalist 'developmentalism' that places economic growth at the centre of visions of progress. These artworks all reveal the violence underlying claims that the colonial global economy is oriented towards producing 'plenty', but also point to possibilities for thinking about co-existence through visual productions that stretch space, challenge linear disruptions of time and share stories of the interdependence that can be found within the colonial global economy and what Bhattacharyya calls 'racial capitalism'.

While we have grouped the chapters to facilitate the exploration of particular themes or visual forms, and to feed neatly into possible teaching session plans, we also encourage you to read across the entanglements that draw chapters from *different* sections into dialogue. Thus, for instance, numerous chapters consider questions of asylum, predatory finance and racialized borders – primarily the chapters in Part III, 'Borders', but equally Ferrini's (Chapter 13) contribution in Part V, 'Gestures'. Similarly, playgrounds and childhood are clearly central to Stork (Chapter 17) and Nir (Chapter 16) in Part VI, 'Play', but are also key to Dickson et al. (Chapter 8) in Part III, 'Borders'. Both Rossipal (Chapter 9 in Part III, 'Borders') and Kish (Chapter 15 in Part V, 'Gestures') consider the particular 'humanitarian aesthetics' used to justify the expansion of indebtedness in the name of ethical, humanitarian interventions. Oil infrastructures are central to the chapters in Part I, 'Blowouts', but also to Schubert (Chapter 11 in Part IV, 'Emergence') and Ferrini (Chapter 13 in Part V, 'Gestures'). Offshore jurisdictions, tax avoidance and Britain's 'second empire' of tax havens – which emerged as a specific response to the need that white settlers had to get their wealth out of newly independent African nations (Ogle 2020) – are central threads in the stories told by Dickson et al. (Chapter 8 in Part III, 'Borders') and Styve (Chapter 21 in Part VIII, 'Imaginaries'). Styve connects offshore financial flows to the 2013 murder of protesting mineworkers at Marikana in South Africa, while Alami (Chapter 10 in Part IV, 'Emergence') examines the decontextualized image of Marikana mineworkers used as a cover image by *The Economist* to depict a generalized, unruly Black African workforce. We invite you to explore your own connections as you unpick and identify the manifold entangled legacies which make an appearance in this collection.

What you need to know: terminology and vocabulary

Our aim with this book is that it is accessible for students and teachers working in and around anthropology, cultural studies, development studies, geography, media studies, political economy and sociology – within and without the academy. We have therefore flagged a number of terms which might be considered 'jargon', or which are contested and most easily understood as part of specific academic debates and dialogues. The remainder of this introduction is given over to providing background to some of these key terms, many of which appear in *italic* type. Readers may consult this book's index for the location of other sections where these terms are addressed.

It is perhaps worth starting with a note on the specificities of *settler colonialism*, which is the focus of a number of chapters throughout the volume focusing on Canada, the US, Australia, New Zealand and Israel/Palestine. Settler colonialism is often understood in terms of the 'logic of elimination' (Wolfe 2006). That is, settler colonialism entails a *structure* of genocidal elimination of Indigenous people from their land, and is organized through the grammar of race; it is not a one-off event but a persistent reality for colonized Indigenous people. For Tuck and Yang (2012) settler colonialism can also be understood as a combination of 'external' colonialism (through which fragments of Indigenous wealth and indigenous plants and resources are extracted and fed to the metropole) and 'internal' colonialism (through which Indigenous people and their land are managed within the borders of a nation through schooling, imprisonment and ghettoization).

Tuck and Yang caution against enthusiasm for 'decolonial' projects on the part of settlers who have no intention of relinquishing colonized land but merely wish to metaphorically 'decolonize' their curricula and themselves – in some cases through 're-colonial' occupations and homesteading. Financial innovation has been central to settler colonialism too. Where English common law protected families from losing land due to indebtedness, English colonizers in the Americas developed a new form of 'foreclosure'. This initially applied only to Indigenous people, and enabled the manufacture of debts and subsequent appropriation of land (Park 2021; see Cordes, Chapter 5, and Comyn, Chapter 4). Despite the influence of Patrick Wolfe's model of settler colonialism as elimination, there are indeed cases where the logic of settler colonialism seems to be one of exploitation rather than elimination (Englert 2020) – as for example in the case of white settlers in South Africa exploiting Black mineworkers (see Alami, Chapter 10 and Styve, Chapter 21). An emphasis on elimination should indeed be approached with caution, as it can contribute to the erasure of Indigenous scholarship and discussions of what it means to decolonize ongoing settler colonialism (Curley et al. 2022) The entanglements of race, finance and inequality that emerge through settler-colonial projects can also be approached through the lens of *racial capitalism* – a term that many authors in this collection use (on settler colonialism and racial capitalism, see Randell-Moon, Chapter 14). Before reviewing thought on racial capitalism in more depth, let's take a look at the two terms that make it up.

Capitalism

Capitalism is an economic system based on (1) the private ownership of the 'means of production' and (2) the exploitation of labour, and that is (3) driven by profit. An economic system is an overarching framework for organizing labour and distributing goods. Different civilizations have developed diverse economic systems, many of them exploitative, where some people do most of the work and get little rewards and a few people do very little work (or only managerial work) and reap the benefits. Capitalism is, by its nature, exploitative, but, unlike any other system, its exploitation is based on a small number of people (capitalists) owning the factories, the plantations and the infrastructure that society uses to create wealth. Unlike any other system, in capitalism money runs the show: its acquisition is what drives capitalists to compete with one another for profit, it is what capitalists use to pay workers and it is what workers use to survive by buying back goods and services from capitalists.

Because capitalism is so adept at motivating certain kinds of action, we often talk about the system capitalism as if it had a life or mind of its own: we speak of 'capital' and its desires (to move around the world freely) and drives (to transform anything of value into a commodity to be traded for money) or its logics (its laws of motion). But, in actual fact, capitalism is driven forward by a kind of collective momentum created by conflicts – much as wind, while it can appear to have its own force, is actually created in the atmosphere by the tension between pressure zones. While capitalism does create a small, very wealthy and powerful elite, it is *not* a conspiracy: it is driven forward by *competition* between capitalists as they seek market share and to better exploit workers to gain profit.

The competition might be between firms in the same industry (Apple vs Google, Ford vs Tesla, HSBC vs Goldman Sachs) or by capitalists in one country or region against those of others (Chinese vs American; Brazilian vs South African). This competition, alongside the resistance of workers to capitalism at every point (demands for higher wages, better conditions or even a different system), creates contradictions within the system, and these contradictions can easily become crises, as for instance when several firms competing in the same industry all try to cut wages so deeply that workers leave or starve.

To manage these contradictions, capitalism often relies on a state (government) to regulate and create universal rules. States also use militaries and police to suppress workers' and oppressed people's uprisings. Through colonialism and imperialism, states aim to gain access to resource or new markets for their local capitalists. But, over the past centuries, workers and oppressed people have organized to also influence or sometimes take over the state, including using it to defend their rights to adequate wages, social services and protections from capitalism or using it to replace capitalism with other economic systems.

Because this book approaches its topics from a critical perspective, most of the authors in this book are sceptical towards capitalism and would propose that, in order to produce greater equality and fairness in the economy, the capitalist system must be either heavily regulated to prevent excesses and abuses or abolished altogether. They are generally sceptical towards neoliberal claims that greater and freer markets lead to peace, human rights and the possibility of universal prosperity.

Race and racism

Historically, capitalism has never existed without colonialism and imperialism and has always depended on racism in order to divide workers and justify the exploitation of some by others. But to understand 'racial capitalism' we also need to understand race. It is plain enough for anyone to see that humans are a very diverse species, genetically and culturally. But what is the story we should tell about those differences? Race names a very specific way of categorizing humans, a specific story about what makes us different from one another. It's also a fiction, with very dark origins and terrible consequences.

Its roots go back to early modern Europe, but it really consolidated in the eighteenth and nineteenth centuries because it was an essential ingredient in the ideology of imperialism and colonialism by which capitalism expanded during that time. It is based on the bogus idea that people's *phenotypical* appearance (i.e. traits like skin colour or hair type that can be observed with the naked eye) are somehow demonstrative of a person's inherent qualities (like intelligence, morality, capacity or character), often tied to a person or a group's (presumed) region of origin. So, racial ideologies try to understand qualities that unite *all* people whose ancestors came from Africa, a region with huge diversity, or from Europe, also a diverse region and one only imagined as a unified 'culture' or race in recent times. Racism is *not* simply another word for prejudice. It is, specifically, the construction of a mythical hierarchy based on the categories of race and has its roots in the way Western European thinkers and scientists began to dream up rationales for colonialism and empire: it helped them to argue that those 'races' of people who were being subjugated were inherently inferior.

Race is a fiction that makes itself real through violence. For instance, in the transatlantic slave trade, Europeans pointed to the fact that Africans were enslaved and Europeans were not so as to suggest not only that Europeans were superior to Africans but that such a thing as 'Europe' or 'Africa' even existed: though indeed these describe more or less distinct landmasses, they are each home to vast cultural and human diversity and have never been homogeneous. The idea that either is a coherent civilization that has specific inherited qualities is a pure invention.

Over the centuries, theories of race take on different forms. At an earlier moment, race was largely a story told in religious language: the conquistadors justified their subjugation and enslavement and destruction of Indigenous people in the Americas because the latter were not Christians. Later, as religion gave way to the modern thinking of the Enlightenment, race and racism cloaked themselves in the mantle of science. Vast resources were dedicated to 'proving' that races were biological fact and that phenotypical differences were indeed reflections of inherent character based on ancestral origin. After the Second World War such scientific theories fell out of favour, partly because of how the Nazis used scientific theories of race to justify genocide, partly because of struggles for decolonization and anti-racism and partly thanks to the development of the study of genetics that has proven that 'race' as we tend to imagine it is a bogus concept. But racism has shifted again.

Today, it is common for us to imagine that the world is broken not into genetic groups but distinct 'cultures'. This argument has justified a new wave of imperialism and neocolonialism, for instance in the wake of the 2001 terrorist attacks on New York which led to a two-decades long War on Terror, presented as a 'clash of civiliza- tions'. Today, white supremacists in Britain, the US and Europe no longer necessarily publicly espouse a belief that white people are inherently superior but do suggest that all people with white skin share a distinct culture that is under threat from migration. But this lumping of a huge diversity of peoples and cultures under 'whiteness' is a dangerous fiction.

From the critical perspective that informs this book, racism persists not because humans are naturally xenophobic but because it remains useful for reproducing divisions between people that serve the interests of colonialism, imperialism and capitalism. It is an ideology which supports existing power relations. We call the process by which people are categorized into races 'racialization'. We speak about the dominant beliefs about racism as racial imaginaries.

On the other hand, today it is common to hear politicians and pundits tell us that we live in a society that has overcome racism, a '*post-racial*' society that is '*colour blind*' because, today, at least in capitalist democracies in the Global North, there are supposedly no longer any legal barriers preventing racialized and non-white people from participating in society and competing in the marketplace. This is a pernicious myth, but even when one presents the irrefutable evidence that, in the US and UK and on a global level, non-white people suffer lower wages, fewer opportunities, higher rates of poverty, poorer health indicators and more, the response is often (a) outright denial or (b) the argument that this is a residual effect of past racism that will soon be eliminated or (c) outright racism that claims that these statistics prove that these people must indeed be inferior because the impartial market has spoken. The reality is more complex.

Centuries of colonialism and racism have undermined the wealth, achievement and security of non-white peoples both in nations that were colonized and also in colonizing nations. But we also need to pay attention to the ways that seemingly universal policies, when they fail to account for the histories of racism and colonialism, can participate in their perpetuation without anyone intending it to be so. For instance, privatizing, commodifying or cutting funds to public school lunch programmes may seem to affect all children equally. But we live in a world where it will impact on poorer families more severely, and many poor children will go hungry and have poorer academic performance, which will lead to poorer competitiveness in the capitalist economy. In a context like the UK or US, where non-white people are much more likely to be poor, thanks to generations of racism and colonialism, this seemingly *universal* policy is *functionally* racist: it will tend to impact on racialized people the hardest. These forms of institutional and systemic racism are much more common than a racist taunt or joke, but are arguably much more damaging, in large part because they are made invisible. While race thinking is often the foundation for dehumanizing ideologies and forms of organization, acting 'as if' race no longer matters because we live in a putative post-racial society does nothing to chip away at institutionalized and structural forms of racism: instead, it simply makes them harder to combat.

Imagination

Before finally turning to define racial capitalism, it is worth noting here the power of the imagination, a theme that recurs in this book. Even though 'race' properly speaking is not real, it becomes real because of its power over our imaginations. Racism is real, and it's deadly, but it is *made* real because of the way it shapes how we imagine the world and who and what we imagine are valuable. When you think about it, this is true of many things: money, for instance, usually takes the form these days of paper bills or digital numerals that only really have value because we, as a society, agree to a kind of mutual hallucination. Even the idea of nationhood is an 'imagined community' that is constantly being recreated. For this reason, many authors in this volume will speak of different *'imaginaries'*, which refers to shared structures of the imagination, ways of envisioning and understanding the world. For these authors, the imaginary and the material are two sides of the same coin: systems of exploitation and inequality produce imaginaries that justify them. Speculative investments require people to buy into convincing imaginaries of what future development (or future technologies) might look like: perhaps an imaginary of 'world-class cities' justifies slum clearance, or an imaginary of 'decarbonized transport by 2030' could justify destructive extraction of the battery metals required for 'green' electric vehicles. The justifications provided by certain imaginaries help to shape people's and government's behaviours and so help to reproduce systems of exploitation and inequality. For this reason, many of the chapters in this book are dedicated not only to explaining reality but also to helping us understand these imaginaries so that we can help to break the cycle.

Racial capitalism

Perhaps the most commonly used term throughout this collection is *racial capitalism*, a term that has spread through academia with renewed vigour and entered journalistic and online discourse, particularly in the wake of the 2020 Black Lives Matter uprising. The widespread use of this term has perhaps only added confusion, since not everyone is specific about *how* they use 'racial capitalism', even though its meaning is by no means fixed or traceable through one particular genealogy. We welcome the democratization of such powerful analytical language, of course, but feel that it may be useful to provide an orientation to how contributors to this book – as well as notable historical writers – have used the term. Many authors (including several in this volume) trace the use of 'racial capitalism' to Cedric Robinson. Robinson's ground-breaking work challenged what he saw as Marxist orthodoxy's pretention to universalism, all while it ignored racism in the history of capitalism and treated the white European worker as the agent of history. Robinson instead argued that capitalism was simply an extension of European feudalism, which carried with it already the ideologies and imaginaries of racist hierarchy.

Yet Robinson barely actually used the term 'racial capitalism' in his own writing. And, in his outright rejection of European Marxism, steered away from concrete, context-specific inquiries into the racial foundations of capitalist exploitation – and the possibility for pursuing projects of anti-racist socialism (Burden-Stelly 2020). As Hudson (2018) has shown, earlier (and highly contested) uses of the term 'racial capitalism' can be found, particularly among anti-apartheid activists in 1970s South Africa. Still, Robinson has been something of a touchstone for most writers on racial capitalism. More recently, Jenkins and Leroy (2021), and Gargi Bhattacharyya (2018), have emphasized that describing the system we live in as *racial* capitalism is an important part of pushing against either a 'race first' or 'class first' approach to social justice. Both Jenkins and Leroy, and Bhattacharyya, treat racial capitalism as something of a question more than an answer: it is our job to tease out the entanglements between forms of economic exploitation and the racial terms and racial hierarchies through which that exploitation is organized *in specific settings* – always with an eye on the past forms of racism and racial hierarchy on which capitalism and colonialism have relied.[11]

Finance and inequality

A number of other contributors refer to some aspect of *sovereign debt*: whether that be *donor conditionalities*, *structural adjustment programmes*, or *oil-backed credit lines*. Sovereign debt takes the form of bonds 'issued' by governments, which they must then pay back to their creditors (or lenders) in full, plus interest or what is termed bond 'yield'. Some bonds are referred to by specific names, such as the old British *Consols* discussed by Kalba (Chapter 18). Heavy sovereign debt burdens limit the amount of spending that is available for social infrastructure, because of the cost of 'servicing' debt (i.e., paying interest or the bond yields to creditors). This became a particular burden during the first wave of the COVID-19 pandemic (Munevar 2020), and the capacity of credit-rating agencies to 'downgrade' the quality of a given country's bonds (i.e., make it more expensive for them to borrow, or force them to pay more 'yield' to creditors willing to lend to them) has both demonstrated the extent of private analysts' control over international financial markets (Mutize 2020) and raised questions about the racist imaginaries underpinning bond downgrades (see Alami, Chapter 10). Oil-backed credit lines are a specific type of borrowing where a government offers either natural resources or the revenue from those as repayments: in other words, future delivery of resources is promised, potentially mortgaging a nation's resource future to its borrower.

Donor conditionalities, on the other hand, refer to requirements that states open their economies to imports, privatize state-owned industries, remove subsidies (even for vital subsistence commodities) and otherwise liberalize their economies in exchange for donor support. Most often associated with the Structural Adjustment Programmes imposed to disastrous effect by the International Monetary Fund (IMF)/World Bank in the 1980s and 1990s, donor conditionalities never went away, and in effect undermined possibilities for deliberative governance by predetermining huge swathes of government policy (Adesina et al. 2021; Mkandawire and Soludo 1998). Concerns have been raised about a return of Structural Adjustment accompanying IMF loans made to countries struggling to respond to the COVID-19 crisis.

Numerous contributors also refer to *offshore, tax havens, profit shifting, Britain's Second Empire*, as well as specific tax abuse scandals like the Panama Papers. In using terms like 'offshore' or 'tax havens' it's worth bearing in mind that a great deal of tax abuse takes place nominally 'onshore' in places like London, because what matters is the capacity to *structure* a financial transaction such that you do not pay tax in high-tax jurisdictions, by 'shifting your profits' on paper to (or through) a low-tax jurisdiction. Campaigners and economists at the Tax Justice Network prefer the language of 'secrecy jurisdictions' to the language of 'offshore' or 'tax havens' for this reason (Cobham et al. 2015). In addition, the focus on offshore or tax havens often conjures up images of 'treasure islands', small island states that are, for various historical reasons, often Overseas Territories or Crown Dependencies of the UK. Perhaps understandably, representatives of these nations have resisted the framing of 'treasure islands' as the problem, when it is firms in London, New York and Singapore who act as the brokers and nodes in networks of tax abuse and profit shifting. Still, the degree to which London has acted as a hub for shifting profits and hiding wealth 'offshore' in the vestiges of its empire has led a number of analysts to term this network (taking in the Cayman Islands, British Virgin Islands, Bahamas, Gibraltar, Bermuda as well as Singapore and Hong Kong) Britain's 'second empire'. To consider the bridge between questions of sovereign debt, donor conditionality and 'offshore' financial flows, it is worth bearing in mind that between 1970 and 2018, *capital flight* of around $2 trillion 'disappeared' from thirty African countries, exceeding the $720 billion of debt owed by the same countries, as well as the donor aid they have received over the same period (Ndikumana and Boyce 2021). As Ndikumana and Boyce show, while it might be argued that money was flowing out of African countries during economic downturns as investors (including African investors) sought opportunities elsewhere, the opposite is true: the more economic value is produced in African economies, the more capital flight is registered leaving the continent.

Unsurprisingly too, a number of authors refer to *financialization*, *speculation*, *securitization* and *liquidity*. Each of these terms is widely used, but not always in the same way, depending on the user's theoretical orientation. The term 'financialization' has been used variously to describe how companies come to rely on financial products for their income, even more than they do on selling commodities as part of their 'core' business. In some cases, financialization is used to refer to the proportion of a country's economic activity that takes place in the financial sector as opposed to other 'productive' sectors. For others, the financialization of everyday life is a question of how far even our imaginations are subordinated to the need to think about the future in terms of punctuated rhythms of debt repayment and personal investment in the absence of collective welfare (Haiven 2011). It has also been used to refer to firms being run according to financial imperatives, rather than those of their other 'stakeholders'. Not only private sector firms, but nominally 'public' services and organizations can change their organizational form when they are run with the interests of creditors rather than users and workers in mind (Hildyard 2017).

'Speculation' is a term perhaps more widely used than financialization, and in general comes along with some kind of moral judgement: speculative investments may be unsound, reckless, contributing merely to financial return rather than 'real' or 'productive' growth, industry and jobs. In truth though, it can be hard to pin down what exactly counts as speculative investment and what counts as investment in the 'real' economy: since almost all valuations of companies and investment products are 'forward looking', or based on future earning potential, they are all to a degree speculative. It may thus be more productive, in engaging with speculation, to think about how speculative projects rely on specific imagined futures, and how successfully drawing money in to fund a speculative endeavour reshapes our lives and landscapes (Gilbert 2019; see Ly, Chapter 12).

Securitization carries two terms in academic and more common use, both at play here, and it is worth a brief note of clarification. In the financial sense, securitization refers to the process of taking a commodity or asset and selling the rights to income from that commodity or asset. You can therefore trade a 'security' that gives you the right to income from a specific mining company, for example, or that gives you the right to income from someone's mortgage (or thousands of peoples' mortgages, as was the case with some of the products implicated in the 2008 financial crisis). In the other sense, securitization refers to matters of violence, conflict and military control, and the act of not only making something 'secure' but making something a 'security problem'. Particular racially marked or religious groups might be 'securitized' by governments that treat them as a certain risk, subjecting them to additional restrictions and surveillance. Or specific places might become 'securitized', subject to a set of controls and restrictions on movement. 'Liquidity', also a common term heard in the financial press, refers for the most part to the ease with which something can be sold: 'liquid' assets being those that can be turned into cash, with less liquid assets being those that might be difficult to price or sell. As Nesvetailova (2010) has shown, financial practitioners' understanding of 'liquidity' has come to be in terms of 'liquid markets' (i.e., how can we keep trades going by creating more and more new products, often by 'securitizing' old ones?), rather than understanding liquidity as a property of specific assets, and, as such, a 'liquidity illusion' is often at play when high turnover is mistaken for robust and resilient markets.

Finally, numerous contributors engage with *neoliberalism* and the associated notion of *accumulation by dispossession*. Neoliberalism has perhaps become used to describe such a vast array of capitalist and market-based ills that advocates of market-based reform often point to this profusion of meanings to deny there is such a thing as 'neoliberalism'. Yet a more or less coherent consensus has emerged among critical scholars: neoliberalism is *not* and never was about the state 'getting out of the way' for markets to work, but about the organization of more and more aspects of our lives (from education, to welfare services, to local government) around the principle of competition, where a 'winner takes all' vision of markets is used as the template for organizing these competitions. Such competitions require endless resources from the state, and are perhaps related to the arch-neoliberal Hayek's philosophy, to the degree that he viewed states (fascist and socialist alike) as tending towards totalitarianism and saw market competition as a way to retain uncertainty (i.e., avoiding excessive control) while providing order in society (Davies 2016). The irony being that increasing financialization, often welcomed by advocates of neoliberalism, exerts ever more control on us through our debt-laden financial futures, and finds comfortable bedfellows in authoritarian, populist-nationalist governments around the world (see Medien, Chapter 7, and Nir, Chapter 16).

Several contributors refer to David Harvey's widely read and widely cited works on neoliberalism, as well as to Harvey's notion of accumulation by dispossession, a term that he uses to extend Marx's 'primitive accumulation'. For Marx, primitive accumulation was the brutal, force-based appropriation of resources that came before capitalism set into motion, as 'extra-economic force' was used to push rural peasants into the workforce through 'proletarianization'. Harvey argues that such dispossession continues to this day, and was not so 'primitive' after all. Harvey's work and concepts are a useful guide for many students, but we would, in closing this Introduction, encourage the readers of this volume to equally turn beyond the amplified voices of the Global North in seeking to engage with the entangled legacies of empire. Behind some of the most highly cited work on neoliberalism is, as Moyo, Yeros and Jha (2012) show, a separation of contemporary 'neoliberal' accumulation by dispossession driven by the logic of capital, and past Scrambles for Africa in the nineteenth century, which Harvey sees as driven by a territorial logic of control. We must come to understand the legacies of empire fully if we are to make sense of the present as a continuation of the colonial global economy – albeit one whose form we cannot always predict. This is not merely to ensure analytical correctness but, as Moyo et al. (2012) argue, because we cannot understand the unity of struggles against racialized borders, land dispossession, indebtedness, extractive violence and putatively humanitarian forms of investment without recognizing the colonial structure against which these struggles are mobilizing. We hope that the chapters in this book can help you to understand, engage with and visualize possibilities for these struggles.

Works cited

Adesina, J., Fischer, A. and Hoffman, N. (2021) 'Speak of me as I am: Reflections on aid and regime change in Ethiopia'. *The Elephant*, 16 January. www.theelephant.info/features/2021/01/16/speak-of-me-as-i-am-reflections-on-aid-and-regime-change-in-ethiopia/ (accessed 12 September 2022).

Beckles, H. McD. (2007) '"Slavery was a long, long time ago": Remembrance, reconciliation and the reparations discourse in the Caribbean'. *Ariel* 38(1): 9–25.

Bhambra, G. K. (2020) 'Accounting for British history'. *Discover Society* 82. https://archive.discoversociety.org/2020/07/01/focus-accounting-for-british-history/ (accessed 12 September 2022).

Bhattacharyya, G. (2018) *Rethinking Racial Capitalism: Questions of Reproduction and Survival*. Lanham, MD: Rowman & Littlefield.

Bourne, C. (2017) 'Sensemaking in an online community after financial loss: Enterprising Jamaican investors and the fall of a financial messiah'. *New Media and Society* 19(6): 843–60.

Burden-Stelly, C. (2020) 'Modern U.S. racial capitalism: Some theoretical insights'. *Monthly Review*, July. https://monthlyreview.org/2020/07/01/modern-u-s-racial-capitalism/ (accessed 12 September 2022).

Cobham, A., Jansky, P. and Meinzer, M. (2015) 'The Financial Secrecy Index: shedding new light on the geography of secrecy'. *Economic Geography* 91(3): 281–303.

Curley, A., Gupta, P., Lookabaugh, L., Neubert, C. and Smith, S. (2022) 'Decolonisation is a political project: Overcoming impasses between indigenous sovereignty and abolition'. *Antipode* 54(4): 1043–1062.

Davies, W. (2016) *The Limits of Neoliberalism: Authority, Sovereignty and the Logic of Competition*. London: SAGE.

Draper, N. (2014) 'Helping to make Britain great: The commercial legacies of slave-ownership in Britain'. In C. Hall, N. Draper, K. McClelland, K. Donington and R. Lang (eds), *Legacies of British Slave-Ownership: Colonial Slavery and the Formation of Victorian Britain*. Cambridge: Cambridge University Press, pp. 78–126.

Englert, S. (2020) 'Settlers, workers, and the logic of accumulation by dispossession'. *Antipode* 52(6): 1647–1666.

Fourcade, M. and Healy, K. (2013) 'Classification situations: Life-chances in the neoliberal era'. *Accounting, Organizations and Society* 38(8): 559–572.

Fowler, C. (2020) *Green Unpleasant Land: Creative Responses to Rural England's Colonial Connections*. London: Peepal Tree Press.

Gilbert, P. R. (2019) 'Bangladesh as the "next frontier"? Positioning the nation in a global financial hierarchy'. *Public Anthropologist* 1(1): 62–80.

Gilbert, P. R. (2020) 'Speculating on sovereignty: "Money mining" and corporate foreign policy at the extractive industry frontier'. *Economy and Society* 49(1): 16–44.

Guermond, V. and Sylla, N. S. (2018) 'When monetary coloniality meets 21st century finance: Development in the Franc zone'. *Discover Society* 60. https://archive.discoversociety.org/2018/09/04/when-monetary-coloniality-meets-21st-century-finance-development-in-the-franc-zone/ (accessed 12 September 2022).

Haiven, M. (2011) 'Finance as capital's imagination? Reimagining value and culture in an age of fictitious capital and crisis'. *Social Text* 108: 93–124.

Haiven, M. (2012) 'Can Pikachu save Fannie Mae? Value, finance and imagination in the new Pokéconomy'. *Cultural Studies* 26(4): 516–541.

Hancox, A. (2021) 'Lieutenants of imperialism: Social democracy's imperialist soul'. *Review of African Political Economy*, 15 July. https://roape.net/2021/07/15/lieutenants-of-imperialism-social-democracys-imperialist-soul/ (accessed 12 September 2022).

Harvey, D. (2017) 'A commentary on *A Theory of Imperialism*'. In U. Patnaik and P. Patnaik (eds), *A Theory of Imperialism*. New York: Columbia University Press, pp. 154–72.

Hildyard, N. (2017) *Licensed Larceny: Infrastructure, Financial Extraction and the Global South*. Manchester: Manchester University Press.

Hopkins, A. G. (1970) 'The creation of a colonial monetary system: The origins of the West African Currency Board'. *African Historical Studies* 3(1), pp. 101–132.

Hudson, P. J. (2017) *Bankers and Empire: How Wall Street Colonized the Caribbean*. Chicago: University of Chicago Press.

Hudson, P. (2018) 'Racial capitalism and the dark proletariat'. *Boston Review*, 20 February. https://bostonreview.net/forum_response/peter-james-hudson-racial-capitalism-and/ (accessed 14 September 2020).

Hudson, P. J. and Pierre, J. (2021) 'Haiti: On interventions and occupations'. *Black Agenda Report*, 4 August. www.blackagendareport.com/haiti-interventions-and-occupations (accessed 12 September 2022).

Huxtable, S.-A., Fowler, C., Kefalas, C. and Slocombe, E. (2020) *Interim Report on the Connections between Colonialism and Properties now in the Care of the National Trust, Including Links with Historic Slavery*. Swindon: National Trust.

Jenkins, D. and Leroy, J. (2021) 'Introduction: The old histories of capitalism'. In D. Jenkins and J. Leroy (eds), *Histories of Racial Capitalism*. New York: Columbia University Press, pp. 1–26.

Keenan, S. (2018) 'A prison around your ankle and a border in every street: Theorising law, space and the subject'. In A. Philippopoulos-Mihalopoulos (ed.), *Handbook on Law and Theory*. Abingdon: Routledge, pp. 71–90.

Koelble, T. and LiPuma, E. (2006) 'The effects of circulatory capitalism on democratization: Observations from South Africa and Brazil'. *Democratization* 13(4): 605–631.

Landricina, M. (2020) *Nkrumah and the West: 'the Ghana experiment' in the British, American and German archives*. Hamburg: Lit Verlag.

Meier, L. (2016) 'Dwelling in different localities: Identity performances of a white transnational professional elite in the City of London and the Central Business District of Singapore'. *Cultural Studies* 30(3): 483–505.

Mkandawire, T. and Soludo, C. (1998) *Our Continent, Our Future: African Perspectives on Structural Adjustment*. Dakar: CODESRIA.

Montgomerie, J. (2013) 'America's debt safety-net'. *Public Administration* 91(4): 871–888.

Moyo, S., Yeros, P. and Jha. P. (2012) 'Imperialism and primitive accumulation: Notes on the new scramble for Africa'. *Agrarian South: Journal of Political Economy* 1(2): 181–203.

Munevar, D. (2020) 'Covid-19 and debt in the Global South: Protecting the most vulnerable in times of crisis I'. Eurodad, 12 March. www.eurodad.org/covid19_debt1 (accessed 12 September 2022).

Murphy, M. (2018) 'Against population, towards alterlife'. In A. Clarke and D. Haraway (eds), *Making Kin not Population. Chicago: Prickly Paradigm Press*, pp. 101–124.

Mutize, M. (2020) 'Downgrading the economies of developing countries in a time of crisis is a very bad idea'. Quartz Africa, 2 May. https://qz.com/africa/1850033/coronavirus-moodys-fitch-downgrades-devastating-for-africa/ (accessed 12 September 2022).

Ndikumana, L. and Boyce, J. (2021) 'Capital flight from Africa 1970–2018: New estimates with updated trade misinvoicing methodology'. Political Economy Research Institute, University of Massachusetts-Amherst.

Nesvetailova, A. (2010) *Financial Alchemy in Crisis: The Great Liquidity Illusion*. London: Pluto Press.

Nkrumah, K. (1965) *Neo-colonialism: The Last Stage of Imperialism*. London: International Publishers.

Ogle, V. (2020) '"Funk money": The end of empires, the expansion of tax havens, and decolonization as an economic and financial event'. *Past & Present* 249(1): 213–249.

Park, K.-S. (2021) 'Race, innovation and financial growth: The example of foreclosure'. In D. Jenkins and J. Leroy (eds), *Histories of Racial Capitalism*. New York: Columbia University Press, pp. 26–51.

Patnaik, U. (2017) 'Revisiting the "drain", or transfers from India to Britain in the context of global diffusion of capitalism'. In S. Chakrabarti and U. Patnaik (eds), *Agrarian and Other Histories: Essays for Binay Bhushan Chaudhuri. Tulika Books, New Delhi.*

Patnaik, U. and Patnaik, P. (2017) *A Theory of Imperialism.* New York: Columbia University Press.

Pigeaud, F. and Sylla, N. N. (2021) *Africa's Last Colonial Currency: The CFA Franc Story*. London: Pluto Press.

Ralph, M. and Singhal, R. (2019) 'Racial capitalism'. *Theory and Society* 48: 851–881.

Stoler, A. L. (2016) *Duress: Imperial Durabilities in Our Times*. Durham, NC: Duke University Press.

Tanoh, G. (2019) *Resource Sovereignty: The Agenda for Africa's Exit from the State of Plunder*. Dossier no. 16. Tricontinental: Institute for Social Research.

Traces of Nitrate (2009) 'Oficina Alianza and Port of Iquique 1899'. https://tracesofnitrate.org/filter/Nitrate-Geographies/2009-Oficina-Alianza-and-Port-of-Iquique-1899 (accessed 12 September 2022).

Traces of Nitrate (2011) Gibbsiana. https://tracesofnitrate.org/filter/Nitrate-Geographies/2011-Gibbsiana

Tuck, E. and Yang, K. W. (2012) 'Decolonization is not a metaphor'. *Decolonization: Indigeneity, Education & Society* 1(1): 1–40.

Wolfe, P. (2006) 'Settler colonialism and the elimination of the native'. *Journal of Genocide Research* 8(4): 387–409.

Yates, A. (2021) 'Rise of the rentier'. https://sites.manchester.ac.uk/riseoftherentier/2021/01/17/defending-the-haitian-debt-bondholder-activism-in-19th-century-france/ (accessed 12 September 2022).

Notes

1 In British, French and Portuguese Africa between the 1950s and 1990s; in Spanish and Brazilian South America during the nineteenth century and the British and Dutch Caribbean between the 1960s and 1980s; in French Asia during the 1940s and 1950s, British Asia between the 1940s and 1990s and Portuguese Asia between the 1960s and 2000s. Asia here is understood as inclusive of West Asia or the 'Middle East'.

2 Chapters in this collection engage with settler colonialism as well as the afterlives of colonialism – and the colonial present – from a variety of localities across the globe, although the workshops and networks through which this volume emerged have resulted in an undeniable emphasis on Anglophone, North Atlantic scholarship.

3 The terms 'colonial' and 'imperial' are often used interchangeably, and they are of course interconnected. Colonization and colonialism are often associated more with settlement, annexation and conquering of territories, whereas imperialism tends to be used to highlight (largely economic) forms of domination by external powers.

4 See also the history of the West African Currency Board, founded in 1912 without any African involvement or consideration of how the Currency Board might 'enlarge internal economies' but, rather, to resolve disputes between expatriate traders to ensure that benefits accrued to Britain rather than the colonies (Hopkins 1970).

5 In the UK, the 2021 Sewell Report has been a key moment in the Conservative government's attempt to deny racial inequality, denounced by the UN Working Group of Experts on People of African Descent as an attempt to normalize white supremacy. The then culture secretary Oliver Dowden's response to a National Trust report on colonial and slave-owner links to country houses was also a meeting point for self-proclaimed 'anti-woke' sentiment in government, media and higher education. In France, the Observatoire du Décolonialisme has curated hostility to scholars concerned with race and decolonialism. In the US, organized opposition to (an imagined version of) Critical Race Theory has also fed into white supremacist politics. A tangential current is running through the supremacist movement in India, where the language of 'decoloniality' has instead been co-opted by some on the Hindu far right, and repurposed towards supremacist ends – including providing justification for the targeting of non-Hindu minorities.

6 Utsa Patnaik has revived an earlier anti-colonial, Indian nationalist strand of economics concerned with accounting for the 'drain' of wealth from colonized India, previously associated with R. C. Dutt and Dadabhai Naoroji – an economist and also Britain's first Indian MP. Patnaik and her predecessors frequently use the term 'loot' to describe the drain of wealth from India to Britain. Though now widely used, this term's history also lies in colonized India. Loot comes to English from the Hindi *lut*, but was originally used by British colonizers and Anglo-Indians to denigrate the actions of Indian soldiers rising up during the Sepoy Rebellion in 1857. It was subsequently turned against the colonizers by nationalist economists, but use of 'loot' to denigrate unruly racialized protestors continues today on both sides of the Atlantic.

7 Brazil, Russia, India, China and South Africa. Goldman Sachs' Jim O'Neill – now Lord O'Neill – created the acronym 'BRICs' (with a small 's') in 2001 in an attempt to break the distinction between developed and developing nations. His focus was on investment opportunities arising from the export of Brazilian and Russian raw materials to Indian and Chinese manufacturers, who then sold to US and European consumers. South Africa later joined the BRICS as a formal political grouping who have at times sought to break away from the Bretton Woods system (the World Bank and International Monetary Fund), setting up the 'New Development Bank' in 2017 as a possible rival to the World Bank. While sometimes claiming to speak for 'the Global South', the BRICS often operate – especially, for instance, in African mining investments – as 'sub-imperialists' if not imperialists. The work of Ana Garcia, Vijay Prashad and Patrick Bond is particularly helpful in getting to grips with 'the rise of the BRICS'.

8 Benin, Burkina Faso, Ivory Coast, Guinea-Bissau, Mail, Niger, Senegal and Togo (UEMOA group); and Cameroon, Gabon, Chad, Equatorial Guinea, Central African Republic and Republic of Congo (the CEMAC group).

9 https://tracesofnitrate.org/

10 Kish focuses on the image of a child in blue from the cover of the HarperCollins edition of Novogratz's book, since it resonates with her story of finding 'her' blue sweater in Rwanda. In the PenguinRandomHouse edition, the cover photo by Susan Meiselas/Magnum is of 'a Tanzanian girl stand[ing] in her doorway behind a curtain made from an insecticide treated bednet manufactured by an investee of the Acumen Fund', and so is as much an advert for the Acumen fund as it is a representation of 'connectedness' that might give rise to personal humanitarian-entrepreneurial obligations.

11 This approach overlaps somewhat with what Ralph and Singhal (2019: 866) – who are somewhat sceptical of the vagueness of racial capitalism scholarship – term the 'forensics of capital', which allows us to consider 'how, in every society and throughout history, people establish institutional protocols for determining ... which forms of difference are salient and how they shape access to capital and to political possibilities'.

Part I

Blowouts

Oil, notes David McDermott Hughes, is 'most dangerous when it behaves ordinarily and when people treat it as ordinary ... Only the abnormal event – the spill – brings a black goo into view and into contact with human flesh' (McDermott Hughes 2017: 2–7). In this part, Tracy Lassiter (Chapter 2) and Imre Szeman (Chapter 1) take as their starting point the banality of oil infrastructure in settler-colonial landscapes. Lassiter's focus in *Boom!* is an 1859 image of Drake's Well in Titusville, Pennsylvania. While Drake's Well was not particularly productive (the oldest continuously productive oil well was drilled in 1866 in Trinidad), the gushing forth of oil on the eve of Drake's investors deciding that they would pull out of his speculative effort to commercially harvest 'Seneca oil' has profoundly shaped the colonial global economy. The enormous wealth of the Rockefellers was built by selling kerosene for heating and lighting in the 1870s, but the appearance of the internal combustion engine prompted a global search for oil. The imperial practice of mapping unruly territories so that they could be ruled, and their riches extracted, was now applied to the subsurface, as soon-to-be oil giants sought to build infrastructure that could profitably extract oil with a range of chemical and physical properties from a variety of territories under imperial control (Shafiee 2018).

For all the work that goes into mapping territory, categorizing the qualities and properties of different types of oil and folding considerations of profitability into drill, derrick and pipeline design, most of us experience oil infrastructure 'in the background'. Often you may find yourself engaging with such extractive infrastructure through an *aesthetic* mode. This is not to say that oil infrastructure is 'art', but that infrastructures 'produce the ambient conditions of everyday life: our sense of temperature, speed, florescence, and the ideas we have associated with these conditions' (Larkin 2013: 336). If you've ever lived near an oil rig or a refinery, how does it make you feel when you walk or drive past it? How does the air smell? What do cinematic images of oil infrastructure conjure up for you? Does oil infrastructure make you feel close to a kind of unnervingly fast, loud and bright 'modernity'? Or do you feel yourself living in the shadow of a poorly maintained, soon-to-be relic of a foolhardy fossil fuel dependency? It is the sheer banality of oil infrastructure in Alberta's landscape that Imre Szeman (Chapter 1) takes as the focus in 'Pumpjacks, playgrounds and cheap lives'. It is not only the banality of an oil derrick outside a McDonald's in Alberta, but the sense of playfulness and loyalty to a regional oil industry that Szeman uses as his jumping-off point for exploring the relationship between cheap food, cheap oil and cheap lives.

A pumpjack near a McDonald's playground domesticates the oil industry, makes it an unthreatening part of the landscape, and of *family* life and household reproduction. The image of Drake's Well – copies of which can be purchased from the Drake's Well Museum and Park – functions as a kind of heritage artefact, valuable because of its 'pastness' (Kirshenblatt-Gimblett 1995), which also removes any sense of threat, immediacy or extractive violence from a cosy history of oil in the American landscape. Yet the setting for both Lassiter (Chapter 2) and Szeman (Chapter 1) is stolen land: the settler colonies of Canada and the US. Lassiter draws a line from Drake's Well to contemporary First Nations' struggles against violent extraction and pipeline construction on Native lands. Idle No More was founded in 2012 by three Indigenous women (Jessica Gordon, Sylvia McAdam and Nina Wilson) and Sheelah McLean to protest the attack by Stephen Harper's Conservative government on Canadian environmental protections, and violations of Indigenous land and treaty rights. Indigenous women have also been at the centre of the caretaking of land, water and community as part of #NoDAPL protests against the Dakota Access Pipeline at Standing Rock Sioux Reservation (TallBear 2019).

Indigenous organization against extraction, pipeline construction and treaty violation is rooted in an ethical framework of solidarity with 'other-than-human relations' (TallBear 2019: 17). When environmental review processes are undertaken, for example in relation to Shell's expansion into Alberta's tar sands on Athabasca Chipewyan territory, relations with other-than-human relations are forcibly reduced to measures of the 'use value' available from hunting, fishing and access to territory. As Zalik (2015) shows, Shell was able to successfully argue to the Canadian state that accepting Athabasca Chipewyan demands to protect the Muskeg river would have 'sterilized' oil resources by rendering them unrecoverable. Visual representations of the ease with which oil can be 'recovered' (or why environmental and other protections might impede this 'recovery') have been developed by the American Petroleum Institute since the 1920s. These representations rely upon the language of 'proving up' oil (rather than extracting it); doing surveys to increase the probability that there is oil present, and altering financial agreements and commitments to make it financially feasible to 'recover' the oil. This language of 'proving up' is in fact borrowed from the homesteading legislation which governed the settler colonization of America's frontier: white men and their wives could claim land as their own by 'proving it up' (Hughes 2017: 80). The very ideology of settler colonialism is hardwired into the technical language of oil extraction.

In 'Spillcam', Alysse Kushinski (Chapter 3) moves to consider not the aesthetics of infrastructure's 'background' presence but the aesthetics of *transparency*. BP's *Deepwater Horizon* spill, and the attempts to cap it, was livestreamed in real time. Here we have the spill that brings oil into view, brings black goo into contact with human and other-than-human bodies. Kushinski shows, however, that oil infrastructure can be just as dangerous when its volatile, leaky nature is made transparent. Rather than just revealing the ecological destruction and risky subcontracting arrangements through which oil extraction proceeds, Kushinski argues that making the *spill* visible in fact gave BP an opportunity to make the resealing of the well, and the return to 'business as usual', even more salient in viewers' minds. This 'aesthetic of accountability' draws upon our familiarity with disaster footage, and the experience of relief and comfort that can be derived from feeling like we have overseen a process of repair and recovery. Live-stream over, and oil infrastructure can blend back into the background of settler-colonial landscapes. Unless, perhaps, we learn to use our familiarity with the aesthetics of oil, finance and empire to cultivate scepticism and mobilize against Big Oil's self-representation.

Works cited

Kirshenblatt-Gimblett, B. (1995) 'Theorizing heritage'. *Ethnomusicology* 39(3): 367–380.

Larkin, B. (2013) 'The politics and poetics of infrastructure'. *Annual Review of Anthropology* 42: 327–343.

McDermott Hughes, D. (2017) *Energy without Conscience: Oil, Climate Change and Complicity.* Durham, NC: Duke University Press.

Shafiee, K. (2018) *Machineries of Oil: An Infrastructural History of BP in Iran.* Cambridge, MA: MIT Press.

TallBear, K. (2019) 'Badass Indigenous women caretake relations: #Standingrock, #IdleNoMore, #Black lives matter'. In N. Estes and J. Dhillon (eds), *Standing with Standing Rock: Voices from the #NoDAPL movement.* Minneapolis: University of Minnesota Press, pp. 13–18.

Zalik, A. (2015) 'Resource sterilization: Reserve replacement, financial risk, and environmental review in Canada's tar sands'. *Environment and Planning A* 47: 2446–2464.

1

Pumpjacks, playgrounds and cheap lives

Imre Szeman

This was one of the first pictures I took when I moved to Edmonton, Alberta, Canada. An oil pumpjack, erected on the edge of a McDonald's parking lot, is front and centre. Visible just behind the jack are the colourful letters designating the restaurant's Playspace, while off to the left is the globally recognizable double arch of the fast food empire's sign. In Alberta, where I grew up, the pumpjack is not an unfamiliar sight. Indeed, in my three-hour drive up from Calgary to Edmonton during the move, I passed a number of them, silently bobbing up and down in fields just off the side of the road, patiently carrying out their assigned task of pulling oil out of the ground. In Alberta, oil matters. The province produces 80% of Canada's fossil fuel output, even though it has only 11.6% of its total population; and since oil represents 7% of the country's GDP (not including any support services), it makes sense that pumpjacks would be a ubiquitous feature of the landscape. But this was the first time I had seen a fake pump jack, and the first time, too, that I had seen anything like it near the golden arches.

McDonald's is more than a fast food restaurant. It is *the* fast food restaurant – not just an example of the process of global consumer standardization, but one of the institutions that led the way in making this happen. There are now more than 37,000 McDonald's locations in 120 countries around the world. As it has spread across the planet, the company has been careful to adapt to the religious and dietary differences among its clientele: in India, for example, you cannot buy a beef Big Mac, but you can get a McSpicy Paneer.

The McDonald's in Edmonton was the first that I had come across that included some sign of local industry on its property. Although

Figure 1.1 *Pumpin'!* A model pumpjack operates in the playground of a McDonald's near Edmonton, Alberta.

New Mexico is the third-largest crude oil producer in the United States, the McD's restaurants in Sante Fe resemble nearby adobe buildings rather than oilfields. So why a pumpjack here in Edmonton? And why this fake approximation of the real thing – a child's version of the complex mechanical apparatus found on oil fields around the world?

There are things that this photo cannot say on its own. This pumpjack *moves*, up and down, slowly and patiently pretending to carry out the work that it has to do, and with a speed approximating the actions of the real thing. This McDonald's is not hidden away, but is located at the corner of two major arteries, one running across the city and the other into and out of it. Thousands of commuters use both daily, as do visitors rushing from the airport into the core of the city. In an otherwise drab and ugly part of Edmonton (though there are many such parts) made up of little more than chain stores and light industrial parks, the pumpjack stands out, a strange sentinel. Its very existence seems to insist on its importance and necessity. Even so, its presence at McDonald's domesticates it, making it an object safe for everyday life, a landmark to use to mark one's progress through the day. The aesthetic and political reality of most of the extractive activity being undertaken in Alberta involves nothing like the calm and safety depicted by this bobbing pumpjack. Instead, we would find extractive firms seeking to circumvent the resistance of First Nations to the expansion of the 'unconventional', landscape-scarring extraction of fossil fuels from the Alberta tar sands.

What the photo also cannot say is that Alberta is a province that has determinately tied its identity to oil. The continued life of oil extraction has come to be viewed by many in the province as an economic necessity, even if it exposes it to the vagaries of oil prices and overstates the actual number of jobs in the industry. The place of oil in the broad cultural imaginary, developed by successive Conservative governments in thrall to the oil industry, has played a crucial role in shaping a provincial populism designed to keep far-right Conservatives in power. In Canada, the introduction of any kind of energy transition has been limited by the need for federal parties of all stripes to massage the bruises which fossil fuel-producing provinces – which include British Columbia and Saskatchewan alongside Alberta – believe other parts of the country have inflicted on them. The victory of federal parties depends on votes from these Western provinces, which make up a quarter of the total number of seats in the country.

The presence of the pumpjack at this McDonald's is a symbol of the complex politics that troubles and unnerves environmental and political change. Its predictable place in the Alberta landscape and its strangely comforting presence next to a child's playground acts as a weight on the present, making it very difficult to imagine any real movement of the province and the nation into the future. To take just one example: Canada's commitment to the 2015 Paris Agreement was to limit greenhouse gas production to 511 megatonnes of CO_2 by 2030. As of January 2020, best-case estimates by the federal government were that Canadian emissions would be 673 megatonnes of CO_2 – more that 30% over its target. Notwithstanding an 8% drop in emissions during the COVID-19 pandemic in 2020, the energy intensity[1] of Canada's economy has been decreasing at a lower rate than that of the other twenty-nine member countries of the International Energy Agency. The McDonald's pumpjack has more to do with this failure that one might ever imagine.

A history of McDonald's in seven cheap things

In *A History of the World in Seven Cheap Things* (2018), Raj Patel and Jason Moore argue that the current global economy runs on cheap things. One might think that cheap things do not matter much, except perhaps to line the shelves of the dollar stores that have proliferated all over the planet. In reality, however, understanding just what cheap things are and what they represent is the way to make sense of the global system of extraction, exploitation and profit, all of which is driven by the need to *make* things cheap for the operations of capitalism. Patel and Moore boil this process down to seven cheap things: nature, money, work, care, food, energy and lives.

All seven things, and the chains of power that link them, can be seen in this image of a faux pumpjack plopped down on the lawn of a McDonald's in Edmonton.

Nature: The manicured grass and the plotted and planned bushes, trees and plants around the restaurant are as artificial as the pumpjack. The delicate prairie landscape that used to exist here, south of the North Saskatchewan River, is long gone and forgotten. In its place: lawn grass, the most widespread crop in North America after maize and wheat. It has little real use, except to soften the harshness of the concrete commercial landscape a little bit.

While pumpjacks are the quintessential symbol of oil extraction, they do not really capture how oil is extracted from nature in Northern Alberta. Just a few hours north, bitumen in the Athabasca tar sands is accessed by surface mining, a process of extraction that leaves vast scars on the surface of the planet, easily visible from satellites, which are impossible to truly 'recover', i.e., to return to the boreal forest that once graced the landscape. Equally hard to deal with are the toxic tailings ponds left behind. These are lakes made up of the water used in the extraction process – good for little more than bringing about the deaths of migratory birds during pauses in their long flight north.

By comparison to these brutal, ugly images of extraction, pump-jacks offer a calm, controlled and domesticated view of oil extraction.

The pumpjack in the photo minimizes worries about the true impact of oil on nature by reducing the footprint of extraction to the work of a small, patient device. It is meant to be as inoffensive and harmless as grasshoppers, which is what pumpjacks are colloquially called.

Money: Fast food is *cheap.* That's the central attraction, and it sometimes results in the disruption of local agro-food systems as Samaniego and Mantz (Chapter 20) discuss. But the purchase of a lot of cheap food adds up. Even in what was an off year, in 2017 McDonald's made $5.2 billion profit on sales of $22.8 billion (all figures in US dollars). In January 2022, the market capitalization of McDonald's was up to $189.15 billion. Its annual revenue was $19.2 billion in 2020, greater than the GDP of more than ninety countries, including Georgia, the West Bank and Gaza, or Jamaica in the same year.[2] Cheap money has helped McDonald's to expand globally. Since 1986, the financial magazine *The Economist* has published a 'Big Mac Index' to measure purchasing power parity. The scale of McDonald's operations means that comparing Big Mac prices around the world offers a better sense of currency valuation than the figures offered by big banks.

The pumpjack speaks to a very different economy. The extraction of oil and gas has generated a staggering amount of wealth over the past century and a half. At the present time, the totality of oil and gas firms listed on stock exchanges around the world are worth more than $4.5 trillion dollars. We like to think that we are living in an age defined by tech companies like Apple and Google. Yet we continue to generate much of the money in the world by ripping into rock and soil, and drilling deep into the bottom of the ocean. In the popular imagination, tech companies are often imagined as the clean alternative to extractive economies – the shiny future which arises out of a dirty industrial past. But tech companies need energy too, to run their servers and to provide their services. Collectively, the information technology (IT) industry trails only five countries in total energy use. Much of this energy is now from renewables, but not all of it. And tech needs plastics for its products and processors, which are shaped out of petrocarbons. There is yet another link between clean IT and dirty oil. Amazon, Google and Microsoft have developed artificial intelligence (AI) tools to help the oil industry develop better extraction methods (the bad public relations led Google in May 2020 to pledge to stop this practice). The planetary costs of tech, big data and AI are immense (Crawford 2021).

Work: With 1.7 million employees, McDonald's is the world's second-largest (private) employer. It is also one of the largest employers of minimum-wage workers. The work they are tasked with is tedious and routine, and dangerous too, due to workplace injuries and robberies. As with other fast food companies, the company's profit depends on the suppression of workers' wages. A job at McD's is one sure way to puncture the deluded hopes and fantasies that have long shaped rags-to-riches stories.

One social fantasy of living in an oil-rich province like Alberta is that everyone can become wealthy, just by putting in a few years of hard work out in the field. The pumpjack is a sign and symbol of what might still be possible for workers to achieve through their labour. And it *is* true that the average salary in Edmonton is higher than in the rest of Canada, even if these high average salaries disguise high numbers of 'unskilled temporary foreign workers' on lower salaries. What is also true is that this makes everything else more expensive, especially housing. Despite the oil wealth in the province, McDonald's employees still make minimum wage, and many find it impossible to live on what they earn.

The idea that these workers should earn more is anathema to many. One of the first acts of the newly elected Conservative government in Alberta in 2019 was to reduce the minimum wage for workers under eighteen, from $15 per hour to $13 per hour. 'This is still a very generous wage,' Premier Jason Kenney told a news conference. '$13 an hour is a lot more than $0.'

Labour at McDonald's is cheap, but evidently not cheap enough for the company and its shareholders. McDonald's has been one of the service industry firms that have most aggressively experimented with automation. Every dollar that is not spent on workers is more money for shareholders. Machines also come with an added benefit: they cannot unionize, as some of McDonald's workers have attempted to do.

As for work in the oil field: like fast food work, much of it is tedious and routine, and also dangerous. The hours are long; and the work demands that labourers live away from home for weeks and months at a time. In Fort McMurray, the city at the heart of the Alberta tar sands, the high cost of housing and everything else can quickly eat up the extra dollars that workers see on their pay cheques.

Care: McDonald's cares for its workers. Or, at least, it wants them to believe it does. To emphasize the importance of education over work, it has established a scholarship system for its youth employees (though its own figures suggest that it has given out only 160 per year for the past twenty-five years – a tiny number for such a large employer). Like other large employers, it has established all manner of mechanisms and processes to keep workers happy and manage behaviour, for the good of all involved (or so it believes). For instance, each of its locations names 'Employees of the Month' to reward hard work and motivation.

There is an entire network of care that takes places at a typical McDonald's. The Playspace that can be found at most McD's is designed to attract pre-teens, who cannot wait to slip down its slides and jump around in its ball pits. It attracts tired parents and caregivers too, who come to feed their kids on the cheap, while taking a well-deserved mental break from the constant care they require. The care of children is disproportionately taken on by women, and the women who end up at McDonald's represent socio-economic inequities tied to class and ethnicity. The more than one billion Happy Meals sold per year are the surest evidence of cheap Playspace care to which all too many parents need to turn.

The pumpjack, too, is a signal of care. It tells the commuters driving by that this restaurant cares about the place where it is located. McDonald's has identified itself with the most important industry in Edmonton. It is on the right side, it shouts out: the side of the extraction industries, the side of the people who, in this city and in this province, have been told repeatedly over decades to link their lives and livelihoods with these industries.

Food: Is there anything that needs to be said about cheap food and McDonald's that is not already obvious? Despite the tales now told by the company of good food sourced responsibly, the golden arches signal factory farming done on a massive scale, which generates cheap food offered on the cheap to any and all who want it. Physicians and nutritionists worry about fast food and the decline of healthy eating. The calorie counts now listed by law in some polities on the illuminated menu boards of fast food restaurants tell us that a single meal can add up to more calories than most of us need to eat over a whole day. (It is worth noting that the Alberta government has not enacted such a law.)

Cheap food is made possible by the presence of oil. Factory farming and food transport via shipping and trucking was built on the back of stuff that pumpjacks make sure to keep bringing to the surface of the earth. And cheap food wouldn't be possible without fossil-fuelled fertilizers, which slowly kill the life of soil by dragging every possible calorie out of it.

Energy: It is not love that makes the world go around, but cheap energy. Nothing works without the dirty liquids dragged out of the earth by the pumpjack, tilting slowly up and down. Fast food restaurants could not be supplied and we certainly could not drive around in our cars without oil. The automobile is indelibly linked to McDonald's and its fast food kin: on its original trademark application, McDonald's was described as offering 'drive-in restaurant services'. The link between oil fields and fast food is deep, though it can be hard to grasp this. The pumpjack at the McDonald's in my picture is perhaps the unconscious of energy culture come to life. The golden arches can shine only because of the dark energy of fossil fuels; and the money spent here, in Edmonton, is no doubt somehow, and at some point, connected to the labour of those stripping away the soil to get at the oil underneath it.

Cheap lives: everyday settler colonialism

There is one last cheap thing to which this photo points that I haven't yet discussed: *lives*. Cheap life abounds here – the cheapness of lives defined by cheap nature, money, work, care, food and energy. Life is cheap in fossil-fuelled modernity, which drains the energy of workers' bodies and the will of consumers. In Alberta, as in so many other polities, the dynamics of cheap life today obscure the brute history of cheap life. Pumpjacks can generate wealth only because of a settler-colonial logic premised on the disposability of Indigenous bodies. The entanglement of extractive capitalism and brutal settler colonial logics is revisited by Comyn (Chapter 4), Cordes (Chapter 5) and Ly (Chapter 12) in this volume.

There is something even more important about the life captured by this photo. In many respects, this is an utterly banal photo about

– well, what else might we call it? – *everyday life*. A quirky object spotted next to a McDonald's – hilarious! A quick pic to show one's friends about the new place that one has moved to, which captures in a flash its peculiarities!

But to see it like this would be to miss this photo's force and meaning. It *is* about the everyday. It is here, in this everyday space, a fast food restaurant next to a commuter road, like so many other burger joints alongside similar strips in all too many parts of the world, where tales of cheap life are played out. It is in spaces like this one where cheap life becomes normal life, something drained of history and very hard to imagine differently, and so seemingly impossible to do anything about. It is where the desire of a small child for the toy that comes in a kid's meal comes into contact with the forces of globalization, neoliberalism, colonialism, extraction, financialization and debt. The stubborn insistence of the legitimacy of the everyday life captured in this photo, despite the violence of its varied cheapness, constitutes perhaps the biggest challenge in doing something to change it.

I arrived in Edmonton in the summer of 2009, in the wake of the financial crash that messed up lives everywhere. Some economists have argued that it was the triple-digit price of oil – the highest price of oil ever recorded – that pushed things over the edge. It was the last straw, making it impossible for consumers to manage already high living costs and heavy household debt. For fast food purveyors, the financial crash turned out to be as golden as the ubiquitous arches. When budgets are tight, where else can one go to get cheap food, especially when out and about in an automobile? The oil culture named by the conjunction of McDonald's and its plastic pumpjack robs us of any sense of other possibilities, of lives and things whose very existence need not be empty, meaningless and cheap.

Further resources

Burtynsky, E. (2003–10), *Oil* [photographic series]. www.edwardburtynsky.com/projects/photographs/oil (accessed 2 September 2022).

Food Inc. (2008) Directed by Robert Kenner [Documentary]. https://watchdocumentaries.com/food-inc/ (accessed 2 September 2022).

H2 Oil (2008) Directed by Shannon Walsh [Documentary]. www.youtube.com/watch?v=IZGYQdIiJSM (accessed 2 September 2022).
Super Size Me (2004) Directed by Morgan Spurlock [Documentary]. www.youtube.com/watch?v=S9__23-zjh (accessed 2 September 2022).

Works cited

Crawford, K. (2021) *Atlas of AI: Power, Politics and the Planetary Costs of Artificial Intelligence*. New Haven, CT: Yale University Press.
Patel, R. and Moore, J. (2017) *A History of the World in Seven Cheap Things*. Oakland: University of California Press.

Notes

1 Energy intensity is a measure of the ratio of energy consumption (coal, oil, gas, nuclear and renewables) to economic growth (GDP). More efficient energy production and use – as well as technological change and changing use patterns – can reduce the energy intensity measure for a given national economy. Because energy intensity measures may include renewables, they can change at different rates to measures of the CO_2 intensity of electricity generation.

2 While comparisons between market capitalization and GDP are often made in economic journalism and academic writing, and such comparisons are rhetorically powerful, the two measures are not *strictly* comparable. Market capitalization is a snapshot measure of the *present* value of a corporation's shares (with that value being based on future earning potential). GDP is a measure of the economic 'output' in a country, or the monetary value of all economic activity across a year. A more precise comparison may therefore be between GDP and the annual *revenues* earned by a given corporation.

2

'Boom!'

Tracy Lassiter

It's an innocuous enough image: two men standing before a wooden structure with another group of (white) men in the background. The two men in the foreground, Peter Wilson and Edwin Drake, in fact stand before the first oil well, drilled on 27 August 1859 in present-day Titusville, Pennsylvania. In the century and a half since this well was drilled, the oil industry has turned into a global economic juggernaut, causing rampant worldwide political, economic and racial exploitation – but it almost didn't happen. The oil industry's history, and what it has become, is vastly complicated. It is an economic boon for some people, an exploitative totality for others. Leaders worldwide today consider warnings regarding climate change, social activism related to equity, the costs of war and other socio-political concerns; they should place a critical lens on resource extraction, namely the oil industry, for its central position in these issues.

Throughout history, different civilizations – ancient Mesopotamia and China, the European Middle Ages, the indigenous peoples in North America – used oil that bubbled from rocks for various purposes: as medicine, in warfare, for fire. But in Pennsylvania in the 1850s, this resource became a commodity. Originally, European settlers didn't think much of this 'rock oil' until a Seneca leader, namely Chief Red Jacket, told them of its reputed medicinal value. Later, the residents considered petroleum and its by-products (such as the waxy substance that coated their salt-well drilling equipment) to be an impediment. But, in time, some of them capitalized on those by-products and on petroleum's reputation as a medicine. In the 1850s, a druggist named Samuel Kier was one of the more infamous

Figure 2.1 Edwin L. Drake, right, stands with friend Peter Wilson of Titusville, Pennsylvania, at the drilling site – but not the original derrick – of America's first commercial oil well of 1859 (Mather 1861).

entrepreneurs to bottle 'rock oil'. He called it 'Kier's Medicinal Petroleum' and sold it as a cure for maladies ranging from toothaches to rheumatism, stomach upset, even deafness. Of course, his panacea didn't deliver the remedies to desperate customers, and soon 'Seneca oil' became known as 'snake oil', or what we call a quack remedy (Yergin 2008: 4; Miller 2008 17–18). This inauspicious start to oil's history is metaphoric; once it was commodified, falsely advertised and widely distributed, its demerits became all too obvious.

Petroleum's value, though, stemmed not from its medicinal uses but from its energy value. Entrepreneurs like Kier and, later, George Bissell realized petroleum's potential as an illuminant. Bissell and a consortium of New York-based investors commissioned Professor Benjamin Silliman to study petroleum's potential uses in lighting and as an industrial lubricant; when Silliman's report confirmed oil's commercial viability, the results became 'nothing less than a turning point in the establishment of the petroleum business' (Yergin 2008: 6). From there, Bissell and his cohort needed to know whether oil was in an abundant-enough supply to make larger-scale drilling a worthwhile undertaking. They hired Edwin Drake to look for oil in Pennsylvania. At first Drake attempted to dig wells by hand, but after about a year of fruitless searching using this method, Drake hired a blacksmith by the name of William Smith to make the tools and other equipment they would need to build a salt-well-style derrick and drill. They established an operating drill in the spring of 1859, but by early August it hadn't produced any oil. The investors felt the search was taking too long; their funds were quickly running out. By August, even Drake's personal bank account was nearly empty. As noted, the photograph above shows Peter Wilson and Edwin Drake; it's significant because Wilson loaned Drake money, gambling that his cash infusion would pay off. Meanwhile, the investors sent a letter to Drake telling him to halt his enterprise; their money was depleted. On Friday 26 August Drake and Smith left the pump working on a hole they had dug, and on Saturday, Smith saw oil bubbling from the pipe. He and his sons stored the oil in tubs, basins and barrels, guarding it until Drake returned that Monday. Drake used a hand pump to help them collect the surging oil. As Fate would have it, that same day he received the New York investors' letter, enclosing his 'final' payment and telling him to quit the venture (Yergin 2008: 11).

As these events demonstrate, the oil industry almost didn't happen; the zero-hour oil discovery from the Drake Well seems like a Hollywood movie script. Perhaps petroleum would have become the global commodity it is today anyway, discovered by a different driller at a different time. Nonetheless, what had at first been called 'Drake's Folly' quickly turned into a 'boom', a sound that echoes into today's energy discussions. 'Boom' is onomatopoeic, referring to the sound of a gusher when drillers strike a deposit; thereafter, it describes the flush of activity occurring upon an oil strike. The 1859 'boom' meant an influx of people moving to the Titusville area, all to capitalize somehow on oil. Boom towns like Titusville needed surveyors, drillers, barrel-makers, and teamsters to haul the oil to trains; they needed housing, food and other supplies. Soon, other boom towns like Pithole and Oil City (formerly known as 'Corn Planter' for another Seneca chief) burgeoned in Pennsylvania, practically overnight. The problem with a boom cycle, though, is that it's later followed by a 'bust'; once a resource – like coal, like oil – is depleted from a region, the town empties, leaving economic loss, environmental damage and other devastation in its wake.

The industry begins

The Drake Well kicked off what over time became a global search for oil, a geopolitical and economic phenomenon so vast that it inspired a neologism, petrocapitalism, for 'a form of capital accumulation founded on the extraction, distribution, and consumption of petroleum' (oxfordreference.com). With the booming oil towns in Pennsylvania, a host of other industries, such as refineries, subsequently arose. One of the most famous names in this regard was John D. Rockefeller, who became notable – and notorious – as the first oil 'baron' through his Standard Oil Company. Rockefeller's father, William, was infamously known as 'Devil Bill' for his reputation as a schemer and 'flim-flam man'; like Kier, he was a 'snake-oil' salesman who tried to profit from petroleum's curative reputation (Juhasz 2008: 25). While John Rockefeller in some respects was more reputable than his father, in other ways he wasn't. He established Standard Oil initially as a refinery, but over time he expanded his company 'vertically', meaning that he controlled every aspect of the oil production, refining and selling process, from buying timberland so that Standard could build its own barrels to buying railroad tank cars, warehouses and boats. It became such an enormous company that it could negotiate discounts on railway freight charges and buy smaller, competing refiners and producers. It even became a controlling interest in the pipelines throughout Pennsylvania's Oil Region. A famous journalist at the time, Ida Tarbell, grew up in the Oil Region and her family members worked in the industry; nonetheless, the exposés she and Henry Demarest Lloyd wrote for the Chicago *Tribune* brought to light Standard's monopolistic control and shady dealings to maintain its dominance. Antitrust authorities began investigating Standard Oil, and in 1911 the Supreme Court ordered Standard Oil to dissolve. It was divided into seven different companies established in different regions around the US, at last bringing 'competition back into the transportation, refining, and marketing of oil' (Yergin 2008: 94).

These companies, plus the remaining smaller producers, soon had a great deal of competition as other countries began discovering their own deposits. Oil fields in Baku, Russia, in Persia (modern-day Iran) and other locations started to produce and affect the nascent global oil market. Furthermore, by the early twentieth century, tensions between Germany and England had increased, namely around who had a superior navy. Winston Churchill, then First Lord of the Admiralty for the Royal Navy, appointed a committee to look into converting Britain's naval ships to burn oil instead of coal. Churchill was concerned about whether it was wise to do so. He had the same question that Drake's investors had asked about sixty years earlier: was there a large enough worldwide supply of oil to fuel the ships? If so, Churchill noted, Britain would have the better ships, and with better ships came 'better crews, higher economies, more intense forms of war power' (Yergin 2008: 140). After his investigations revealed that vast deposits existed, namely in the Middle East, Churchill successfully argued before Parliament that the Royal Navy should commission with the Anglo-Persian Oil company; doing so, he argued, would mean that Britain would not have to rely on any institution beyond the government for its fuel. The House of Commons voted to commission with Anglo-Persian; good timing, as eleven days later the First World War began.

Repercussions

This short account oversimplifies a complex system and past, which is detailed at length in places such as Daniel Yergin's book, *The Prize*. Nonetheless, even this short summation reveals what we should learn from history in order to create a more equitable and climate-friendly future.

Today, oil is a dominant force in the global economy. The consortium of Middle Eastern oil companies known as OPEC (Organization of Petroleum Exporting Countries) alone were estimated to have earned $595 billion in 2019 (EIA 2021). Reliable sources like the US government's Energy Information Administration or the international collaborative Worldometer reveal that every continent has some oil reserves. Venezuela, Saudi Arabia and Canada have the world's largest reserves. A country's oil reserves translate into political power. As energy author Yergin says, after the Saudi Arabian oil embargoes occurring in 1967 and 1973, 'Petroleum had become the province of presidents and premiers, of foreign and finance and energy ministers, of congressmen and parliamentarians, of regulators and "czars", of activists and pundits ...' (Yergin 2008: 595).

Indeed, since Churchill successfully argued for working with a British-based oil company so that Britain wouldn't be reliant on outsiders for its fuel supply, the rhetorics of 'national security' and oil drilling have become intertwined. Today in the US, it appears in calls to 'Drill, baby, drill' and it serves as justification for ongoing wars, such as its Iraq war. As oil industry author Antonia Juhasz notes, 'Oil is also about more than oil company profits. Control over the world's oil is an unparalleled source of regional and global hegemony' (Juhasz 2008: 325). Obtaining and maintaining that power is an impetus for many governments' political and militaristic actions. One agency reports that 'between one-quarter and one-half of all interstate wars since 1973 have been linked to oil, and oil-producing countries are 50% more likely to have civil war' (Oil Change International n.d.).

Yet, over time it has become more difficult for companies to access oil deposits. While many deposits remain, they are located deeper in the ground and farther below the sea. Companies must drill in hitherto nearly inaccessible areas, bringing great risk to employees, residents and ecosystems. For example, in 2010, BP's offshore *Deepwater Horizon* drilling platform experienced a massive blowout and leak. The initial explosion – a massive boom – killed eleven platform workers and subsequently released millions of gallons of oil into the Gulf of Mexico. The *Deepwater Horizon* blowout, and the political consequences of livestreaming various attempts to cap the well, are the focus of Kushinski (Chapter 3). It took roughly two and half months for BP and subcontractors Transocean Ltd. and Halliburton to cap the well. A subsequent US governmental investigation discovered that the profit-seeking companies had ignored warning signs of the wellhead blowout. The spill caused lasting damage to the Gulf of Mexico's wildlife and ecosystem and wiped out the livelihoods of fishermen and other residents who relied upon the waterway. Despite this devastation and loss of human life, one year after, BP posted first-quarter earnings of $5.48 *billion*. Worse, Transocean Ltd. awarded its top executives with bonuses for attaining the 'best year in safety performance in [the] company's history' (Robertson 2011: B1).

The spills, leaking pipes, gas flaring, untreated waste and runoff, and many other industry-related hazards depicted in fictional texts often go unresolved in real life, leaving residents to face environmental and health-related consequences, such as respiratory illnesses.

These risks will increase as countries permit farther and deeper searches for the oil that will allow them political influence, national security, economic power or all three. Yet pushback on Big Oil's influence, incursion and destruction is underway – in fact, it has been for decades. In many cases, the places where oil companies wish to drill for, refine or pipe oil happen to be where historically marginalized populations live. Nigeria is an oil-rich nation, yet it is rife with petro-problems, not the least of which is the roughly 1.5 million tons of oil spilled in the Niger Delta. Abuses have long been documented by its domestic and international agencies. One writer and activist, Ken Saro-Wiwa, was particularly outspoken against Shell Oil's destructive practices in his home area, Ogoniland. Yet members of Nigeria's larger and more dominant tribes, in places of political leadership, allied with Shell. Saro-Wiwa and other members of his activist group, MOSOP, were brought up on false charges, tried in a rigged trial and subsequently found guilty. All members of the 'Ogoni Nine' were hanged in a case that brought international rebuke (Kahn 2009: 7). Even so, pollution, lawlessness, corruption and fighting persist. The historical colonialism that occurred in West Africa exists in Nigeria today as collusion between multinational corporations and local elites (see Dickson et al., Chapter 8 this volume).

In South America, the lawsuit *Aguinda v. Chevron*, depicted in the 2009 *Crude* documentary, describes the nearly thirty years of struggle and legal action taken by the Cofán, Huaorani and other Amazonian tribes against Chevron for the rampant pollution caused by the company (and its predecessor company, Texaco). The destruction caused in the Amazon has been called 'one of the greatest oil-related disasters in history' (Juhasz 2008: 251). However, the case continues today, due to the company's challenges to the $19 billion judgment against it.

In North America, various Indigenous groups likewise have begun acting against drilling and pipeline installation on their lands. As Szeman shows (Chapter 1), oil infrastructure has become a banal, comforting presence in settler-colonial landscapes, even as First Nations and Indigenous people resist the violence of extraction on their lands. In the Arctic, across both the US and Canadian borders, First Nations groups like the Gwich'in are fighting oil developers to keep areas like the Arctic National Wildlife Refuge intact for hunting, fishing and other aspects of their culture. Other activist groups like Canada's Idle No More challenge certain types of resource extraction, particularly those on indigenous peoples' lands, when the extraction won't benefit those peoples. Similarly, various US Native American tribes banded at the Standing Rock Sioux Reservation in North Dakota to fight the Dakota Access Pipeline. One argument against it is that it violates the Fort Laramie Treaty, which was meant to guarantee 'undisturbed use and occupation' of the land for the Sioux. The pipeline still operates, despite lawsuits filed by the tribe; in April 2021, US President Joseph Biden allowed the pipeline to carry oil while the government reviews its environmental impact.

The Drake Well photo depicts an innocuous enough scene, but from that location a vast geopolitical, economic force emerged that impacts worldwide on communities 150 years later. Who could have predicted the profiteering and exploitation that this small Pennsylvania patch would unleash? From the Drake Well we can trace out manifold oil-based legacies. In the chapter by Ferrini (Chapter 13), oil extraction is shown to be entangled with abortive attempts at postcolonial reparation between Italy and Libya. In Schubert's work (Chapter 11), we see how the promise of future oil production gets entangled with Angola's new debts to China. Even Drake didn't know, that August weekend in 1859, that the first well had produced oil. It probably came in quietly, with something that sounded like a gurgle, but which has grown over time into an alert, a warning, a sounding boom.

Further resources

Estes, N. (2019) *Our History Is the Future*. London: Verso.

Juhasz, A. (2008) *The Tyranny of Oil*. New York: HarperCollins.

Miller, D. (2010) *Current Controversies: Oil*. San Diego: Greenhaven Press.

Miller, S. (2008) *Pennsylvania's Oil Heritage: Stories from the Headache Post*. Charleston, SC: History Press.

Yergin, D. (2008) *The Prize*. New York: Free Press.

Works cited

Juhasz, A. (2008) *The Tyranny of Oil*. New York: HarperCollins.

EIA (2021) 'OPEC Revenues Fact Sheet.' US Energy Information Administration. 14 January. www.eia.gov/international/analysis/special-topics/OPEC_Revenues_Fact_Sheet (accessed 30 May 2021).

Kahn, C. (2009) 'Shell settles human rights lawsuit'. *Indiana Gazette*, 9 June, p. 7.

Mather, J. (1861) 'The original Drake Oil well in 1861'. Library of Congress, www.loc.gov/item/2007678590/ (accessed 27 May 2021).

Miller, S. (2008) *Pennsylvania's Oil Heritage: Stories from the Headache Post*. Charleston, SC: History Press.

Oil Change International (n.d.) 'War and militarization.' http://priceofoil.org/thepriceofoil/war-terror/ (accessed 30 May 2021).

Robertson, J. (2011) 'Transocean gives safety bonuses despite deaths'. *Indiana Gazette*, 3 April 2011, p. B1.

Yergin, D. (2008) *The Prize*. New York: Free Press.

3

Spillcam

Alysse Kushinski

On 19 May 2010 the public gained access, via internet live feed, to the sea floor of the Gulf of Mexico. The feed was focused on a site nearly 5,000 feet below the water's surface: at the Macondo Prospect, 66 km off the south-east coast of Louisiana, on the sea floor of Mississippi Canyon Block 252, an oil well was leaking into the Gulf. The image in Figure 3.1 is a still-capture from this feed showing the steady plume of oil that resulted from the explosion of the *Deepwater Horizon* oil rig. On 20 April 2010, just prior to the well's being sealed for later extraction, a methane gas bubble travelled up the drilling column and ignited at the platform. The blowout resulted in a day-long fire and the eventual sinking of the rig. On 24 April 2010 an unencumbered stream of oil, gas and mud was discovered flowing from the well. Nearly five million barrels of oil were released into the Gulf basin until the well was capped, eighty-seven days after the initial event.

Many media forms and media outlets captured the unfolding disaster. News agencies, artists, activists, environmental monitors, as well as government and corporate actors circulated video footage, still images, reports, graphs and measurements documenting what was happening in the Gulf. Moreover, the affected sites and enduring effects of the *Deepwater Horizon* disaster, to this day, continue to be mediated through blockbuster movies, documentary productions, ongoing monitoring and information leaks, amongst a variety of other forms. This reflection focuses on just one of these enduring mediations – Spillcam – and asks how the operations of capital and its imperial entanglements can be glimpsed through this real-time feed, a century and a half after the first still image of an oil well

Figure 3.1 A still from the Spillcam which livestreamed BP's attempt to cap the *Deepwater Horizon* well.

was circulated (see Lassiter, Chapter 2). Whose interests are served by making visible the aftermath of an extractive disaster? Can real-time feeds of extractive operations and their failures produce accountability, or merely shore up 'business as usual'?

Mediating the spill

While news media regularly featured aerial footage of the burning rig, video coverage of the clean-up efforts, images of oil-slicked beaches and maps of spill projections, the public was without images of the leak – at its source on the sea floor – for the first twenty-three days following the disaster. Real-time access to the site resulted from a request made by then US Congressional representative Edward Markey to BP (formerly British Petroleum) following suspicions that the company had severely underestimated the flowrate of the leaking well. By 3 June 2010, BP provided twelve different views of the site, accessible to the public via the US Select Committee on Energy Independence and Global Warming website. Observation via Spillcam's multiple vantage points allowed for new flowrate estimates from government officials, engineers and independent scientists totalling anywhere from 25,000 to upwards of 80,000 barrels per day (bpd), far above the initial 1,000, then 5,000, bpd estimates reported by BP during the first weeks of the spill.

Near the end of 2010 'Spillcam' was announced as one of Global Language Monitor's top words, phrases and names of the year. The wide use of the feed's name across social media, journalism and news coverage also placed 'spill-cam' on the New York Times's list of top words – though Meriam Webster opted for 'austerity' instead, and the American Dialect Society only referenced the events in short-listing 'spillion' and 'spillionaire' for 'most creative' words of 2010. Spillcam's livestream of the leak became a common element of television news chyrons and was eventually featured on more than 3,000 websites receiving several million views over the feed's life.

The *Deepwater Horizon* disaster itself provides a fruitful opportunity to critically engage the forces at work in the creation of capital, commodities and legacies of empire. While Spillcam might appear to offer a means for accountability, I argue that it upholds a notion of responsibility entangled in processes of financialization, risk mitigation, capitalism and exploitation. The livestream of the leaking well gives the impression that BP's responsibility for the disaster in the Gulf is finite and measurable, and thus the damages of the spill are within industry's own ability to reconcile, control and mitigate. The gushing well of oil and gas into the Gulf of Mexico was a material manifestation of violent flows of empire, regardless of how, and if, the spill was ever witnessed – the documentation of the leaking well, and its eventual sealing, did not simply allow us to witness the disaster as it unfolded at the sea floor and alert us to the risks of resource extraction, but it also helped BP to cultivate an aesthetic of accountability.

Extractive economies are speculative economies – they require speculation on geological sites and commodity prices – deploying an arithmetic that operates without regard for social, cultural and environmental risks, or, at best, accounts for these factors by assigning them a cost-value. This speculation of profit potential and risk utilizes financial instruments and other technologies of imagination to propagate an imagined future of worthwhile resource extraction. And while theorists such as Anna Tsing (2000) and Paul Gilbert (2020) have demonstrated the necessity of cultivating these imagined futures for the promotion of exploration-phase extraction projects, mediations of completed and ongoing projects, even when disastrous, can render risk as limited and tolerable. Mediations of catastrophes of capital are just as integral for animating speculative activities (Gilbert 2020). To these ends, I argue that Spillcam is a technology of imagination. In capturing the eventual sealing of the Macondo project well and then eventually going offline, Spillcam allowed the public to envision themselves as overseeing the remediation of the spill, but it also acted as a means for industry to impress on us its ability to mitigate its own risks. Though the opportunities and threats that come along with extractive industries are always already implicated in the long history of colonial logics and resource exploitation, so too are the media that facilitate them – here we must consider how technologies of mediation are utilized as technologies of imagination in the name of capital.

Framing business as usual

Spillcam represents a particular means through which finance capital can be glimpsed. Visual evidence of leaks may provide opportunities to witness dynamics that often elude us – the ecological toll of capitalism, the banality of disaster in late modernity and the unaccountability of private enterprise. Sprung leaks are often indications of poorly functioning systems – they can call into question an entire network of pipelines, flows and currents and are rarely isolated occurrences. And while the live feed of BP's defunct well represents a distinctive moment in imagining the unseen, a literal vantage point that is often invisible to the public, Spillcam also captured and reified the reality of 'business as usual'. The feed scrutinized a single site and a sole endeavour – the execution of a 'top kill' procedure that would secure the oil in reserve.

While the feed allowed for a degree of public scrutiny, it did little to clarify the complex layers of extractive networks. More, it rendered them simple – the risk and threat of extractive capitalism was simply the uncontrollable escape of the commodity from the well. The live feed of the leaking well is, in some sense, antithetical to capturing the enduring effects of exploitation. In spite of this limitation, there is a potential offered through Spillcam for a more radical figuration of accountability. If we look closely, at play in Spillcam is a constellation of actors: natural, technological and political. Through its images, we see the literal entanglement of elements, technologies and a range of actors. Spillcam does not merely capture these dynamics in all of their significance, but it does provide a diagram through which these assemblages can be traced.

While Spillcam allowed the public the opportunity to witness the incredible volume of oil flowing from the Macondo well, it also shored up an overly simple image of accountability. The live feed of the oil geyser enabled several seemingly contradictory narratives. On one hand, Spillcam helped us to visualize the real risk of resource extraction and the impotence of corporate responsibility, but, on the other, it operationalized an aesthetics of accountability that collapses the act of 'making visible' with public-facing corporate responsibility. This is not to suggest that the end of Spillcam's live feed was the end of accountability measures faced by BP – indeed, as of early 2020 the company had paid out more than US$50 billion dollars in settlements and fines for its role in the disaster – but, rather, that Spillcam was, literally, a limited frame of capital's exploitation of the Gulf, and one that suggested a symbolic exchange that concluded with the sealing of the well.

The problem of a 'limited frame' is of course not unique to the operation of Spillcam but, rather, a concern of media more generally. The role of media in the witnessing of events, as well as media's entanglement with notions of evidence, further complicates the power dynamics that underlie certain forms of representation. From the role of aerial photography in the First and Second World Wars, to the framing of the war in Vietnam as the first televised war, media's potential to capture and evidence has long been a fruitful exploration for scholars and journalists as well as for governments, policy makers and legal councils, especially with regard to accountability. Like the decades before, the 2000s marked new capabilities for information and communication technologies – benefiting from expanded network infrastructures throughout the 1990s and 2000s, real-time media and live-feed video were increasingly common by the end of the first decade of the twenty-first century. While closed-circuit television had long allowed for the surveilling of property, employees and the public by specific entities, live feeds hosted online seemingly provided an opportunity for publics to return this gaze. However, the use of video for acts of witnessing requires particular attention to the way concepts such as objectivity, veracity and evidence are cultivated and communicated (Gates 2013).

The aesthetics of accountability

While activism and art practice have developed means for using media to critical ends, media often operate through the same colonial logics that enabled imperial domination, extractive industries and real violences. From mapping and charting to photography and networked technologies, many media share roots in colonial pursuit, warfare and domination. In fact, Spillcam, as a technological assemblage, was born as a device of extraction. Spillcam was not a single 'cam' but, rather, the feed that shared the leak to the public. The components that captured the images of the well, the plume of oil and the many attempts to cap it were the figurative eyes of a series of remotely operated underwater vehicles (ROVs). While the livefeed of the ROVs' cameras allowed for the government, the scientific community and the public to observe the status of the well, these technological capabilities were also those that facilitated the site to be found, the placement of extractive equipment and the drilling of the well in the first place. Moreover, it is the same technology utilized in surveillance, target location and remote bombing. Arguing that this material history is relevant to media's presents and futures is not to suggest that media cannot be used counter to their designed purpose, but is simply a reminder that the ability to 'make visible' is as integral to colonial pursuits and extraction as it is to evidencing and accountability. While ROVs are utilized to at once develop oil and gas exploration and facilitate the accountability of these industries, so too are the fibre optic networks that make their video feeds accessible to the public. As Nicole Starosielski demonstrates in *The Undersea Network* (2015), these cable technologies allow for measurement and observation of the effects of climate change, while aiding the oil and gas sectors in the very activities that drive global warming. This feedback loop between capital, its violent effects and media technologies cannot be neglected when considering the relationship between documentation, mediation and accountability.

Spillcam should not be read as a neutral agent 'making visible' the effects of extractive capitalism – rather, extractive capital (BP) made Spillcam visible as a means to appear effective in the eyes of the public. It is in this regard that I frame Spillcam as a practice in an aesthetics of accountability. An aesthetics of accountability operates on the neoliberal premise that 'bearing witness' is a sufficient measure for assigning responsibility – it seeks to deliver proof that industry, capital and institutions can effectively address the outcomes, risks and consequences of their own contradictions. Certainly, solutions such as the one witnessed by Spillcam – the eventual capping of the well – are imperative for remediation, but they also serve to maintain broken systems. The permitted observation of these 'fixes' facilitated by capital's beneficiaries do not function to instigate further redress or the rejection of the system altogether. In fact, observation is as much about keeping systems functioning as they are, as it is a means of facilitating critique. To these ends, it is worth interrogating how devices such as Spillcam play into French philosopher Michel Foucault's (1995) assertion that 'visibility is a trap'.

The socio-technological developments leading up to the capability for real-time public access to Spillcam are particularly important for considering the material and discursive functions of this variety of accountability measures. While I gestured earlier to the intersections between media and war, what has yet to be accounted for here is the particular nature of media, communication technologies and accountability in the 1990s, especially in relation to the (Persian) Gulf War. The US mission to protect oil reserves in light of Iraq's invasion of Kuwait was the first combat to be broadcast in near real time. The use of media outlets to strategically illustrate a perfect campaign was integral in the US' attempt to secure positive public opinion for their first Gulf War. And while media theorists have pointed to the Gulf War as an example of a new real-time politics, the socio-economic conditions of the 1990s were such that capital, too, could benefit from the neoliberal imaginaries being operationalized by real-time mediation.

The aesthetics of accountability at play in Spillcam, however, can be traced and radicalized. The shifting entanglements of politics, capital and media and information technologies in the 1990s did not mark the end of the modernity rooted in imperialism, colonial pursuits and exploitation, as theorists such as Francis Fukuyama (2002) have suggested, but, rather, obscured them as phenomena such as globalization. The neoliberal, post-Cold War world imagines accountability and good governance as being derived from individuals' ability to participate in networks regardless of outcome – an underlying argument of Thomas L. Friedman's *The World Is Flat* (2005). The aesthetics of accountability, then, facilitates the sensation that individuals can participate equally – in this case, by logging on to bear witness of what was happening on the ocean floor of the Gulf. But what is obscured in this interaction is the absence of an ability to participate – to verify or further demand that the interests beyond capital are being attended to. The material realities of real time and livestreaming counter the impression of inclusion that these technologies sometimes seem to convey. Only capital can reach the Macondo prospect, only capital can drill that reserve and only capital can harvest from a hydrocarbon target 130,000 feet beneath the sea floor. Here, we can be invited to bear witness only to whether capital will succeed in protecting itself.

Glimpsing capital, debt and empire

So, how might capital, debt and its empire be glimpsed through Spillcam? The specific frame in Figure 3.1 is from the camera of one of the ROVs for the *Skandi Neptune*, a multipurpose offshore support vessel owned by DOF Subsea and operated by Subsea. *Skandi Neptune* was a component part of the technological assemblage that was Spillcam; however, it was also a component part of the standard operations of extractive industries. This is true also of the other actors and objects entangled in the Spillcam feed, such as Oceaneering International's Satellite ROV *Sea Maxx* that was operated on board a vessel they leased from Island Offshore. All of these components and entities serve to maintain the functioning of the offshore oil and gas industry, literally, through offshore support services. While noting a handful of the deep sea oil exploration entities involved in imaging the leaking well may not be a spectacular revelation, it troubles the impression of Spillcam as a measure for accountability. Spillcam can serve to remind us that there is no such thing as an inherently critical gaze. BP's agreement to provide the stream for hosting on the US Select Committee on Energy Independence and Global Warming website was a strategic decision to make themselves appear answerable to the American public and not just their shareholders. What Spillcam made visible was the severity of the leaking well which we would not have otherwise seen – but it, in itself, did not facilitate a radical witnessing. Rather, where we might derive a real potential is not from the act of witnessing but from the recognition of what 'business as usual' looks like through the eyes of capital. In the chapter by Szeman (Chapter 1), we see how important the domestication of oil infrastructure can be in creating a sense of ordinariness and safety, in contrast to the toxic leakiness that often accompanies oil infrastructure and the violent eruptions that characterize briefly visible moments of failure. To these ends Spillcam offers us an example of a representational frame of what an aesthetics of accountability might look like. In this, we might be able to cultivate scepticism to the totalizing narratives and aesthetics offered to us by capital.

Further resources

Appel, H., Mason, A., Watts, M. and Huber, M. T. (eds) (2015) *Subterranean Estates: Life Worlds of Oil and Gas*. Ithaca, NY: Cornell University Press.

Black, B. C. (2010) 'On BP's Deepwater Horizon live video feed'. *Environmental History* 15(4): 741–745. https://doi.org/10.1093/envhis/emq089 (accessed 27 February 2020).

Cochrane, D. T. (2020) 'Disobedient things: The Deepwater Horizon oil spill and accounting for disaster'. *Valuation Studies* 7(1): 3–32. doi:10.3384/vs.2001–5992.2020.7.1.3 (accessed 1 April 2020).

Cowen, D. (2020) 'Following the infrastructures of empire: Notes on cities, settler colonialism and method'. *Urban Geography* 41(4): 469–486. https://doi.org/10.1080/02723638.2019.1677990 (accessed 11 May 2019).

Ferguson, J. (2005) 'Seeing like an oil company: Space, security and global capital in neoliberal Africa'. *American Anthropologist* 107(3): 377–382. https://doi.org/10.1525/aa.2005.107.3.377 (accessed 1 June 2019).

Jue, M. (2019) 'Fluid cuts: The anti-visual logic of surfactants after Deepwater Horizon. *Configurations* 27(4): 525–544. 10.1353/con.2019.0034 (accessed 24 February 2020).

Works cited

Foucault, M. (1995) *Discipline and Punish: The Birth of the Prison*. New York: Vintage Books.

Friedman, T. L. (2005). *The World Is Flat: A Brief History of the Twenty-first Century*. Farrar, Straus and Giroux.

Fukuyama, F. (2002) *The End of History and the Last Man*. New York: Perennial.

Gates, K. (2013) 'The cultural labor of surveillance: Video forensics, computational objectivity, and the production of visual evidence'. *Social Semiotics* 23(2): 242–260. https://doi.org/10.1080/10350330.2013.777593 (accessed 14 October 2020).

Gilbert, P. R. (2020) 'Speculating on sovereignty: Money mining and corporate foreign policy at the extractive industry frontier'. *Economy and Society* 49(1): 16–44. https://doi.org/10.1080/03085147.2019.1690255 (accessed 12 October 2020).

Starosielski, N. (2015) *The Undersea Network*. Durham, NC: Duke University Press.

Tsing, A. (2000) 'Inside the economy of appearances' *Public Culture* 21(1): 115–144.

Part II

Circulations

'Circulation' is a popular way to describe how money works. One metaphor suggests that money irrigates economies as water irrigates land. This metaphor is so popular that someone even built a machine to illustrate the flow of money. If you ever happen to be in the city of Wellington, you can visit the MONIAC machine on display at the Reserve Bank of New Zealand.

In this part, our three contributors press you to consider deeper meanings circulated by coins, banknotes and other financial assets. Catherine Comyn (Chapter 4) gets right to the heart of matters in 'Te Peeke o Aotearoa', rereading New Zealand's colonial history to unearth a paradox beneath the idea of money as circulation. We think of money, especially cash, as something that circulates easily and widely. But in colonial New Zealand cash was not the medium of exchange for the Indigenous Māori populations; it was not how they circulated value. For the Māori, value was held in land; every parcel of land represented complex, interrelated layers of value. Yet land stays put; it cannot circulate like water. For colonizers, this dilemma was easily solved by asserting property rights, as stipulated by English common law. This allowed land to circulate in asset form. New Zealand is just one location in the former British empire where Indigenous populations were forcibly separated from their land through the aggressive use of English law. Thereafter, Indigenous populations were frequently 'brought into circulation' as financial citizens through the imposition of entrenched cycles of debt. Comyn shines the spotlight on a little-known and short-lived Māori currency, an important symbol of Māori political activism, which helped circulate resistance to colonial power. Traces of these Māori banknotes still rest in a museum, whispering their ghostly message of resistance to whoever might listen.

Ashley Cordes (Chapter 5) engages in an equally important revisionist history project, this time highlighting the Coquille nation in Oregon, US. Like Comyn (Chapter 4), Cordes explores a painful history of settler colonialism, an ideology that seeks to replace original populations with a new society of settlers. In 'Both Sides of the Coin', Cordes examines coinage struck in the 1850s, featuring iconography of Lady Liberty, represented first in Greco-Roman form. A year later, the colonial coins were restruck to feature Lady Liberty framed as an 'Indian princess', culturally appropriating a feather headdress. Cordes traces how early coinage across settler America circulated colonial fantasies of bravery and superiority, ideas of American nationhood, myths of the American dream and economic success through enslavement. Yet the iconography on these coins masked brutal genocides, stolen lands, broken treaties and debts owed to indigenous American peoples.

Syahirah Abdul Rahman (Chapter 6) dissects the colonial extraction and circulation of the mineral ore tin, a circulation of finance capital that haunts Malaysia to this today. Rahman's contribution is simply entitled 'Milo'. The name will conjure up happy memories for those who grew up with this milky chocolate ready-mix drink, sold in highly recognizable green tins across the Global South. Here, Rahman gets us to think about 'circuits of capital', a concept made famous by Karl Marx (1885/2014) when analysing the dynamic movement of value in capitalist production. Abdul Rahman uses the Milo tin to weave together her discussion of Malaysia's ongoing position in postcolonial circuits of capital. A straightforward economic analysis might simply have traced Malaysian tin from its extraction as mining ore using Indigenous labour, to Malaysia's role in a complex circuit of global and regional trade and investment. However, Rahman digs far deeper, tackling British colonialism head on, to reveal the uncomfortable haunting of Britain's harmful, far-reaching policies of racial capitalism.

The notion of racial capitalism as an analytical framework is often traced to Cedric Robinson in his ground-breaking work 'Black Marxism' in 1983. Other authors, including Gargi Bhattacharyya (2020), a contributor to this volume, use the term racial capitalism to explain the role racism has played in enabling key moments of capitalist development. This includes capitalism's coercion of people to participate in economic arrangements that consign them to the social margins. Abdul Rahman explores the coercion of the Malay population into the arduous extraction of tin from colonial Malaysian mines for trade throughout Britain's empire. Rahman then shows how Malays were repeatedly kept out of 'circulation', denied full financial citizenship through restricted education, social mobility and access to investment markets. She further highlights the momentary circulation of Malaysian nationhood and self-reliance through its creation of the Proton automobile. The Proton and other icons highlighted in these three chapters no longer circulate the same meanings, but we can learn so much from them.

Works cited

Bhattacharya, G. (2020) *Rethinking Racial Capitalism: Questions of reproduction and survival*. London: Rowman & Littlefield.

Marx, K. (1885/2014) *Capital: A critique of political economy*. Baltimore MD: Project Muse.

Robinson, C. J. (1983/2019) *Racial Capitalism*. London: Pluto Press.

4

Te Peeke o Aotearoa: colonial and decolonial finance in Aotearoa New Zealand, 1860s–1890s

Catherine Comyn

The familiar narrative of the British colonization of Aotearoa New Zealand is one of military violence and legal coercion that stripped Māori of their communally held lands and left them impoverished, ravaged by disease and, by the end of the nineteenth century, apparently destined for oblivion (Te Rangi Hiroa 1924). A banknote issued by the Kīngitanga, the Māori King movement, in the 1880s, however, hints at a less linear, more complicated regime of financial colonization waged by the British in Aotearoa New Zealand. The kotahi pāuna (one pound) note is one of few existing examples of currency issued by Te Peeke o Aotearoa, The Bank of Aotearoa, and is, indeed, one of few testimonies to the bank's existence. Very little is known about the bank, save that it operated as an exclusively Māori alternative to prevailing colonial financial institutions for approximately twenty years (1885–1905). In this chapter, I take the banknote as an artefact that reveals historical and material entanglements of finance and colonization and that, moreover, points towards political potentialities of finance for decolonial struggle.

Reportage on Te Peeke o Aotearoa is scarce and, of the few news articles that give mention to it in the 1880s and 1890s, much is inflected with the racialized, often patronizing tone of the Pākehā (New Zealand European) journalists who penned it. Details of the bank's establishment and dissolution are particularly unclear, and where certain claims are posited as fact in one article, in others they are called into question. Yet, with such accounts constituting some of the most substantial sources on the bank, they cannot be discounted. As Andrew Clifford notes in one of the only recent studies of the bank, 'Ko Te Peeke o Aotearoa (Bank of Aotearoa) is cloaked

Figure 4.1 Kotahi pāuna (one pound) note issued by the Kīngitanga bank, Te Peeke o Aotearoa.

in the mists of time' (Clifford 2017: 290). The contribution in this chapter is, on one level, a patching together of a lost history in an attempt to recover Te Peeke o Aotearoa from those mists. In this endeavour, colonial news sources provide necessary but problematic pieces of the puzzle, and are best consulted with a degree of caution.

An exact date for the founding of Te Peeke o Aotearoa is unknown, but an article in the *Waikato Times*, dated 12 December 1885, suggests that 'a Maori bank at Maungatautari' was operating 'in full swing' at that time. The bank at Maungatautari and Te Peeke o Aotearoa are believed to be either the same institution or branches of the same institution, with cheques issued under each name that appear identical in style and printing (Park 1992: 164). Te Peeke o Aotearoa was established by King Tāwhiao, leader of the Kīngitanga from 1860 to 1894. Kīngitanga secretary, T. T. Rāwhiti of Ngāti Hauā, played a major role in the bank and 'was probably its organiser and manager' (Park 1996: 97). The bank provided retail functions including deposits, chequing, note issue and lending, offering loans at an interest rate of a penny a day per pound sterling. It is likely that Te Peeke suffered a major fire in 1886; however, dated cheques suggest that the bank survived the fire and was functioning in 1894 and even as late as 1905 (Clifford 2017).

Although little can be discerned about the bank's daily operations, Te Peeke left material traces of its existence in the form of cheques and notes. I take these traces as a prompt to further understand the political and economic conditions of the bank's emergence. The kotahi pāuna note pictured in Figure 4.1 is a historical artefact that both was embedded within and reveals much about a broader regime of financial colonization enacted by the British in Aotearoa New Zealand (Comyn 2022). This was a regime within which financial institutions, instruments and practices were not incidental to the materialization of the colonial project but centrally enabled and even impelled it, from the first waves of settler emigration in the 1840s to the formation of the colonial state and beyond. Indeed, the effort to settler-colonize Aotearoa New Zealand was not, at least initially, a national undertaking but a joint stock speculation pursued in direct defiance of the British government (Cumming 2019). This was part of a broader push towards colonialism from the early nineteenth century that was motivated by a particular strain of political economy that viewed colonialism as a solution to Britain's economic troubles – in particular, the coincidence of the increasing poverty of the masses with the increasing concentration of wealth in a few hands.

The circulation of currency plays a significant role in the establishment of, and resistance to, settler colonialism as we also see in the chapter by Cordes (Chapter 5). The banknote issued by Te Peeke o Aotearoa provides an entry point from which to explore both the workings of the financial–colonial regime in Aotearoa New Zealand and the forms of Māori political organization that developed in response to it, powerfully subverting its mechanics to challenge the logic of division explicit in the colonial project.

Colonial finance: debt as a means of expropriation

The political potency of Te Peeke o Aotearoa can be appreciated only when measured against the sustained centrality of finance, and particularly credit, to the colonial regime as a means of securing Māori land, resources and political and economic subordination in the decades immediately preceding the bank's establishment. Situated within these conditions, the advent of the bank may be grasped as a powerful subversion of reigning financial–colonialist logics towards new, decolonial ends.

Pākehā credit networks and the debt relations they fostered in Māori communities were immensely damaging in their effects on whānau, hapū and iwi[1] from the 1860s through to the 1900s. These relations fuelled a self-perpetuating system of colonization by binding Māori into networks of dependency on the colonizer that could be dissolved only through the alienation of land. Taken together, the Native Lands Acts of 1862 and 1865 were a key driver of this system of financial colonization. The Acts, whose effect upon Māori land tenure is often understood as one of 'individualization', must also be grasped as means of enacting a profound *financializaton* of Māori land, realized fundamentally through the transformation of land into a security against debts. For, what the land Acts implemented first and foremost – inseparable from and prefiguring the individualization of Māori land tenure – were particular debt relations. It was these relations, rather than the legislation directly, that crippled Māori economically, wresting the base from them piece by piece, repayment by repayment. (The role that securitization of land and housing plays in contemporary settler colonialism is also a central focus of Nir (Chapter 16).

According to customary tenure, Māori land claims (or take) were held communally by hapū and iwi, and could derive from a range of factors including discovery, ancestry, conquest and gift. This made them unrecognizable in terms of English property relations, which are founded upon exclusive ownership rights vested in individuals. Hence, in order to expedite land sales and the progress of colonization, the New Zealand government implemented the Native Lands Acts, which enabled for Māori land rights to be 'ascertained, defined and declared' and provided for the establishment of a Native Land Court, presided over by Europeans, for this purpose. Māori were required to apply to the Court, which opened in 1865, in order to have their interests recognized and certified, a process that rendered them 'claimants' with respect to their own lands. Any individual could notify the Court of their interest in a particular piece of land, and no more than ten individuals could be named on a certificate of ownership.

The Native Lands Acts were expressly intended to assimilate Māori customary title into English property law, in doing so fracturing the economic and political bases of Māori social relations. As minister of justice Henry Sewell stated in 1870,

> The object of the Native Lands Act was two-fold: to bring the great bulk of the lands of the Northern Island which belonged to the Natives, and which, before the passing of that Act, were *extra commercium* [...] within the reach of colonization. The other great object was, the detribalization of the Natives, – to destroy, if it were possible, the principle of communism which ran through the whole of their institutions, upon which their social system was based, and which stood as a barrier in the way of all attempts to amalgamate the Native race into our own social and political system.[2]

The political motives of the legislation were clearly articulated by F. D. Fenton, key architect of the Native Lands Acts and chief judge of the Native Land Court from 1865 to 1882, who wrote in 1871: 'in the destruction of the communal system of holding land is involved the downfall of communal principles of the tribe, and the power of combination for objects of war or depredation'.[3]

The Acts' effect was to individualize land title formerly vested in the collective mana of the iwi or hapū. Instead of land being managed by a community, each 'owner' was granted a particular share of land that they could individually decide to hold, lease or alienate to government agents or directly to settlers. The scale of this operation is seen in the example of Hawke's Bay, where ownership title was granted to 558 individuals for 569,220 acres of land that properly belonged to 3,773 people (Ballara 1982). Every one of those individuals was empowered without restriction to alienate land that properly belonged to the iwi or hapū. This system prefigured the alienation of four million hectares of Māori land within the first thirty years of the Court's operation (Walker 1990). By the end of the century, only 15% (or seven million acres) remained of the more than sixty-six million acres in Māori ownership in 1840 (Sorrenson 1976). As Judith Binney (1990: 143) and other important historians see it, the Native Lands Acts were 'an act of war' that aimed to complete what the colonial administration set out to achieve with its invasion of the Waikato in 1863–64: large-scale land acquisition and the concomitant fracturing of the communal economic base of Māori society.

The Native Lands Acts' dramatic effectiveness as a means of expropriation cannot wholly be attributed to the legislation itself, nor even to the colonial legal system at large. A major factor in this effectiveness was the concurrent fostering of debt relations between Māori 'landowners'[4] and Pākehā storekeepers. The creation of debt relations is not only a structuring feature of settler colonialism, but becomes entangled with attempts to create a hostile environment for racialized subjects of former colonies in contemporary Britain, as the chapters by Medien (Chapter 7) and Dickson et al. (Chapter 8) reveal. Legislation, and in particular the Native Lands Acts, was a powerful instrument of colonization in Aotearoa New Zealand, but its fulcrum was finance.

For the majority of Māori claimants, indebtedness was a precondition for simply commencing the process of obtaining land title. In order to be heard before the Native Land Court, the 1865 Act obliged claimants to meet the costs of employing a government-appointed surveyor. Māori, however, being overwhelmingly based in rural areas away from commercial centres, lacked access to cash. They had to pay for survey costs on credit, with the land functioning as security, and because of this 'often pa[id] double what it cost a European' (Heale 1867). The Waitangi Tribunal notes that, 'From the outset there was a legislative expectation that survey costs would be paid in land.' In order to extinguish the debts owing to surveyors – which under further Land Acts in the 1880s and 1890s became subject to a 5% interest rate – claimants were forced to sell off portions of land once title was eventually ascertained. To take Ngāti Whakaue as an example, Kathryn Rose notes that for three of the iwi's blocks in the Rotorua district, 'the compounding interest and administration fees increased the total debt [...] by 30 per cent in the five years from 1893 to 1898' (Rose 2004: 271). Indeed, the Native Lands Act 1865 provided for the direct transfer of title to surveyors whose services were conducted on credit, who would 'have a lien thereon' until the charges were paid. As Angela Ballara (1982: 532) summarizes, 'Land rather than money became the Maori means of exchange.'

The expense of surveys could consume large portions of the proceeds accruing to Māori from land sales. According to one report, in the central North Island the average proportion of sales revenue taken up by survey costs was 21% (Macky 2004: 64). In some cases, survey costs consumed almost the entire sale value of the block. Often, the payment was made in land. In the case of the Tahorakuri block, for instance, 36,362 acres out of 50,000 (73%) were surrendered to 'defray survey costs' (Stirling 2004). Ngāti Tūwharetoa, a central North Island iwi, sold an estimated 300,000 acres of land to the government in order to cover court costs and survey costs incurred in securing its title. Under the Native Lands Acts, immense amounts of land passed out of Māori hands in lieu of surveying fees – that is, in merely servicing debt. Debt relations embroiled iwi and hapū in a paradoxical cycle of alienation wherein, ultimately, 'the Māori people paid in land for the privilege of selling land' (Ballara 1982: 534).

Debt relations were, then, in place at the very outset of the legal process for 'ascertaining' Māori land title. A creditor–debtor relation that mapped onto, qualified and entrenched the relation of colonizer and colonized was, in fact, foundational to the legislation used by the Crown to progressively deplete Māori of their material wealth. Many claimants entered the courts in a position of indebtedness that predetermined their outcomes and foreclosed possibilities for the future.

Moreover, the Native Land Court hearings themselves were designed in such a way as to entrench claimants into cycles of debt. Any member of an iwi could apply for investigation of title, and anyone with interests in the land in question had to attend court if they wanted these recognized. Evidence towards a claim could be presented only at the appointed hearing, notice of which was posted in the national newspaper. This meant that entire communities had to attend court hearings, often in Pākehā towns located at great distances from their lands. In 1883, for instance, Taupo claimants protested against travelling 100 miles to Cambridge for the hearing on the Tatua block. With some hearings lasting several months, large expenses were incurred on accommodation, transport and rations, not to mention the cost of the longer-term food shortages arising from the neglect of cultivations in claimants' absence: 'Rations (food) for 200 people for six weeks cost about £300, the equivalent of five years' wages for a single agricultural worker' (Waitangi Tribunal 2008: 516). In addition to survey costs, fees paid to lawyers and interpreters were incumbent upon the claimants. These additional costs meant that, upon receipt of title, grantees often sold off portions of land to discharge debts owed to a network of creditors comprising lawyers, interpreters, surveyors, hoteliers and publicans.

The transformation of the land into security for debts, a pivotal moment in the financialization of Māori land tenure, is highlighted by M. P. K. Sorrenson (1956: 186) as 'a fundamental factor that sooner or later coerced even strong opponents of sale into disposing of land'. Once the land was registered in the names of ten or fewer individuals, it was easy for government land agents to pick off the often indebted grantees and coerce them into selling their shares. They did so, Sorrenson explains, by engaging 'the assistance of the local storekeeper or publican, who often acted as "Native land agents" and who offered the Maoris liberal supplies of goods and liquor on credit' (Sorrenson 1956: 186). According to Ballara, individual grantees were offered unlimited credit by Pākehā storekeepers. This would continue 'until their debts had mounted to such proportions that they could only be settled by mortgaging or selling the land that was theirs, at least on paper' (Ballara 1982: 536). An 1872 government land commission found that storekeepers engaged in many duplicitous practices, including withholding from Māori customers the true extent of their indebtedness and falsifying accounts (Richmond 1873: 2).

The commission, which looked into 301 disputes from Māori landowners concerning purchases in the Hawke's Bay area, found that 'Nearly all the sales which we investigated were made to dealers. The land was in fact taken in discharge of a previous debit balance.' The debts accrued by Māori vendors were so significant that, upon selling the land, the balance owed to them often came to nothing. In the few cases where a credit did favour the vendor, purchasers (chief among them government agents) consistently refused to pay in cash and insisted Māori take the payment in goods, chiefly alcohol. Putting such outcomes down to the 'careless and extravagant expenditure' of the 'natives', the commission did not recommend a return of land to the claimants (Richmond 1873: 2–3).

Credit was, therefore, a crucial facilitator of the colonial legislative project to expropriate Māori land and destroy the communal relations identified as foundational to Māori society. This was a regime of financial exploitation that was premised upon and systematically reinforced the lack of access Māori had to cash. In Ballara's (1982: 527) terms, it 'inveigled them into an inflationary spiral of trading, debt-incurrence, land-alienation, further purchasing, further debts and further land sales or leases'. This cycle of debt, mediated by purchase agents, storekeepers, publicans and the courts, could be settled only with the alienation of the only asset Māori had: the whenua (land). Under the Native Lands Acts, thousands of acres of Māori land were alienated to the colonial regime via transactions that were not simply enabled by credit networks but were, in turn, necessitated by them, as Māori became entrapped in relations of debt dependency upon the colonizer.

Viewed in the context of this financial-colonial regime waged against Māori in the 1860s and 1870s – decades in which the latter experienced a ruthless depletion of communal lands mediated by cycles of debt – it is easy to understand why, by the mid-1880s, some wanted to develop their own financial institutions.

Decolonial finance: the Kīngitanga and Te Peeke o Aotearoa

Certain Māori in the central North Island refused to engage with the Native Land Court from 1867, when its first hearings were held in the district, through the 1870s and beyond. Chief among those who remained steadfast in their opposition to the Court was Tāwhiao, Waikato rangatira and leader of the Kīngitanga, a pan-tribal Māori movement aimed at protecting the land and recovering economic and political autonomy, or mana motuhake. Tāwhiao maintained his refusal to engage with the Court even as five iwi applied in 1886 for the investigation of title to Te Rohe Pōtae, an area comprising an estimated 3.5 million acres in the central North Island and which included Kāwhia, 'a bastion of Kingitanga strength and refuge to many of the King's Waikato supporters' (Husbands and Mitchell 2011: 101–121).

These iwi had resisted the Native Land Court for twenty years because of their alignment to the Kīngitanga and the fear that engagement with the Court would result in land loss. At a major Kīngitanga hui at Te Poutu in 1885, which was attended by more than 1,000, resolutions reportedly included the withdrawal of iwi lands from the Native Land Court and the refusal of land surveys, leases and sales (Marr 2011). However, in 1886, Ngāti Maniapoto, Ngāti Raukawa, Ngāti Tūwharetoa, Whanganui and Ngāti Hikairo made a tactical decision to apply to the Court in order to have the boundaries of Te Rohe Pōtae recognized and protected (Marr 1996).

Despite the intentions of the iwi not to alienate, simply engaging with the Court resulted in 91,000 acres of land being transferred to the Crown in lieu of survey fees and other court-related costs (Husbands and Mitchell 2011). The subsequent subdivision of the land, once the boundaries were ascertained, paved the way for individuals to be picked off by land agents and, by 1910, more than half of Te Rohe Pōtae had passed out of iwi hands.

Credit was integral to the 'opening' (Adams, Te Uira and Parsonson 1997) of the King country in the late nineteenth century, functioning as a key driver in the transfer of immense amounts of Māori land into Pākehā hands. But, just as finance was employed by the colonizer as an instrument for partitioning and assimilating Māori social relations, so too was it identified and mobilized by some Māori as a potential means of securing autonomy within a decolonial framework. In 1885, Tāwhiao and the Kīngitanga established Te Peeke o Aotearoa – the first and only bank built by Māori for Māori. For the Kīngitanga to develop its own banking facilities at this particular historical moment was to lay the foundations for a financial network that was disengaged from, and could exist outside of, the creditor–debtor relation that drove the seizure of land. The Kīngitanga's actions may be viewed as a refusal of the terms of credit proffered by the colonizer, a refusal to partake in a relation of dependency, which not only asserted the economic autonomy of iwi aligned with the Kīngitanga but, given the centrality of credit to the colonial project, threatened to weaken its very fabric.

The bank's emergence was shaped by and must be understood in relation to the development of the Kīngitanga. Founded in 1858 in the central North Island, the Kīngitanga sought to unify iwi in the creation of a polity that represented and embodied Māori sovereignty. It intended to govern in parallel with the British Crown, which, for its part, would preside over the Pākehā population. The colonial government, however, refused to recognize any entity other than the Crown as sovereign in the country and, in the 1860s, did its utmost to quash the Kīngitanga in the Waikato Wars. In 1863, Tāwhiao and his followers were declared rebels under the New Zealand Settlements Act and the Crown proceeded to confiscate 1.2 million acres of their fertile lands. Even this, according to Matthew Wynyard (2019: 4) 'paled in comparison' to the amount of land lost through the Native Land Court.

After the raupatu (confiscations) of the 1860s, Tāwhiao and his people retreated into Ngāti Maniapoto lands and he remained itinerant for the next twenty years. In 1884, he travelled to London, where he failed to gain an audience with Queen Victoria, before resolving 'to look for Maori solutions to Maori problems through Maori institutions, and to attempt to do so on a national basis' (King 1977: 29–30). His vision, according to R. T. Mahuta (1996: 60), was 'the rebirth of a self-sufficient base, supported by the strength and stability of the people'. Te Peeke o Aotearoa would provide support for a range of social institutions intended to promote mana motuhake (autonomy) and kotahitanga (unity). In the 1880s and 1890s, Stuart Park (1996: 179) writes, Tāwhiao's 'drive for Maori autonomy led him to establish a separate government, with parliament, treasury, licences, courts, justices and constables, with power to levy fines for the treasury, and a bank to house the treasury'.

As storehouse for the Kīngitanga treasury, Te Peeke o Aotearoa was inseparable from the development of Te Kauhanganui, the Kīngitanga parliament that opened in May 1891 and raised revenue by collecting taxes. Financial autonomy was essential to a project aiming to restore the self-determination of Māori in all aspects of social and political life. In practical terms, as Clifford (2017: 290) writes of Te Peeke o Aotearoa, 'A functional state within a state would require this type of institution.' The harakeke (flax bush) pictured on the lower left of the banknote is particularly apposite here. Harakeke is a symbol not only of whānau but also of industry and exchange. The motif also has associations with self-sufficiency and sustainability, with Māori tikanga (practice) being to harvest only the outer (tupuna or 'grandparent') leaves of the bush and allow the inner, younger shoots to develop.

As noted earlier, many Māori vendors were not paid cash in exchange for lands 'sold' as a result of engaging with the Native Land Court but, rather, in credit. However, by the late nineteenth century, those who did receive cash needed a secure location for it. To some extent, then, the establishment of Te Peeke o Aotearoa may be understood as a practical response to an inflow of cash into previously cashless communities. As well as wanting to consolidate and protect the sums acquired through land sales, Kīngitanga leaders likely saw opportunities in providing deposit and lending services for communities in the central North Island, services which would otherwise be provided by the Pākehā banks. Notwithstanding the patronizing tone of his *Hawke's Bay Herald* article, J. F. Edgar (1891) spoke a certain amount of truth when he wrote that the bank's founders reasoned that, 'as the Europeans were making a profit by keeping the Maoris money, there was no reason why the Maoris should not be their own bankers, and enjoy the profit themselves'. Indeed, the potential threat posed by Te Peeke for the colonial economy is evident in Edgar's claim that news of its opening precipitated 'an immediate run on the European banks', which, had it become general, would have caused widespread closures.

Beyond the immediate and practical motives for its establishment, Te Peeke o Aotearoa also signified broader possibilities for Māori in terms of the decolonial futures whose imaginings it was entwined with, and for which it could provide economic support. This claim is fair in light of the bank's conditions of emergence; namely, that it was conceived within a transformative political movement engaged in a broad (re)imagining of the future that cut across Māori social, political and economic organization – a reimagining necessitated by the colonial project, which was, by this time, entrenched. A bank is not merely a storehouse for money but a means of consolidating, redistributing (via credit) and augmenting it (via interest). The productive power of money centralized in a bank is more than the sum of its parts; transformed into interest-bearing (loanable) capital it can support capitalist enterprise on a scale unachievable when resources are scattered across a disparate population.

Te Peeke o Aotearoa was a way of centralizing iwi wealth and rendering it available for (re)distribution. In the context of a brutal undermining of the Māori economic base, this was in effect a pooling of resources. In this way, Te Peeke should not be seen as a capitulation to but, rather, a subversion and repudiation of the financial-colonial regime. The colonial administration employed credit as an instrument of division specifically intended to fracture and disperse the communal economic base of Māori society. It was a key weapon mobilized as part of a strategy of 'divide and conquer'. Yet, whereas in the hands of the colonizer credit signified and enacted a logic of division, the Kīngitanga sought to mobilize it as an instrument of integration and consolidation within a broader political project founded on a logic of pan-iwi solidarity. For the Kīngitanga, banking represented a means of reorganizing the existing material resources of iwi that was concomitant with, and facilitated, a broad restructuring of Māori social relations to build a united front against colonization. It is not known what, if any, grand ventures were pursued or envisaged by Tāwhiao and the directors of Te Peeke o Aotearoa. But what is clear is that for the Kīngitanga to establish its own, exclusively Māori banking institution at this moment in history was not simply a practical response to newly obtained cash reserves. The formation of Te Peeke o Aotearoa was a political decision that aimed to regain financial independence for Māori by establishing credit systems – the means to consolidate and (re)distribute community assets – outside the financial-legal infrastructure of the colonizer. It was, moreover, a powerful symbolic assertion of rangatiratanga (sovereignty) that reminded Pākehā of the right of Māori as tangata whenua to self-determination. For Māori to conduct their financial transactions with Te Peeke, to make deposits and draw loans in a network that excluded predatory Pākehā lenders, was a subtle way of claiming and demonstrating fidelity to an authority outside of colonial rule.

(Re)reading colonial histories in terms of finance

Undertaking to critically reread colonial histories so as to render the pivotal role of financial institutions, instruments and practices explicit has important implications for knowledge. One of these is that it provokes a reconsideration of the centrality typically accorded to government entities and influential individuals as the agents of history. In orthodox narratives of the colonization of Aotearoa New Zealand, finance tends to name a passive technical apparatus operating in the background, the utility of which is largely assumed. To instead document the material ways in which finance has effected colonization – and not incidentally to its otherwise purely technical activities, but through the realization of a logic of division and reproduction that is immanent in it and is mobilized for particular ends – reveals it as an agentive and highly political entity that can, moreover, be contested.

(Re)reading colonial histories in terms of finance has implications not only for knowledge but for contemporary politics. It brings new emphases and complexities to debates in the settler-colonial context regarding, for instance, where responsibility lies for the (ongoing) social, cultural and economic destruction wrought by colonization, or by what means the reparations owed to indigenous peoples should be paid. And looking to a specific example of decolonial finance like Te Peeke o Aotearoa not just in terms of what it achieved, but in terms of the broader possibilities it represented within a movement of building indigenous political autonomy, contains further insight for contemporary decolonial movements in its suggestion of the potential utility of finance as a means of moving beyond the restrictions of the colonial-capitalist present.

Further resources

Adams, T., Te Uira, N. and Parsonson, A. (1997) '"Behold, a kite flies towards you": The Kiingitanga and the "opening" of the King Country'. *The New Zealand Journal of History* 31(1): 99–116.

Bhandar, B. (2018) *Colonial Lives of Property: Law, Land, and Racial Regimes of Ownership*. Durham: Duke University Press. See especially 'Propertied abstractions', pp. 77–113.

Lazzarato, M. (2012) *The Making of the Indebted Man: An Essay on the Neoliberal Condition*, trans. J. D. Jordan. Amsterdam: Semiotext(e). See especially 'The genealogy of debt and the debtor', pp. 37–88.

Sorrenson, M. P. K. (1956) 'Land purchase methods and their effect on Maori population, 1865–1901', *The Journal of the Polynesian Society* 65(3): 183–199.

Wynyard, M. (2019) '"Not one more bloody acre": Land restitution and the Treaty of Waitangi settlement process in Aotearoa New Zealand', *Land* 8(162): 1–14.

Works cited

Adams, T., Te Uira, N. and Parsonson, A. (1997) '"Behold, a kite flies towards you": The Kiingitanga and the "opening" of the King Country'. *The New Zealand Journal of History* 31(1): 99–116.

Ballara, A. (1982) 'The pursuit of mana? A re-evaluation of the process of land alienation by Maoris, 1840–1890'. *The Journal of the Polynesian Society* 91(4): 519–541, at 537.

Binney, J. (1990) 'The Native Land Court and the Maori Communities'. In J. Binney, J. Basset and E. Olssen (eds), *The People and the Land:*

Te Tangata me Te Whenua: An Illustrated History of New Zealand 1820–1920. Wellington: Allen & Unwin, pp. 143–164.

Clifford, A. (2017) 'Unofficial issuers: Ko Te Peeke o Aotearoa'. In *New Zealand Trading Banks and Early Paper Currency*. Auckland: New Zealand Banknote Guild, pp. 287–291.

Comyn, C. (2022) *The Financial Colonisation of Aotearoa New Zealand*. Auckland: Economic and Social Research Aotearoa.

Cumming, C. (2019) 'How finance colonised Aotearoa: A concise counterhistory'. *Counterfutures* 7: 40–72. Wellington: Rebel Press.

Edgar, J. F. (1891) 'The Maungatautari Bank'. *Hawke's Bay Herald*, 11 April.

Heale, T. (1867) 'Report by Mr Heale on the Subject of Surveys under the Native Lands Act', Appendix to the Journals of the House of Representatives, 1867, session I, A-10B, pp. 3–5.

Husbands, P. and Mitchell, J. (2011) *The Native Land Court, land titles and Crown land purchasing in the Rohe Potae District', 1866–1907: A Report for the Te Rohe Potae District Inquiry (Wai 898)*. Wellington: Ministry of Justice.

King, M. (1977) *Te Puea: A Biography*. Auckland: Hodder and Stoughton.

Macky, M. (2004) *Crown Purchasing in the Central North Island Inquiry District, 1870–1890*. Wellington: Crown Law Office.

Mahuta, R. T. (1996) 'Tāwhiao'. In A. Ballara (ed.), *Te Kīngitanga: The People of the Māori King Movement – Essays from the Dictionary of New Zealand Biography*. Auckland: Auckland University Press, pp. 55–60

Marr, C. (1996) 'The Alienation of Maori Land in the Rohe Potae (Aotea Block), 1840–1920'. Working paper. Wellington: Waitangi Tribunal Rangahaua Whanui Series.

Marr, C. (2011) *Te Rohe Potae Political Engagement 1864–1886*. Report commissioned by the Waitangi Tribunal for the Te Rohe Potae district inquiry. Wellington: Ministry of Justice.

Park, S. (1992) 'Te Peeke o Aotearoa: The bank of King Tawhiao'. *New Zealand Journal of History* 26(2): 161–183.

Park, S. (1996) 'T. T. Rāwhiti'. In A. Ballara (ed.), *Te Kīngitanga: The People of the Māori King Movement – Essays from the Dictionary of New Zealand Biography*. Auckland: Auckland University Press, pp. 97–100.

Richmond, C. W. (1873) 'Report by the Chairman of the Hawke's Bay Native Lands Alienation Commission 1872', Appendix to the Journals of the House of Representatives, 1873, session I, vol. III, G-07, pp. 1–9.

Rose, K. (2004) *The Fenton Agreement and Land Alienation in the Rotorua District in the Nineteenth Century*. Wellington: Crown Forestry Rental Trust.

Sorrenson, M. P. K. (1956) 'Land purchase methods and their effect on Maori population, 1865–1901', *The Journal of the Polynesian Society* 65(3): 183–199.

Sorrenson, M. P. K. (1976) 'Colonial rule and local response: Maori responses to European domination in New Zealand since 1860'. *Journal of Imperial and Commonwealth History* 4(2): 127–137.

Stirling, B. (2004) *Taupo-Kaingaroa Nineteenth Century Overview*, vol. 2. Wellington: Crown Forestry Rental Trust.

Te Rangi Hiroa (P. H. Buck) (1924) 'The passing of the Maori'. *Transactions and Proceedings of the Royal Society of New Zealand* 55: 362–375. Wellington: W. A. G. Skinner, Government Printing Office). http://rsnz. natlib.govt.nz/volume/rsnz_55/rsnz_55_00_003930.html (accessed 17 August 2022).

Waikato Times (1885) 'A Maori bank at Maungatautari'. *Waikato Times*, 12 December, p. 2.

Waitangi Tribunal (2008) *He Maunga Rongo: Report on Central North Island Claims*, Stage 1, Volume 2, Part III [Wai1200v2III]. Wellington: Ministry of Justice, pp. 413–880.

Walker, R. (1990) *Ka Whawhai Tonu Mātou: Struggle without End*. Auckland: Penguin.

Wynyard, M. (2019) '"Not one more bloody acre": Land restitution and the Treaty of Waitangi settlement process in Aotearoa New Zealand', *Land* 8(162): 1–14.

Notes

1 Whānau refers to an extended family group. Hapū refers to a larger kinship group consisting of a number of whānau sharing descent from a common ancestor. It was the primary political unit in traditional Māori society. Iwi refers to an extended kinship group, tribe, nation or people – often descending from a common ancestor and associated with a distinct territory.

2 Mr Sewell, *cited in* New Zealand Government, New Zealand Parliamentary Debates (Hansard), vol. 9 (Wellington: G. Didsbury, Government Printer, 1870), p. 361, accessible at www.parliament.nz/en/pb/hansard-debates/historical-hansard/ (accessed 15 September 2022).

3 Judge Fenton to the Hon. D. McLean, 28 August 1871 (No. 2) in Papers Relative to the Working of the Native Land Court Acts, AJHR 1871, Session I, A-2A, p. 10.

4 The concept of owning whenua (land) did not exist in tikanga Māori.

5

Both sides of the coin: Lady Liberty and the construction of 'the New Native' on currency in Oregon's colonial period

Ashley Cordes

Coins are far more than tiny denominations of money made of malleable metals. They are collectibles, good luck charms, repositories of stories, sentiments of nationhood, remembrances of violence and storers of possibility. In this chapter, I analyse two aged coins in the context of settler colonialism in America, specifically in the state of Oregon. The first is an 1853 half dollar coin and the second is an 1854 full dollar coin, both decorated with the face of Lady Liberty and other significant symbols. Between 1853 and 1854, the coin designer gave Lady Liberty a costume change – replacing her headwear of a coronet with an Indigenous headdress. Reading (i.e., analysing) these coins' design elements is important because it allows for the unravelling of settler-colonial imperatives and provides clues into their socio-technical journeys – from g*** metal belonging to the earth to antique tokens of American imperialism.[1] How does Lady Liberty's change of headwear reflect the complex relationships between settler-invaders and Indigenous peoples in America's early history? What can coins like these reveal about the intersections of currency, settler colonialism and contemporary debts to Indigenous peoples? The question of how to understand and repay debts to Indigenous peoples is a concern of Randell-Moon (Chapter 14), as well as of Comyn (Chapter 4), which also takes the circulation of currency as its central concern.

Figure 5.1 Half dollar coin.

The Rogue River War and settler colonialism in Oregon

In the 1850s, in what is currently known as Oregon, American imperialism was accelerating. The fur trade and the G*** Rush ushered thousands of settler-invaders into Indigenous homelands, supported by the Oregon Donation Land Claim Act of 1850 that sanctioned American white men to each steal 320 acres of land, or 640 acres for white men with wives. This Act was consistent with the broader sweep of settler colonialism in America, what Patrick Wolfe (2006) describes as structural, multidimensional elimination of Indigenous peoples and homeland takeover. The Rogue River War (1853–56) in Oregon was designed to eliminate, precipitated by ongoing tensions between Indigenous peoples and settlers. Settlers committed acts of genocide and sexual violence, and spread diseases to Indigenous peoples.[2] Ultimately, the war ended with federal reservation policies that removed most Indigenous people in Oregon to reservations such as the Grande Ronde and Siletz reservations by 1856.

Oregon Territory's Superintendent of Indian Affairs, Joel Palmer, who was white, and others had brokered an arrangement known as the Coast Treaty. Leaders of many tribes along the Oregon Coast signed with X-marks to safeguard a million-acre reservation for their peoples. However, other treaties were never ratified, acreage promised to tribes was reduced and government entities conveniently claimed that a 'lost map' was needed to process treaties and thus they could not honour them.

This land that was promised – the rivers that sparkled with salmon and served as meeting places for tribes to forge diplomacy, the rock formations that protect them, including one that has since been destroyed by the government called 'Grandmother Rock', the ground that each generation of our families has stood on since time immemorial – are all wanted back. This is the true debt of the American empire. The debts of settler colonists cannot be settled while Indigenous relations with land continue to be violently interrupted, as Randell-Moon (Chapter 14) shows in the chapter on Gurindji Country in Australia. All else that was lost – lives, Indigenous epistemologies and technologies, ideas of land as sacred and not a commodity, are all immeasurable. For example, Oregon is potlatch territory, where gifts from the sovereign earth were given between tribes in ceremonies to honour notions of reciprocity, obligation and relationship building. The loss of potlatch practice (though potlatches have been revived in limited contexts), largely supplanted by capitalist systems, resulted in mass environmental damage, the ruthless pursuit for capitalist gain and alienation of community bonds for individualism. When an Indigenous community endures methods of cultural elimination their ability to steward the land, speak their languages and engage in traditional exchange is stolen. It is not just past generations but present and future generations that are impacted. It can be hard to regain even parts of what has been lost, but when Indigenous nations engage in cultural revitalization, reflection and emancipatory research, it is sometimes possible.

Archaeological considerations

In the summer of 2016, I was invited to participate in a Southern Oregon University project that archaeologically and ethno-historically reconsiders sites of importance during Oregon's colonial period. This project was brought to my attention by Southern Oregon University professor of anthropology Dr Mark Tveskov and the Coquille Tribal Historic Preservation Officer (THPO). I am an enrolled citizen of the Coquille Nation, located around Coos Bay Oregon, and I serve as chair of the Coquille Culture and Education Committee. This archaeological excavation presented a unique opportunity to work with my nation to learn more about the Rogue River War, which has had intergenerational effects on Coquille families. It also provided opportunities for me to connect and correct biased histories that are framed by settler-colonial storytelling (Cordes 2020). What I learned was that loss of sovereignty was categorically based on the value placed on the land as property, as well as value placed on people. Those are mediated through notions of ownership, cash, commodity, currency and the significance ascribed to them. Thus, I found myself most interested in artefacts/belongings related to currency. They are the mechanisms and systems that drove settlers to displace Indigenous peoples and commit genocide, and for that, the ghosts of colonialism will forever haunt each generation of Americans who must reckon with their complicity, historical amnesia and ultimate responsibility to engage in comprehensive reparation, including, but not limited to, the return of lands to Indigenous nations.

About a month into excavations, where I was primarily responsible for film-recording belongings and interviews, and helping to sift through layers of earth, one of the lead archaeologists announced the uncovering of a full, unaltered excavated coin. After brushing off, it revealed itself as an 1853 half dollar coin designed by James B. Longacre. This coin is imprinted with elements that when decoded, speak to how America imagined itself in the colonial period and is thus an ideal coin for helping to understand cultural politics. My process of coming to understand the importance of this coin and its agency as a signifier of American imperialism came from dissecting everything about it – its materials, symbols, size, purpose and how it changed in the next iteration of coins, and then zooming back out to see how it fits into America's settler-colonial arrogance.

Understanding Lady Liberty coins

The front of the excavated coin displays Lady Liberty, facing left from the neck up with an expressionless face, curled hair and a coronet. The coin's modelling and type of profile framing, a common generic convention of coin design, is based on Greek and Roman figures as well as nineteenth-century notions of European phrenological and phenotypical aesthetic predilections. The iconography of money frequently projects settlers' self-understandings of the nation in settler-colonial contexts (Mwangi 2002). Lady Liberty's gaze shows that she is conscious of her identity – a hesitant national symbol of freedom and the most prominent piece of the coin's design. She is important because of her ties to American femininity and status. America had consistently been conceptualized as feminine and, in the eighteenth century, under 'captivity' by British rule; metaphorized as colonizable, rapeable, vulnerable and yet still strong. Lady Liberty represented the breaking of captivity and the promise of freedom. She holds symbolic power, but not as a queen, as suggested by her wearing a coronet as opposed to a royal crown. Around her head are thirteen stars and around the stars is a rim, which perhaps signifies her crown accomplishment, the possession of thirteen colonies.

The reverse side of the coin displays 1853 in the centre and is encircled with a wreath and the words 'Half Dol California G***'. Due to its immediate proximity, Southern Oregon was treated as an extension of California's g***fields, as California remains the primary site in the historical memory of the larger G*** Rush. The California G*** Rush was brutally genocidal against Indigenous peoples of California, and settler invaders tried rationalizing their methods of elimination and conquest through myths, including that of the American Dream. This myth that success and happiness are possible for anyone in America, though what they meant is white Americans, is undergirded by settler self-making and entrepreneurial colonial terrorism in the quest for capital. Specifically, California g*** was the ultimate commodity or the token of g*** fever, whose allure superseded acting with humanity toward Indigenous peoples and those that the settlers enslaved.

The thirteen stars on the coin underscore that America was to be comprised of its thirteen colonies, Delaware, Pennsylvania, New Jersey, Georgia, Connecticut, Massachusetts, Maryland, South Carolina, Virginia, New York, North Carolina and Rhode Island, leaving a clear erasure of Indigenous nations, despite diplomatic promises from the government. America's conception of democracy, however, is based on the biased interpretation of structures of the Haudenosaunee

Confederacy and a specific symbolic wampum belt, made of hundreds of pieces of wampum (quahog and whelk shells that also served as currency) woven into elaborate forms (Shell 2013). As depicted in their Great Law of Peace wampum belt, there is an agreement that their Confederacy respects the liberties of each of the Mohawk, Onondaga, Oneida, Cayuga and Seneca clans. Notably, America's so-called founding fathers were inspired by the Confederacy's ability to honour unity among separate powers and various other freedoms with regard to religion and the right to assembly.

These thirteen colonies on the coin were a band that imagined themselves in a particular way and shared the idea of a supposedly justified or godly backed fight for independence and a democratic trial. To be sure, American currency is still saturated with signifiers of these same colonies, ones that were based on federalist principles that are indeed indebted to Indigenous nations. For example, there are thirteen layers of brick on the pyramid that is imprinted on the left side of the reverse one dollar bill, and there are thirteen stars above the eagle seal on the right side of the same bill.

The coin also contains a laurel wreath around the year 1853, a symbol of martial victory based on another enduring Roman symbol. The coin contains laurel to signify triumph over Great Britain in the Revolutionary War. One of the primary grievances of the colonial revolutionaries was the enforcement of British treaties that forbade settlers from their trajectory of stealing more Indigenous lands. The year after the war, the founding fathers of America offered the Olive Branch Petition of 1775 to King George III in hopes that a sense of peace could exist between Great Britain and the newly forming America. The king refused the petition, thereby not accepting the said metaphorical olive branch, and the colonies intensified American nationalism and the dispossession of Indigenous peoples in the years following.

America claims to be peaceful and Christian, and, as such, liberally stamps signifiers of peace and freedom on its coinage. But the irony is that America is rather offensive in wars, especially those waged on Indigenous peoples to steal land. As the line of the frontier moved into more territory, Indigenous peoples were challenged through wars such as the Cherokee–American Wars, the Northwest Indian War, the Seminole Wars and the Rogue River War, among countless others. America rationalizes defeat by appealing to its perceived exceptionalism and desire for a self-serving peace that made the American empire-building project as expedient as possible.

Full dollar coins in 1854

Full dollar coins were also in circulation in 1853. However, from 1854 the dollar coin design was replaced with an updated profile portrait (Figure 5.2). The g*** coin displays a woman's head facing left from the neck up, with rudimentary features, an expressionless face and a headdress. This bears basic similarities to the Lady Liberty coin and is plainly a product of a genre that has staying power. One just needs to dip into one's coin jar to note that faces are a staple feature of many coins. The coin also changes the flora of the wreath on the reverse side to corn, tobacco, maple and cotton agriculture that Americans largely usurped from the lands of Indigenous peoples, and enslaved Black peoples to produce.

The most notable change of the coin design is indeed the switch to Lady Liberty culturally appropriating a feather headdress, Lady Liberty in Indigenous American drag. She becomes framed as an 'Indian princess', adorned with European stylization topped off with the Indigenous symbol as an afterthought. She appears confused about her identity, her symbolic power and the nature of relationships between Indigenous peoples and Americans. Lady Liberty 'taking'

Figure 5.2 Full dollar coin.

the headdress is reminiscent of a common practice for a leader who defeats a nation to take their crown, expunging them of the need to repay their debts through dominance and a 'finders-keepers' mentality. Lady Liberty with a headdress connotes entitlement and the dethroning of Indigenousness in America, illustrating that there is a new power. But there is also simultaneously other cultural work that is being performed on this coin, where a now American icon is simultaneously appropriating markers of Indigenousness.

Lady Liberty, by attempting to look Indigenous, functions to make herself seem as if she actually *is Indigenous* to the land, to America. She is granting herself the power to appropriate, but also foreshadows the belief that many Americans hold, that they are Indigenous to the land or perhaps even descended from an Indigenous person. This reflects the popular misguided adage that Americans are all 'part' Indigenous, have a long lost Indigenous relative or are simply now Indigenous to the land since so many years have passed since colonial imposition. These are settler attempts to move themselves toward legitimacy and even innocence (Tuck and Yang 2012).

Like Lady Liberty in this coin, Americans are historically known to pillage cultural symbols based on tropes of Indigenous peoples to construct a pretence that they are in fact 'the new Native' of the land (O'Brien, 2010). This kind of appropriative symbolism has a longer history, notably in European empires that frequently erect statues and produce art that contains cultural signifiers of lands they have colonized. The 1854 coin is a stylized, recycled jumble of colonial tropes.

Wolfe (2006: 389) states that settler colonialism requires Indigenous peoples to be eliminated or supplemented, yet settlers 'sought to recuperate indignity in order to express its difference'. There are numerous examples of intentionally pejorative appropriations and representations of Indigenous peoples in American culture to express difference (e.g., the media stereotype of Indigenous savagery). However, the coin designer's intention of a sympathetic addition of the headdress on Lady Liberty, though still thoroughly problematic and racist, suggests a strategic attempt to align America's identity with qualities of American views of Indigenous identity. Specifically, settler-invaders desperately wanted their ideas of Indigenous identity such as freedom, competency in and closeness to the land, and bravery projected back upon themselves (Deloria 1999). Drawing on Indigenous motifs was a way for Americans to distinguish themselves from the British. Additionally, in building up Indigenous peoples, Americans could also claim superiority in achieving victory against a formidable yet honourable opponent, and claim that they had absorbed the qualities and practices that could transform them into being capable 'new Natives'. Ultimately, this type of appropriation is rooted in white supremacist nostalgia for the frontier and selective deployment of symbols and ideologies to allow future generations to remain feeling legitimately American. This includes a false sense of entitlement to stolen lands and has led to the contemporary belief that many Americans hold: that non-white peoples and Indigenous peoples are threatening to their settler futurity.

Expanding the scope of this discussion, it is notable that 'Indian heads' and headdresses are present not just on G*** Rush coins but on a number of coins including the one cent coin, minted from 1859 to 1909, and ten dollar coins minted in 1907–8. The first with the 'In God We Trust' motto, the right-facing Indian head buffalo nickel, was designed by James Earl Fraser and minted from 1913 to 1938, along with others. The pervasiveness these representation and appropriation practices, forms of colonial fantasy, can be seen not just on coins but in many American cultural/commodity forms from Cherokee cars to sports teams that were once named R*dsk*ns and Indians.

Coins become colloquially accepted tokens that contain selectively edited imagery of those that were conquered, and they serve as a discursive vehicle to bolster colonial identity formation and maintenance. On the other hand, Indigenous faces decorate coins and are in the company of other coins with revered symbols including Lady Liberty. But it is the self-serving selectivity of signifying that presents historical incongruence that should be carefully considered. These coins can be interpreted to signify settler-colonial righteousness, and directly feed into the mainstream belief that decorating anything with synthetic ideas of Indigenousness 'honours' Indigenous peoples. This instead turns multidimensional Indigenous peoples into fixed images, freezing people in time. This is because dated and narrow representations of Indigenous life create stereotypes of Indigenous peoples as pre-modern, imaginary (e.g., in headdresses, war paint and buckskin loincloths) and defeated, rather than dynamic and contemporary.

Colonial process and coin production

Coins, like those I described, are important tokens of settler coloniality, and their journeys from metal to finished product reveal more. Their mass production, in tandem with the G*** Rush, is what began to transform America as a project into something 'real'. G*** was a substance of capitalist greed for colonizers; a means to claim land, impose power and war on Indigenous peoples in order to extract the natural resource and dispossess them. The extraction of Indigenous resources is a form of colonialism, but the control of Indigenous bodies, representation and cultural disenfranchisement is also part of the larger internal structure of settler colonialism. Stolen g*** is raw material, which was then refined, processed, pressed into coins and stamped with signifiers of a then-forming American nation. After minting they were disseminated, pushing out mass quantities of coins with stamped representations that both valorized and demonized Indigenous people, while methodically racially appropriating them. The coins, in the context of colonialism, are belongings that signify the identity crisis of America, and when placed in the larger story of the G*** Rush and Rogue River War, come alongside genocide in Oregon.

However, to settlers, these coins were ascribed different meanings rooted in futurity and survival. They represented the accumulation of wealth, or the early American dream, backed by the conception of Manifest Destiny. This conception refers to America's false belief that 'God' wanted settlers to invade Indigenous lands and seed ideas of democracy, capitalism, Christianity and white ideals from the East Coast to the West Coast and beyond its borders.

By the mid-1850s, currency was just starting to become more nationally standardized with the establishment of five mints operating in Charlotte, Dahlonega, New Orleans, Philadelphia and San Francisco. The opening of the San Francisco mint in 1854 made g*** bullion the official currency of the area, with the government mandating that private coinage be turned in and melted. Mints, which are factories that serve as a mechanism of government, expressed power and authority as they churned out coins that then trickled up and down the coast, aiming to replace and standardize the various currencies in dynamic circulation. These coins attempted to systematize value, filling a need created by a lack of trust in currency created with the influx of many competing forms.

Other currencies and transformations

There were well over ten types of currency in use in specific markets in Oregon, including Indigenous types referred to as alaquah-chick. These included dentalium, tusk-shaped shells from scaphopod molluscs, and off-white in colour. Indigenous peoples in Oregon even had tattoos on their forearms indicating equidistant lengths to determine value by measuring strings of shells. Olivella shells, fur pelts, beads, baskets, copper and ooligan grease were also common forms. Elsewhere, in what is now known as the East Coast, Indigenous currencies that were widespread in precolonial times were also appropriated by settlers, and significantly influenced the trajectory of American currency (Shell 2013). Wampum, for example, was adopted by colonists as legal tender, allowing for international transactions with Indigenous peoples. Over time, wampum was also counterfeited, devalued and eventually replaced with what was called paper wampum, paper bills that frequently had images of Indigenous peoples designed on them. Indigenous people struggled when colonizers monopolized the wampum that they needed for their holistic well-being. They also became alienated from new currency forms, often forced to sell their lands, if they had not already been stolen, in order to transact in newer, stricter markets to survive. This happened with different Indigenous currencies across the country.

Indigenous peoples were skilled in precolonial international diplomacies and trade cultures, which extended into the colonial era, when they used a variety of different Indigenous forms and colonial forms, including manufactured coins, concurrently. The shift, however, from exclusively Indigenous currencies to an assortment of both Indigenous and settler currencies to exclusively standardized colonial forms is one marked by strategic domination. These currency shifts are representative of a government that sought to control those markets, brand itself in relation to Indigenous peoples, shut out or ban traditional types of Indigenous transactions and practices (such as potlatch) and make Indigenous cultural forms obsolete relics.

Coins circulating in Oregon during the Rogue River War, and the iconography that they express, were likely taken for granted by the people that the coins belonged to, as most people do not carefully examine and perform semiotic analysis on their spare change. Regardless, these were material belongings that connected people to an imagined collective American identity, which was predicated on the elimination of Indigenous peoples. The 1853 and 1854 coins are iconic artefacts/belongings that codify American imperialism and settler colonialism. Moreover, they are important tokens that allow us to retrospectively question settler-colonial histories, Indigenous histories and debts that Indigenous nations in Oregon, and throughout America, are waiting to be rectified.

Further resources

Black, J. E. (2005) 'Sacagawea as commodity, currency, and cipher'. *Journal of Media and Cultural Politics* 1: 226–230.

Cordes, A. (2020) 'Revisiting stories and voices of the Rogue River War (1853–1856): A digital constellatory autoethnographic mode of Indigenous archaeology'. *Cultural Studies ↔ Critical Methodologies* 21(1): 56–69.

Cronon, W. (1983) *Changes in the Land: Indians, Colonists, and the Ecology of New England.* New York, NY: Hill and Wang.

Ganteaume, C. R. (2017) *Officially Indian: Symbols that Define the United States.* Minneapolis, MN: University of Minnesota Press.

Tveskov, M. A., Rose, C., Jones, G., and Maki, D. (2019) 'Every rusty nail is sacred, every rusty nail is good: Conflict archaeology, remote sensing, and community engagement at a Northwest Coast settler fort'. *American Antiquity* 84(1): 48–67.

Works cited

Cordes, A. (2020) 'Revisiting stories and voices of the Rogue River War (1853–1856): A digital constellatory autoethnographic mode of Indigenous archaeology'. *Cultural Studies ↔ Critical Methodologies* 21(1): 56–69.

Deloria, P. J. (1999) *Playing Indian.* New Haven CT: Yale University Press.

Mwangi, W. (2002) 'The lion, the native and the coffee plant: Political imagery and the ambiguous art of currency design in colonial Kenya'.

Geopolitics 7(1): 31–62. https://doi.org/10.1080/714000898 (accessed 13 September 2022).

O'Brien, J. M. (2010) *Firsting and Lasting: Writing Indians Out of Existence in New England*. Minneapolis MN: Minnesota Press.

Shell, M. (2013) *Wampum and the Origins of American Money*. Urbana IL: University of Illinois Press.

Tuck, E. and Yang, K. W. (2012) 'Decolonization is not a metaphor'. *Decolonization: Indigeneity, Education and Society* 1: 1–40.

Wolfe, P. (2006) 'Settler colonialism and the elimination of the Native'. *Journal of Genocide Research* 8(4): 387–409.

Note

1 To protect Indigenous lands from looting, we have rendered all references to the element with symbol Au and atomic number 79 as 'g***'.

2 Ongoing settler colonialism in America, in particular its relation to resource extraction, is also the focus of Szeman (Chapter 1) and Lassiter (Chapter 2), while settler colonialism more broadly is considered by Comyn (Chapter 4), Randell-Moon (Chapter 14) and Nir (Chapter 16).

6

Milo

Syahirah Abdul Rahman

When you type in the terms 'Milo' and 'Malaysia' on Google search, some of the first results you will see are questions such as 'Is Milo Malaysian?' and 'Why is Milo so popular in Malaysia?' Milo, a chocolate malt-powder drink is a staple brand and beverage among Malaysian households. Despite this cultural background, Milo was invented by Australian chemist Thomas Mayne during the Great Depression (1929–32) and is currently produced by Nestlé, a Swiss company that is also the world's largest maker of food and beverages. Despite Milo's international citizenship, the beverage is held dear in the hearts of many Malaysians.

A typical Malaysian childhood involves memories of a Milo truck turning into the driveway of the primary school, kids lining up outside the truck in the hot sun, waiting patiently for Milo's promotional staff to hand out tiny paper cups of the drink. The kids then would sit on the concrete floor in the school corridor, slowly sipping their Milo drinks, savouring every millilitre of their worth. The taste of that memory is so clear that if you were to ask a Malaysian person what is one of the best drinks in Malaysia, they would say Milo, and if you were to ask what was the best-tasting Milo, they would answer, 'The one I had from the Milo school trucks.'

Milo, pronounced 'mee-lo' in Malaysia, comes in green containers. They are sold in corner stores and supermarkets and can be ordered at nearly all food and beverage establishments in Malaysia. There are countless variations on how to enjoy Milo. Children spread the chocolate powder on a slice of bread to make a Milo sandwich. Adults order a glass of Milo *dinosaur* at their local *mamak*[1] restaurant: a glass of iced milo with a heap of undissolved Milo powder on

Figure 6.1 Image of a commemorative Milo tin issued for Merdeka and Malaysia Day 2021.

top. The extent of Milo's entanglement in the livelihoods of Malaysian citizens is such that one refers to the containers' shade of green as Milo green. Despite Milo's popularity and rather expensive price tag, there is a rather peculiar perception of the Milo containers themselves – a reflection not so much of the brand's quality but more of the material that it is made out of: *tin*.

My drive to find connections between Milo, produced by a multinational corporation, and the commodity of its container, extracted from Malaysia – tin – was largely inspired by a growing list of academics who have observed the colonial spirits that haunt present material objects and urban life. For example, Deborah Cowen (2019) has tracked the connections between national infrastructures in Canada and the UK. She mapped the importance of the transatlantic slave trades which assisted in circulating capital around the world, connecting national infrastructures with very different nationalistic narratives through identical histories of Indigenous dispossession and genocide. What Cowen's work reminds me of is the importance of untold stories in the making of capitalism. As economist Kalyan Sanyal (2014) has argued, there is a need to represent the neglected stories of the colonized; those who were integral in the makings of modern capitalism but whose roles have been disposed, marginalized and purposely ignored for the benefit of colonialism and imperialism.

More closely related to my present story of the Milo tin or, more importantly, its underlying commodity, tin, is Simon Naylor's (2000) work on the material culture of colonial commodities. Naylor focuses on tin cans, examining their importance to the networks of the British empire, its imperialism and modern-day globalization. In a similar vein, here I attempt to switch this focus around by highlighting the stories of the neglected in the British empire's conquest of tin, specifically, the stories of Malays in Malaya and, later, Malaysia. I share with Szeman (Chapter 1) a concern with the entangled colonial legacies that can be traced out behind 'ordinary' and 'everyday' consumer objects. In telling this story of tin, I hope to uncover the traces of colonialism in simple, taken-for-granted material objects that you see in your daily life. And thus begins the story of the Milo tin and its place in a small country in South-East Asia, Malaysia.

Kereta tin Milo

Putting aside the physical and chemical qualities of tin, among Malaysian laypeople the perception of tin often comes with a rather negative connotation. Specifically, tin is perceived as a low-quality metal. The reason for this has much to do with the Milo tins themselves. Besides feeding the people of Malaysia, Milo has also made a fascinating cultural mark on a completely different aspect of the country: the production of cars.

One has to go back to the 1950s, before the inception of Malaysia in 1963, and before the independence of Malaya from British colonization in 1957. Then, the majority of the population lived predominantly in agricultural villages. A legacy of this period is the term '*kereta tin Milo*' (trans.: Milo tin cars). The term was derived from a cultural phenomenon in which self-taught mechanics used recycled Milo tins rather than genuine parts to shoddily repair vehicles. The cost of genuine parts was very high and, due to the lack of income, mechanics simply found creative methods to provide their services. They would take recycled Milo tins, repurpose them as replacement panels for the vehicles they were fixing, mostly cars, and shoddily repaint over the panels to hide the material they had used. These shoddy repairs were often exposed when an accident occurred to a repaired car. The damage would scratch off the new paint, thus exposing the original Milo name on the tin replacement panels.

Since then, '*kereta tin Milo*' is used pejoratively to describe cars that are cheaply made or unsafe. The most prominent usage of this term is in fact in relation to Malaysia's own home-brand automotive company, Proton. The stigma against Proton is not always necessarily on account of the technical features of the company's vehicles. Much of the negative connotation actually stems from an idolization of anything European-made, a sentiment that originates from Malaysia's colonial past. During colonial periods, Eurocentrism played an important part in exploiting native communities' wealth by downplaying the value of their skills in business. This, coupled with the lack of economic and development opportunities given to native communities, created a stereotype that anything European-made was immediately of high quality. Alongside this idolization was constant criticism of home brands, especially if they were made by the Malay community. Thus, the stereotype had been that Europeans were well educated, diligent, high class and skilled. Meanwhile, Malaysians, specifically Malays, were uneducated, lazy, low class and unskilled. This stereotype permeated even to non-living aspects of daily life, including brands and companies. As such, European cars were and are parallel to high quality, good engineering, innovation and safety. In contrast, Proton, a Malaysian brand, was simply *kereta tin Milo*.

Proton, short for *Perusahaan Otomobil Nasional* (National Automobile Company) was set up in 1983 as part of the Malaysian government's strategy to enhance Malaysian industries through the development of a national car. The then prime minister, Dr Mahathir Mohamad, saw the lack of technological development in Malaysian industries as a skills-based issue. It could be argued that Dr Mahathir's vision for Proton was personal in nature. The former premier had grown up under three forms of colonial occupation: by the British, the Japanese and the British again. He spoke passionately against colonists and was open about his desire to overthrow the British economically, or at least to claim back from the British what they had taken from Malaya and Malaysia economically.

Despite having lived through Japan's brief occupation of Malaya, Dr Mahathir had a liking for the Japanese work ethic and planned for a national car brand to mimic Japan's success in overtaking American mass manufacturing in the automobile industry. Dr Mahathir saw Japan's success as representative of the ability of Asian countries to do well, and better than their Western, colonial counterparts, specifically the British. As such, the development of Proton was presented to Malaysians through two important policies, first, Look East, and second, Buy British Last. Both policies urged Malaysians to look to growing and successful Eastern countries such as South Korea and Japan as examples of economic success, rather than to the United Kingdom and/or other European countries.

Look East was instrumental in the development of Proton. Behind Look East was a bilateral trade agreement in which Mitsubishi was to invest in Proton as a National Car Project. Initially, Proton was financed through Heavy Industries Corporation of Malaysia (HICOM; a wholly government-owned company), which held 70% ownership of Proton, while Mitsubishi Motors and Mitsubishi Corporation each held a 15% stake, the ownership of which would be given back to Proton on completion of the bilateral agreement (Machado 1989). As part of the bilateral agreement, Mitsubishi would assist Proton in the designs of their first prototype cars, thereby contributing important technical and soft skills development needed for Malaysia's first home-grown automobile industry. Thus, Proton was founded not only as a means to develop a national car to stimulate the country's real economy, but was also used as a training ground to cultivate a generation of local engineers and to turn Malaysia from a consumption-based country into a production-based one. The history of this has much to do with the country's colonial histories, whereby the predominant ethnic group of Malaysia, the Malays, were disadvantaged educationally, due to the discriminatory British colonial policies.

In 2018, when Proton, which was privatized in 2012, was bought out by the Chinese multinational automotive firm Geely, Dr Mahathir lamented that this sale of the national car disrespected Malaysia's painful colonial past and the reasons why Proton existed.

Dr Mahathir's personal concerns had always permeated into his political ideologies, which included wanting to move away from the colonial perception that Malays should remain as farmers. In an interview on the Najib Razak administration's sale of Proton to foreign hands, specifically a Chinese firm, he remarked emotionally that the move had felt like giving the Malays' economy back into the control of the Chinese. He lamented, 'Jika anda mahu jadi negara petani, menanam padi dan menangkap ikan, okey, kita akan buat' ('if you want this country to become a country of farmers, of paddy planters, and of fishermen; then okay, we will do it') (Aw and Goh 2018).

Sejarah tin di koloni British-Malaya. The history of tin in colonial British-Malaya

Dr Mahathir's concerns were not unfounded, of course. Historical accounts have shown that growing up in colonial British-Malaya was unfavourable to non-aristocratic and non-royal Malays. Most Malays, such as Dr Mahathir himself, grew up in rural villages, far away from schools, businesses and other urban amenities. It is through these colonial histories that we may be able to learn about the irony behind the stigma that comes from the so-called low quality of Milo tins – because its underlying commodity, tin, happens to be one of the most valuable commodities in historical and modern times.

Firstly, beyond Milo tins themselves, tin is one of the most flexible and useful metals on Earth. Alloys of tin have various uses and are present in our daily lives in many forms, mostly in tin coatings to protect the surfaces of various household and industrial objects. In Malaya's colonial period, the demand for tin was so great that it assisted the British to attain unparalleled economic growth in the Industrial Revolution, tin being used in various forms of new manufacturing processes. Tin was in such great demand in the nineteenth century that it led to the British colonizing the lands that border present-day Malaysia. It is not so much tin, but the stigma of anything Malay-made that is the true subject of *kereta tin Milo* and Proton.

From colonial times, Malays have been stereotyped as lazy by British colonists who were displeased by Malay communities' reluctance to work in the harsh conditions of the tin mines, set up sporadically across three main states of Malaya. The deep interior of the tin mines made living conditions difficult, exposing miners to diseases such as malaria and smallpox, while open-cast mines were exposed to the blazing hot tropical sun (Leam Seng 2019; Siew 1953). Syed Hussein Alatas (1977) has written that miners were forced into extreme dependency on their employers, through a series of exploitative employment conditions. The tin mine owners often enticed workers with opium, sold on credit in order to keep workers distracted from their hunger and illnesses and, more importantly, dependent on their employers. Employers have also been documented as encouraging miners to gamble their wages in a game of chance stacked against them, thus leaving the miners indebted to their employers and forcing them to work beyond their agreed hours and preferences.

Reflecting the long, entangled histories of racialized distinctions that were activated in the exploitation and indebting of migrant labourers – a theme picked up in Part III, 'Borders' – miners who came from outside Malaya (for example, China) were often displaced from their families, their travel documents withheld by their employers, with the promise that these documents would be returned only after their travel expenses had been paid through hard labour. Prostitution dens and pawnbroking shops were also prevalent at tin mines, to distract miners from the harsh conditions of their employment. Many Malays of Islamic birth did not favour the conditions of the mines, as the consumption of 'earthly pleasures' such as drugs and prostitution is deemed the highest form of sin. As such, they would often reject work in the mines, which earned them the stereotypical epithet of being 'lazy'.

Malaysia, then made up of several Malay kingdoms (now known as the Malaysian states), was referred to as Malaya, and in the late nineteenth century and early twentieth century as British-Malaya. Malaya fell within the South-East Asian Tin Belt, and the tin produced there was categorized as Straits tin, comparable to and competitive against the tin produced in Cornwall in the UK) and Pulau Banka in Indonesia. From the 1800s to the early twentieth century, the South-East Asian Tin Belt was the most important tin-producing region of the world, producing 54% of the world's tin (Schwartz et al. 1995). British geologist Joseph Carne (1839) documented tin production and consumption in Great Britain. He wrote of the East India Company's operations in exploiting price negotiations against Straits tin producers, only to resell to China. It is important to highlight that Chinese tea imports had been integral to the survival of the East India Company, saving the company financially and establishing it as a major political authority over British colonies. Instrumental in the East India Company's control over Chinese tea was the trading of tin with China, produced in colonial British-Malaya.

The Industrial Revolution was also instrumental in Great Britain's decision to make a more prominent colonial mark in Malaya in the nineteenth century. The Industrial Revolution caused a great demand for tin as a material, thus pushing its price up considerably from the late 1840s to late 1890s. Before the Industrial Revolution, the price of tin was fixed, but its extraction in colonial countries such as British-Malaya meant that metal traders needed a faster way to communicate their contract prices to their international trading partners. The London Metal Market and Exchange Company (LME) was set up in 1877 for this purpose. It acted as one of the first advanced international financial institutions, using technologies such as the telegraph to assist in the faster communication of stocks and commodities trading for Great Britain and its international partners.

Demand for tin shot up beyond the needs of domestic consumption (in Great Britain, that is, as domestic consumption in Malaya was ignored in the colonial account of things). As a result, the British established an even greater colonial presence in Malaya, inviting mass migration by their Chinese trading partners to set up enterprises there specifically for tin trading and production. British-Malaya became even more of a lucrative colonial settlement for the British, its tin attracting British general investors to exploit the Malayan tin mines. Malaysia's first stock market, the Singapore Stockbrokers' Association, established in conjunction with Singapore in 1930, was set up specifically to assist global flows of investment into Malayan commodities. Of course, the arrangements of the stock exchange greatly discriminated against Malayan home enterprises, which were not given equal opportunities to trade on the exchange – although the domestic population had been largely displaced from commercial and economic activities, such that few of them could be entrepreneurs in the first place.

Tin, among other commodities extracted from Malaya, was so important to Great Britain that it helped to finance the British during the Second World War. Professor Richard Stubbs, quoted in prominent Malaysian economist Jomo Kwame Sundaram's (1986) *A Question of Class*, mentioned that in 1951 Malaya earned US$400 million in government income, much of this derived from commodities exports. Eighty-three per cent of this amount was redirected to London to finance post-war reconstruction in Great Britain and to service international balance of payment deficits.

Despite the riches that tin brought to Great Britain in the past, and to the UK today, back in the early 1900s the Malay communities were pushed further away from commercial areas of British-Malaya. As part of the British colonial strategy, Malays, who made up the majority of Malaya's population, were purposely left out of economic spaces. This was done through several measures, the most important of which were discriminatory practices in education, which would have provided students with professional skills needed for higher-paid employment and/or entrepreneurial and business opportunities. Instead, the British wanted the Malays to stay in rural areas, focusing on agricultural jobs such as farming and/or fishing. This can be exemplified by the statement of the British Chief Secretary of Federated Malay States, George Maxwell, who said that the strategy to educate Malays was 'to make the son of the fisherman or peasant a more intelligent fisherman or peasant than his father had been, and a man whose education will enable him to understand how his own lot fits in with the scheme of life around him'.

As a result, when Malaya gained independence in 1957, income disparity between the Malays and other ethnic groups of the country was extremely high, with Malays accounting for 75% of poor households. Studying the number of graduates from the University of Malaya, Malaya's only university at the time, is telling with regard to the racial imbalance in education. For example, between 1960 and 1970, the numbers of Chinese and Malay graduates with a Bachelor of Science degree from the university were 1,488 and 69, respectively (Abdul Khalid 2014). For the Bachelor of Engineering, the numbers of Chinese and Malay graduates were 408 and 4, respectively. The disparity is jarring when one considers that Malays made up 70% of the local population, followed by Chinese (20%), Indian (5%) and others (5%).

Against the historical backdrop of tin in Malaysia, it is ironic that tin was and is used pejoratively against Proton, even though the metal had been instrumental in Great Britain's growth as an empire, courtesy of its colonization of Malaya. Although the British made considerable financial gains from the tin mines of Malaya, all that was left domestically was a legacy of racial stereotyping backed by the legacy of discriminatory practices. In 1983, when Proton was set up by Dr Mahathir in his mission to push the Malay communities upwards in income and skills, it is little wonder that the company was stigmatized. How could a Malay-made car be good? They were not like the Europeans, who had years of engineering training. Malays had been farmers and fishermen after all, according to many. How could they possibly make cars?

Tin Milo okay apa ...: Milo tins aren't so bad ...

In 2020, Proton celebrated the thirty-fifth anniversary of its first *kereta tin Milo*, the Saga. Like Malaysia, Proton has grown considerably, from becoming an important skills-growth firm for Malaysian engineers to being one of the biggest producers of cars in the world. Despite the many criticisms, the firm has been instrumental in many Malaysians' lives, as important as the Milo tins that its vehicles are supposedly made of. During its years as a national car company, Proton was protected by government policies in the form of protective barrier taxes against foreign car purchases, the burden of which were borne by Malaysian consumers.

During Dr Mahathir's premiership from 1981 to 2003, tariffs on imported cars were as high as 300% in order to protect Malaysia's national cars, or what the former premier called a 'symbol of national dignity' (Jaipragas and Woon 2018). As P. Gunasegaram (2017) analysed, Proton's protective barrier cost Malaysian consumers additional taxes averaging 30,000 Malaysian ringgit (approximately £5,600 at 2020 exchange rates) per vehicle purchased. As soon as tariffs on imported cars were relaxed following the end of Dr Mahathir's administration, Proton faced a sharp decline in sales, costing dearly in terms of government expenditure to maintain the firm. Proton was privatized in 2012, as the Najib Razak administration found the national car company's maintenance to be a burden on the government. Later, the company was sold to Geely, thus losing its title as Malaysia's national car company.

Despite the changes in Proton, what has remained the same is the global importance of tin as a commodity. From the Milo tins, we have traced the commodification of a simple object that we take for granted, tracing it back into what Simon Naylor (2000) calls the circuits of capital. Today, tin trading is still extremely important to the UK economy. This can be exemplified by the 1.24 million lots (one 'lot' is five tonnes) of tin futures traded on the LME each year. Further, LME Tin (the official trading name of tin on the LME) is listed as one of the most expensive metals among all non-ferrous metals traded on the LME. As of January 2022, LME Tin was traded at the bid price of US$44,190 per tonne. However, the most actively traded tin contracts on LME are the three-month futures contracts, which were established because, when the LME was established, three months was the time that it took for tin to be shipped from Malaysia. As shown by Kalba (Chapter 18), London-based financial exchanges have always been intimately connected to imperial exploitation, despite traders' disavowal of their role in labour exploitation, violence and resource extraction. If one were to ask, however, how much of this wealth can be attributed to a small South-East Asian country called Malaysia, where the name of its national car is viewed derogatorily by its own people, mocked for its quality that is 'as good as a Milo tin', they would simply say 'I don't know'. As we have learned in this story of the Milo tin, the ghosts of colonialism have never really gone away. In fact, its spirits continue to live on, making distinctive marks in the lives of those who have been colonized, those whose stories are often neglected. With this story, I hope to have engaged readers to think of these histories that continue to exist in our daily lives, now in the most trivial forms, in actions as simple as consuming a glass of chocolate drink at a local twenty-four-hour *mamak* restaurant.

Further resources

Ahmad Kamal, I. M. A. (2020) 'One man's incredible "saga" in designing Malaysia's first national car!' *The Star*, 30 August. www.nst.com.my/lifestyle/sunday-vibes/2020/08/620607/one-mans-incredible-saga-designing-malaysias-first-national.

Alatas, S. H. (1977) *The Myth of the Lazy Native: A Study of the Image of the Malays, Filipinos and Javanese from the 16th to the 20th Century and Its Function in the Ideology of Colonial Capitalism*. London: Psychology Press.

Cowen, D. (2020) 'Following the infrastructures of empire: Notes on cities, settler colonialism, and method'. *Urban Geography* 41(4): 469–486.

Naylor, S. (2000) 'Spacing the can: Empire, modernity, and the globalisation of food'. *Environment and Planning A*. 32(9): 1625–1639.

Yamada, H. (1971) 'The Origins of British Colonialization of Malaya with Special References to its Tin'. *Developing Economies* 9(3): 225–245.

Works cited

Abdul Khalid, M. (2014) *The Colour of Inequality: Ethnicity, Class, Income and Wealth in Malaysia*. Kuala Lumpur: MPH Publishing.

Alatas, S. H. (1977) *The Myth of the Lazy Native: A Study of the Image of the Malays, Filipinos and Javanese from the 16th to the 20th Century and Its Function in the Ideology of Colonial Capitalism*. London: Psychology Press.

Aw, N. and Goh, N. (2018) *Mengapa Dr M tetap pertahan kereta nasional ketiga*. www.malaysiakini.com/news/440149 (accessed 4 August 2020).

Carne, J. (1839) 'Statistics of the Tin-Mines in Cornwall, and of the Consumption of Tin in Great Britain'. *Journal of Statistical Society of London* 2(4): 250–268.

Cowen, D. (2019) 'Following the infrastructures of empire: Notes on cities, settler colonialism, and method'. *Urban Geography* 41(4): 1–18.

Gunasegaram, P. (2017) 'The price M'sians pay to prop up ailing Proton'. *Malaysia Kini*, 28 March. www.malaysiakini.com/columns/377219 (accessed 3 October 2020).

Jaipragas, B. and Woon, K. C. (2018) 'Did Najib sell Proton to Chinese because it was Mahathir's brainchild?' *South China Morning Post* 12 February. www.scmp.com/week-asia/business/article/2132772/will-proton-be-political-football-mahathir-uses-against-najib (accessed 6 October 2020).

Leam Seng, A. T. (2019) 'Of magic and opium – hardship faced by early tin prospectors!' *New Straits Times*, 19 May. www.nst.com.my/lifestyle/sunday-vibes/2019/05/489672/magic-and-opium-hardship-faced-early-tin-prospectors (accessed 10 October 2020).

Machado, K. G. (1989) 'Japanese transnational corporations in Malaysia's state sponsored heavy industrialization drive: The HICOM automobile and steel projects'. *Pacific Affairs* 62(4): 504–531.

Naylor, S. (2000) 'Spacing the can: Empire, modernity, and the globalisation of food'. *Environment and Planning A* 32(9): 1625–1639.

Sanyal, K. (2014) *Rethinking Capitalist Development: Primitive Accumulation, Governmentality and Post-colonial Capitalism*. London: Routledge.

Schwartz, M. O., Rajah, S. S., Askury, A. K., Putthapiban, P. and Djaswadi, S. (1995) 'The southeast Asian tin belt'. *Earth-Science Reviews*, 38(2–4): 95–293.

Siew, N. C. (1953) 'Labour and Tin Mining in Malaya'. Southeast Asia Program, Department of Far Eastern Studies, Cornell University.

Sundaram, J. K. (1989) *A Question of class: Capital, the state and uneven development in Malaysia*. Oxford and Singapore, Monthly Review Press, 1986.

Note

1 Mamak restaurants are 24-hour Indian Muslim food establishments institutional to the Malaysian culture.

Part III

Borders

'Not everyone alive in the present is automatically included in its sense of "living" or "present".' This quotation from Esther Peeren's book *The Spectral Metaphor* offers a thought-provoking frame for 'Borders', the theme of our next three chapters, in which migration into the UK and US vividly embodies colonialism's afterlife.

The process of crossing a country's border is experienced very differently by travellers, depending on what part of the world you are from. EU citizens can travel from country to country within the European Union with minimal hassle. If you hold a passport from the UK or the US, you can travel to many countries without restrictions. The situation is quite different for international travellers trying to enter US or UK borders – even trickier if you are a migrant, potentially hazardous if you are an undocumented migrant.

Migrants, particularly undocumented migrants, face many forced interactions with finance capital. Migrants can be driven across potentially unwelcoming borders by indebtedness incurred at home, only to be burdened with new debts on arrival. In this sense, undocumented migrants become living ghosts in constant motion, never arriving, although their journeys are profitable for various entities along the way.

Our first encounter with borders comes from Kathryn Medien (Chapter 7), who portrays the UK border as a lethal apparatus that criminalizes movements through carceral (i.e., related to prisons and policing) surveillance. Here, Medien draws on the notion of carceral capitalism, a concept proffered by Jackie Wang in her 2018 book of the same name. Wang defines carceral capitalism as a very modern and particular form of racial capitalism, encompassing parasitic governance and predatory lending. Parasitic governance engages in several techniques, including automated processing, extractive practices, confinement and gratuitous violence. Medien examines the private debt-collection agencies contracted to collect debt from overseas patients, using all the threatening techniques for which debt-collection agencies are well known. The intended outcome? To deter undocumented migrants from seeking medical attention for fear of Home Office involvement. The unintended outcome? Driving vulnerable people into the shadows, thwarting national efforts to manage public health.

Medien looks at the border erected at hospitals, clinics and sites that form Britain's National Health Service or NHS. The NHS is a much-cherished British institution, funded through general taxation, enabling everyone to receive free healthcare at the point of use. Not quite everyone. Medien examines the new reality for migrants who must prove eligibility for healthcare or face upfront charges – or deportation. The slow marketization of the NHS, and the expansion of a range of managerial reforms, as well as disastrous 'private finance initiatives' (where hospitals lease back buildings at often inflated costs from private developers) introduced since the 1990s, have put strains on the NHS that make it an increasingly stretched public service, even for those who are not forced to endure additional surveillance and charges by virtue of their migration status. In truth, too, the recent turn to an explicitly exclusionary NHS does not come from nowhere; the Commonwealth migrants who were drawn in to staff the NHS after the Second World War were met with racist exclusionary labour and housing markets, and a socialist government comfortable with ongoing colonial trusteeship over their 'sending' countries.

Eve Dickson, Rachel Rosen and Kehinde Sorinmade (Chapter 8) contend that twenty-first-century borders have their own temporality. Many social scientists use the term 'temporality' to refer to the way in which we experience time, and how we organize our lives around those experiences and understandings of time. The temporality of borders for many racialized migrants could mean that your daily life is structured by concerns about debt repayments and the need to constantly keep up with bureaucratic requirements. The three co-authors transport us across the UK's formal borders, setting us down at the school gates, where they demonstrate how the UK's 'hostile environment' erects borders in multiple places.

The 'hostile environment' is a UK Home Office policy introduced in 2012, representing some of the harshest immigration policies in Britain's history, solidified through the 2014 and 2016 UK Immigration Acts. Collectively, hostile environment policies suggest that jobs, benefits and services are the sole preserve of British subjects, where British subjects are constructed as white. In this chapter, the border is erected between migrant parents and their children's education.

Britain's state schools are a local government entitlement for most residents; some families are also entitled to free school meals. Migrant parents whose passports are stamped 'no recourse to public funds' are often forced to pay for school meals, propelling them into more indebtedness to keep their children educated. Children become collateral, as debts incurred by migrant parents in one place must pay back debts in another place. Dickson, Rosen and Sorinmade redefine a modern British empire built on finance capital's continued extraction of 'other' bodies.

Carceral capitalism becomes literal when Christian Rossipal (Chapter 9) examines the US immigration detention system, itself a billion-dollar industry and an extension of the prison-industrial complex. In his chapter, carceral capitalism is manifested through both parasitic governance and predatory lending. Rossipal demonstrates that when undocumented migrants cross the US–Mexican border they soon encounter invisible borders of finance capital. Once detained, some migrants negotiate temporary 'freedom' through monetary bonds offered by immigration bond companies operating in a grey zone opened up by US public policy. Such zones are classic haunting territory, as Rossipal demonstrates in his analysis of immigration bond services and their disturbing appropriation of humanitarian language to promote predatory debt.

All three 'Borders' chapters interrogate the complex symbiosis between private companies and nation-states to facilitate the flow of global capital through public dispossession.

Works cited

Peeren, E. (2014) *The Spectral Metaphor: Living Ghosts and the Agency of Invisibility* Basingstoke: Palgrave Macmillan.

Wang, J. (2018) *Carceral Capitalism*. South Pasadena CA: Semiotext(e).

'The trust will pursue debt through all means necessary'

Kathryn Medien

'The Trust will pursue debt through all means necessary.' This is the response that I received to a Freedom of Information Act (FOI) request that I submitted to a London-based NHS Trust. I had specifically asked the Trust to 'provide details of the Cost Recovery Programme, specifically how outstanding charges are enforced and recuperated by the hospital'. Their response, in many ways, encapsulates the aggressive financialization of NHS secondary care for migrants in Britain. In 2015, later amended in 2017, the UK government introduced the National Health Service (Charges for Overseas Visitors) Regulations, which build on earlier legislation (1982, 2015) in order to place a statutory duty on secondary care NHS providers to establish whether a person is a lawful resident in the UK before providing them with treatment. Justified through narratives of 'health tourism' and austerity, hospitals now have a duty in law to check the immigration and residential status of all patients and make those who are deemed not 'ordinary residents' pay for their treatment at 150% of the cost to the NHS.

The introduction of these charges has led to the attendant creation of Overseas Visitor Manager posts in NHS trusts and the implementation of an Overseas Visitor Cost Recovery Programme. Through a complex system of data gathering and sharing between the NHS and the Home Office, regulations stipulate that if any bills for NHS treatment over £500 are outstanding for two months, hospitals must pass on patient details to the Home Office. This will result in the likely refusal of any future visa applications and, in some cases, detention and deportation. Furthermore, in implementing the Cost Recovery Programme, NHS trusts employ third-party debt-collection

[Attach patient ID sticker here]

NHS
North Middlesex University Hospital
NHS Trust

Pre-Attendance Form

Why have I been asked to complete this form?

NHS hospital treatment is not free to all. All hospitals have a legal duty to establish if patients are entitled to free treatment. Please complete this form to help us with this duty. A parent/guardian should complete the form on behalf of a child. **On completing the form, you must read and sign the declaration below.**

Please complete this form in BLOCK CAPITALS

Family name/surname:		
First name/given name:		Date of birth:

DECLARATION: TO BE COMPLETED BY ALL

This hospital may need to ask the Home Office to confirm your immigration status to help us decide if you are eligible for free NHS hospital treatment. In this case, your personal, non-clinical information will be sent to the Home Office. The information provided may be used and retained by the Home Office for its functions, which include enforcing immigration controls overseas, at the ports of entry and within the UK. The Home Office may also share this information with other law enforcement and authorised debt recovery agencies for purposes including national security, investigation and prosecution of crime, and collection of fines and civil penalties.

If you are chargeable but fail to pay for NHS treatment for which you have been billed, it may result in a future immigration application to enter or remain in the UK being denied. Necessary (non-clinical) personal information may be passed via the Department of Health to the Home Office for this purpose.

DECLARATION:

- I have read and understood the reasons I have been asked to complete this form
- I agree to be contacted by the trust to confirm any details I have provided.
- I understand that the relevant official bodies may be contacted to verify any statement I have made.
- The information I have given on this form is correct to the best of my knowledge.
- I understand that if I knowingly give false information then action may be taken against me. This may include referring the matter to the hospital's local counterfraud specialist and recovering any monies due.

Signed:		Date:
Print name:		Relationship
On behalf of:		to patient:

1. ALL: PERSONAL DETAILS – *Please answer all questions that apply to you*

Do you usually live in the UK?	YES: ☐ NO: ☐	Nationality:	
Address in the UK:		Passport number:	
		Country of issue:	
Telephone number:		Passport expiry date:	
Mobile number:		Dual Nationality:	
Email:		Date of entry into the UK:	
Will you return to live in your home country?	YES: ☐ NO: ☐	If yes, when?	
Address OUTSIDE the UK:		Name and address of Employer (UK or overseas):	
Country:		Country:	
Contact telephone:		Employer telephone:	

Figure 7.1 A copy of an NHS Pre-Attendance Form received in response to a Freedom of Information Request submitted to a London NHS trust.

2. ALL: OFFICIAL DOCUMENTATION		
Please tell us which of the following documents you currently hold (check all that apply):		
☐ Current United Kingdom passport	☐ Current European Union passport	
☐ Current non-EU passport with valid entry visa	Visa No.	
☐ Student visa ☐ Visit visa	Visa expiry date:	
☐ Asylum Registration Card (ARC)	ARC No.	
Other – please state:	BRP No.	

3. ALL: YOUR STAY IN THE UK – *You may be required to provide documentation*		
Please tell us about the purpose of your stay in the UK (check all that apply):		
☐ Holiday/visit friends or family	☐ On business	☐ To live here permanently
☐ To work	☐ To study	☐ To seek asylum
☐ Other – please state:		
How many months have you spent OUTSIDE the UK in the last 12 months?		
☐ None	☐ Up to 3 months ☐ 3-6 months	☐ Over 6 months
Please indicate the reason for any absence from the UK in the last 12 months (check all that apply)		
☐ I live in another country	☐ A holiday/to visit friends	☐ To work
☐ I frequently commute (business/second home overseas)		☐ To study
☐ Other – please state:		

4. ALL: GP DETAILS – *If you are registered with a GP in the UK*	
GP/surgery name:	Address of GP surgery:
GP telephone:	
NHS number:	

5. HEALTH OR TRAVEL INSURANCE DETAILS – *If the UK is not your permanent place of residency*		
Do you have insurance?	YES: ☐ NO: ☐	Name and address of insurance provider:
Membership number:		
Insurance telephone:		

6. EUROPEAN HEALTH INSURANCE CARD (EHIC) DETAILS – *if you live in another EEA country*			
Do you have a <u>non-UK</u> EHIC?	YES: ☐ NO: ☐	If yes, please enter the data from your EHIC below:	
	If you are visiting from another EEA country and do not hold a current EHIC, you may be billed for the cost of any treatment received outside the Accident and Emergency (A&E) dept. Charges will apply if you are admitted to a ward or need to return to the hospital as an outpatient.	3	
		4	
		5	6
		7	
		8	9

7. STUDENT DETAILS – *If you have come to the UK to study*			
Name of college/university:		Telephone:	
Course dates From:	To:	Number of hours/week:	

If you have completed this form in the A&E department, please give it to a receptionist or nurse before leaving. If you are admitted to any ward or referred for further treatment outside the A&E department, charges may apply. Please expect to be interviewed by a member of our Overseas Visitors Team

Figure 7.1 (cont.)

agencies to recuperate healthcare debt 'through all means necessary'. What does the Trust's response tell us about the deepening relationship between finance capital, digital surveillance and internal border controls in Britain? In what ways does this regime of hostility and cost recovery represent a continuation of Britain's colonial logics of population governance in the aftermaths of empire – logics which are discussed in relation to the administration of British empire by Abdul Rahman (Chapter 6)? And how might we understand the introduction of NHS charges as operating as a lethal deterrent for certain racialized migrants who seek access to healthcare in Britain? Indeed, during the COVID-19 epidemic we have seen just how lethal a deterrent this can be.[1]

Entanglements with empire: 'making a fair contribution'

In order to fully understand the context within which the National Health Service (Charges for Overseas Visitors Regulations) (2015, 2017) came about, it is important to situate this policy within Britain's history of empire and colonialism, along with the racially exclusive development of Britain's welfare state. Against notions that Britain is a postcolonial nation-state, Nadine El-Enany (2020: 3) has argued for an understanding of Britain as 'a racially and colonially configured space in which the racialized poor are subject to the operation of internal borders and are disproportionately vulnerable to street and state racial terror'. Within this geography of 'colonial space', El-Enany charts how successive nationality and immigration Acts, including the 1948 British Nationality Act, 1965 Immigration and Nationality Act, 1971 Immigration Act and 1981 British Nationality Act, have redefined post-empire Britain in order to preserve the financial 'spoils of empire' – the wealth derived from centuries of colonialism and enslavement – for Britain's white populace, using immigration law to keep such wealth out of the hands of racialized populations from whom it was derived (El-Enany 2020: 2).

While the creation of the NHS in 1948 is often heralded as creating a universal health system for all, racialized forms of entitlement and control have been present from its inception. In its early years the NHS benefited greatly from the labour of formally colonized populations, particularly through the overseas recruitment of nurses and ancillary workers from the Caribbean (Bryan, Dadzie and Scafe 2018). Yet the provision to charge NHS patients deemed not 'ordinarily resident' is an early and salient feature of the NHS. Arrangements for charging those deemed 'not ordinarily resident' for healthcare have existed since 1977, while notions that the NHS exists to serve and preserve white Britishness date back to its founding. As El-Enany has argued:

> The British welfare state has always embodied the assertion of white entitlement to the spoils of colonial conquest. The 1942 Beveridge Report perhaps captured this spirit best when it declared that 'housewives as Mothers have vital work to do in ensuring the adequate continuance of the British Race and British ideals in the world.' Britain has always been an internally bordered, hostile environment for migrants, with access to welfare made contingent on legal status.
> (El-Enany 2020: 69)

These assertions of white entitlement to Britain and its welfare state, and the attendant construction of racialized populations as underserving of access to it, have become pronounced through the politics of austerity, the 2016 Leave Campaign that preceded Brexit and the hostile environment policies that have emerged out of the 2014 and 2016 Immigration Acts. Arising out of all of these sites is a notion that it is simply not fair for migrants to come to Britain and access the benefits, services and jobs that ought to be the sole preserve of British subjects, who here are constructed as white (Shilliam 2018). In the specific context of the National Health Service (Charges for Overseas Visitors) Regulations (2015), the Department of Health has articulated these regulations as a request for migrants to make a *fair* contribution to health services. Indeed, 'ensuring fairness' and 'making a fair contribution' have been the titles and language used throughout public consultation and in policy documents (Department of Health 2013, 2017). As Sir Keith Pearson, Chair of Health Education England, remarked in a video on the NHS Cost Recovery Programme, 'the NHS is a national health service, not an international one'.[2]

It is within this context of 'fairness' that certain migrants from outside of the European Economic Area, including those with no recourse to public funds (NRPF) and those who have yet to apply for asylum or whose asylum applications have been refused, are now require to pay an upfront charge of 150% of the value of the treatment (Shahvisi 2019). Covering all secondary care services, including maternity and post-natal care, cancer treatment, cardiology, among others, the charges entwine border controls with healthcare and situate vulnerable racialized populations as materially and figuratively indebted to the British state. Through the introduction of these charges, Britain's borders move from airport terminals and ports of entry into healthcare institutions, operating as a lethal 'apparatus that facilitates, regulates, stigmatizes, and criminalizes movements in space and time' (Mitropoulos 2017). The charges install a regime of racial profiling within healthcare institutions, turning healthcare workers into border guards and positioning all of those who appear or sound 'foreign' vulnerable to profiling and questioning. The implications of being categorized as a person with NRPF for school-age children is explored in more detail by Dickson and colleagues (Chapter 8).

Carceral healthcare debt

Since the coming into effect of upfront charging in October 2017, there is significant evidence that the NHS charges operate as deterrent to healthcare access, with migrant women seeking to access maternity and post-natal care being disproportionately affected (Maternity Action 2017, 2018). Everyone seeking to access secondary NHS care is required to fill in a pre-attendance form on visiting a hospital, such as the one shown in Figure 7.1.

This form, which I received in response to an FOI request to an NHS trust, states that the details of patients may be passed on to the Home Office and other law enforcement authorities, and that any outstanding debt may be passed on to debt-recovery agencies for recuperation. The use of third-party debt-collection agencies by NHS trusts has been a recurring theme in my research, with a large number of trusts contracting CCI Credit Management, a debt-collection agency who list 'collecting NHS debt from overseas patients' with the help of their '90 offices servicing 130 countries' as one of their core competencies.

Jackie Wang (2018) has called on us to extend our definition of the carceral – a term that is characterized as anything related to prisons and prison infrastructure – to encompass the various racialized systems of financialization and debt and technologies of surveillance and control that are central to capitalism. The relation between carceral regimes and racialized systems of indebtedness is examined further in the chapters by Rossipal (Chapter 9) on immigration bonds in the US and by Stork (Chapter 17) on predatory lending and Black access to higher education, also in the US. In arguing that instruments of credit are carceral instruments of unfreedom, Wang examines the US practice of debt-financed government, whereby local municipalities increasingly rely on private credit which is then offloaded to their constituents in the form of a fine-and-fee regime for traffic violations, court fees and a privatized court and prison system. Together, for Wang, these modes of 'predatory lending' and 'parasitic governance' form the 'two main modalities of contemporary racial capitalism' (Wang 2018: 69). For the undocumented migrants, 'failed' asylum seekers and other groups who are met with charges under the NHS/Home Office regime, their existence in Britain is already coded by the carceral logic of 'illegality'. The extension of healthcare debt into their lives, tied to an expansive carceral surveillance and border regime, represents a tactic of predatory carceral capitalism that positions certain racialized populations as vulnerable to 'premature death' (Gilmore 2007: 28).

Emerging research has found that undocumented migrants are failing to seek medical attention for fear of Home Office involvement. A report found that three pregnant women had died after being reluctant to access care over fears of costs and immigration enforcement (MBRRACE-UK, 2019), while a study produced by charity Maternity Action (2018) found that new mothers were receiving threating phone calls and letters from debt collectors just weeks after giving birth. In their interviews with women targeted by the charging regime for maternity and post-natal care, they described the kinds of fears and anxieties that shape their lives:

> I am afraid that if I go to the hospital, they will charge me and I'm so afraid what's gonna happen to me if I say that I don't have money to pay for that. If they will detain me, or if after I have delivered the baby if I'm gonna stay at the hospital or in a detention centre or something like that. (Helena, Maternity Action 2018: 46)

> It is not just a bill to me, or not even the bill, the harassment I had to endure all those months because I couldn't pay. So I was very stressed, and that affected the way I look after my children, it affected how confident I was to be able to have a different role in society, like work or study and other things, I basically stopped for a year or so, so I could pay this debt. I felt like I was in debt with the whole country! (Isabella, Maternity Action 2018: 30)

The carceral logics of the state interweave debt, healthcare and border controls, creating a hostile environment for already subjugated populations. If the welfare state is designed to promote and secure the health and vitality of the British populace, then the NHS charging regime places these women and many others on its necropolitical[3] underside, figuratively and materially indebting those deemed 'not ordinarily resident' to the British state.

Financial belonging

The use of credit and debt instruments extends beyond NHS debt and the use of credit agencies and bailiffs. In September 2019 it emerged that Lewisham and Greenwich NHS Trust, who run two hospitals in south-east London, had since 2015 been passing patients' confidential information, including name, date of birth and residential address, to private credit check agency Experian in order to conduct credit footprint checks. As part of an NHS pilot scheme, the algo-rithmic credit footprint checks work to 'confirm residency by matching an individual to an address using a patient's digital footprint and then analysing credit bureaus for other aspects which could "disprove" residency against economic activity' (Lintern 2019). In other words, the footprint checks work to assess the likelihood of lawful residency in Britain through the examination of one's digital economic activity, with the absence of such activity deeming a patient potentially an unlawful resident and thus chargeable for treatment. Taking place without the knowledge of the patients concerned, the credit footprint checks assisted Lewisham and Greenwich NHS Trust in generating £4.2 million in invoices in 2017–18 (Lintern 2019). After coming under public scrutiny, the Trust announced in 2019 that they were suspending their data-sharing agreement with Experian while an independent review was conducted (Lewisham and Greenwich NHS Trust 2019).

The Trust argued that Experian's services acted as a 'non-discriminatory way of potentially identifying patients that are not entitled to free NHS treatment' (Lintern 2019). However, this use of algorithms and big data to detect economic activity arguably ushers in new forms of racialized bordering and surveillance. In their work on smart border technologies, Tamara Vukov argues that the increasing technologization of the border using data-driven, algorithmic technologies, rather than 'postracial', allows 'race [to be] monitored and produced through the tracking of nonnormative movements' (Vukov 2016: 87). Through the algorithmic predicting of immigration status via economic activity, the credit-footprint checks equate those who are not economically active in the UK with the racialized marker of 'health tourism'. As such, they function as a digital mode of surveillance that codes those whose economic activity is deemed 'abnormal' – lacking in direct debits, credit cards, a bank account and so forth – as subjectable to racialized border controls. These checks work in concert with the broader hostile environment policies, which until 2018 required UK banks and building societies to check the identity of every bank account holder against a Home Office database and gave banks the power to close the bank accounts of those deemed 'illegal'.

This chapter has sought to illustrate the role that debt and indebtedness play within NHS migrant care, tied to Britain's expansive carceral border regime. Here the border violently emerges in hospitals, birthing centres and bailiff visits and retains a constant presence in the lives of those targeted by the charging regime and border apparatus. While they are framed as a request for vulnerable migrant populations to make a 'fair contribution' to British society, I have argued that NHS charges and the pursuit of debt through all means necessary should be situated within the afterlives of British empire, whereby immigration controls operate to secure the 'spoils of empire' for Britain's white populace (El-Enany, 2020).

At the same time, I have sought to elaborate on the important role that digital technologies play in surveilling migrant populations and expanding the frontiers and possibilities of debt through the creation of new technological instruments that can be used in the service of state racism and internal bordering. Here, seemingly banal financial products – credit cards, direct debits, a bank account – are utilized as proof of economic activity, which in turn generates data on residency and entitlement to welfare services. Tracing and understanding these deepening and profitable relations between welfare, debt, debt-collection agencies, credit footprint technologies and immigration and border controls is vital both in tracking state racism, border infrastructures and the expanding frontiers of capitalism and in calling for their abolition.

Further resources

Bhambra, G. K. (2017) 'Brexit, Trump, and "methodological whiteness": On the misrecognition of race and class'. *The British Journal of Sociology*, 68: 214–S232. https://doi.org/10.1111/1468–4446.12317 (accessed 9 August 2021).

Button, D., Salhab, A., Skinner, J., Yule, A. and Medien, K. (2020) 'Patients not passports: Challenging border controls in healthcare'. https://fass.open.ac.uk/school-social-sciences-global-studies-sociology/news/patients-not-passports-challenging-border (accessed 9 August 2021).

Corporate Watch (2018) *The UK Border Regime: A Critical Guide*. London: Freedom Press for Corporate Watch.

Okolosie, L. (2020) 'A reignited spirit: Black women's lives in Britain'. Verso Blog. www.versobooks.com/blogs/3949-a-reignited-spirit-black-women-s-lives-in-britain (accessed 6 September 2022).

Works cited

Bryan, B., Dadzie, S. and Scafe, S. (2018) *The Heart of the Race: Black Women's Lives in Britain*. London: Verso Books.

Department of Health (2013) *Sustaining Services, Ensuring Fairness*. https://assets.publishing.service.gov.uk/government/uploads/system/uploads/attachment_data/file/268630/Sustaining_services__ensuring_fairness_-_Government_response_to_consultation.pdf (accessed 6 September 2022).

Department of Health (2017) *Making a Fair Contribution: Government Response to the Consultation on the Extension of Charging Overseas Visitors and Migrants Using the NHS in England*. https://assets.publishing.service.gov.uk/government/uploads/system/uploads/attachment_data/file/590027/Cons_Response_cost_recovery.pdf (accessed 6 September 2022).

El-Enany, N. (2020) *(B)ordering Britain: Law, Race and Empire*. Manchester: Manchester University Press.

Gardner, Z. (2021) 'Migrants deterred from healthcare during the COVID-19 pandemic'. London: The Joint Council for the Welfare of Immigrants.

Gilmore, R. W. (2007) *Golden Gulag: Prisons, Surplus, Crisis, and Opposition in Globalizing California*. Berkeley: University of California Press.

Lewisham and Greenwich NHS Trust (2019) 'Statement on agreement with Experian for identifying overseas visitors'. www.lewishamandgreenwich.nhs.uk/latest-news/statement-on-agreement-with-experian-for-identifying-overseas-visitors-1944/ (accessed 17 November 2021).

Lintern, S. (2019) 'Mass use of credit check firm to find NHS patients to charge'. *Health Service Journal*, 30 September. www.hsj.co.uk/policy-and-regulation/revealed-mass-use-of-credit-check-firm-to-find-nhs-patients-to-charge/7026012.article (accessed 17 November 2021).

Maternity Action (2017) 'The impact on health inequalities of charging migrant women for NHS maternity care'. London: Maternity Action.

Maternity Action (2018) 'What price safe motherhood? Charging for NHS maternity care in England and its impact on migrant women'. London: Maternity Action.

MBRRACE-UK (2019) 'Saving lives, improving mothers' care – lessons learned to inform maternity care from the UK and Ireland confidential enquiries into maternal deaths and morbidity 2015–17'. National Perinatal Epidemiology Unit, University of Oxford.

Mitropoulos, A. (2017) 'Bordering colonial uncertainty'. PoLAR: Political and Legal Anthropology Review. https://polarjournal.org/bordering-colonial-uncertainty/ (accessed 9 August 2021).

Patients not Passports (2020) 'Migrants' access to healthcare during the coronavirus crisis'. Patients-Not-Passports-Migrants-Access-to-Healthcare-During-the-Coronavirus-Crisis.pdf (medact.org) (accessed 17 November 2021).

Shahvisi, A. (2019) 'Austerity or xenophobia? The causes and costs of the "hostile environment" in the NHS'. *Health Care Analysis* 27(3): 202–219.

Shilliam, R. (2018) *Race and the Undeserving Poor: From Abolition to Brexit*. Newcastle, UK: Agenda Publishing.

Vukov, T. (2016) 'Target practice: The algorithmics and biopolitics of race in emerging smart border practices and technologies'. *Transfers* 6(1): 80–97. https://doi.org/10.3167/TRANS.2016.060107 (accessed 6 September 2021).

Wang, J. (2018) *Carceral Capitalism*. Cambridge MA: MIT Press.

Notes

1 Although the British government made COVID-19 testing and treatment exempt from the charges normally levied on migrants seeking NHS treatment in February 2020, the wider regime of charges, and liaison with the Home Office for the purposes of immigration enforcement, has persisted throughout the pandemic. Despite exemptions, fear of Home Office involvement has nonetheless deterred migrants from seeking treatment for COVID-19 (see Patients not Passports 2020; Gardner 2021).

2 This phrase was also used by Health Secretary Jeremy Hunt when he called for 'action to ensure the NHS is a national health service – not

an international one'. Department of Health and Social Care and Home Office (2013) 'New report shows the NHS could raise up to £500 million from better charging of overseas visitors'. Press release, 22 October. www.gov.uk/government/news/new-report-shows-the-nhs-could-raise-up-to-500-million-from-better-charging-of-overseas-visitors   (accessed 12 September 2022).

3 Necropolitics is a term that comes to us from Achille Mbembe. Mbembe developed the term to describe the kinds of deathly sovereign violence exercised against colonized populations and others experiencing racist violence. It has come to be used as a description of how authorities might exercise the right to expose people to death, or the risk of death – for instance, by putting them in a situation where they must choose between ill health, indebtedness and encounters with hostile, racialized border regimes. The chapter by Bhattacharyya (Chapter 22) contains an extended discussion on necropolitics (or the 'necropolis') and racial capitalism.

8

Hunger or indebtedness? Enforcing migrant destitution, racializing debt

Eve Dickson, Rachel Rosen and Kehinde Sorinmade

Unless otherwise stated, the first-person testimonies in this chapter are the words of people we have met through collective activism with North East London Migrant Action (NELMA) and our research at University College London. These multiple voices and experiences weave together into a tapestry of the complex and oppressive conditions of indebted life with 'no recourse to public funds' in the UK. In this way, we hope to evade the 'dangers of a single story' which flatten and simplify. Academic writing often forces a formal distinction between 'authorial voice' and the voices of those with lived experience (e.g., here through the use of quotation marks and italics). However, the various voices in this chapter are entangled in ways that problematize such distinctions. Authorship does not mean lack of lived experience of 'no recourse to public funds', and the analysis here has been informed by those with lived experience and those acting in solidarity. In short, 'voice' and 'authorship' in this piece are more complex than they may seem.

'*A brown envelope. When you see the brown envelope, you know what it means. Everybody knows what it is when they see the letter. They know you are owing. That's what the brown envelope means.*' The brown envelope becomes an object of shame, symbolizing something owing. A child's school lunches have produced a debt: £768.20. It cannot be paid. '*They kept on putting debt on my mum … like "oh you need to pay this", they keep texting her – "oh you need to pay this money, you need to pay this money".*'

This letter, from a school, and many others like it, marks a new chapter in the entanglement of mobility and (neo)colonialism. The letter has been sent to a mother who, because of her immigration

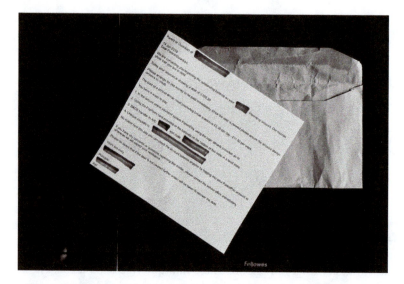

Figure 8.1 Photograph of a brown envelope and the letter it contains, received by a parent with no recourse to public funds. The letter reads: 'You owe £768.20 for school lunches ... If the debt is not cleared further action will be taken to recover the debt.'

status, has no right to work and 'no recourse to public funds' (NRPF). This is a condition linked to being 'subject to immigration control'. While some of the most destitute families in the UK are migrants subject to NRPF, once children from such families reach Year 3 (age 7–8) they are excluded from accessing free school meals, despite the fact that such meals are purportedly intended to mitigate the impacts of poverty.

'*I went to the school. I said please, no more school lunches. If you can allow, I'll make packed lunches. They said no. No packed lunches. So there was nothing I could do.*' In the context of a rapid marketization of education, including the rise of policy-setting neoliberal academies, children can be barred from bringing packed lunches to school. The stark choice thus seems to be: incur debt to eat or go hungry. '*How is my mum going to pay this money? We didn't have anything then, we were just living our lives ... If I kept on not eating food, it's gonna make my tummy – I'm not going to feel well ...*' Meanwhile, school meals are increasingly provided by outsourced companies, including the five largest in the UK, whose chief executives made £81.2 million between 2010 and 2017. Outsourcing giants, including security firms like G4S, are also securing a 20–30% profit margin from the migration-industrial complex through provision of accommodation for asylum seekers – which has been termed 'disgraceful and unsafe' by parliamentary committees – and the management of immigration removal centres.

What does the experience of families who receive these brown envelopes tell us about the way contemporary migration policy in the UK produces indebtedness? How is Britain's 'second empire' generated at the intersection of the UK's 'hostile' migration regime, colonial legacies, sovereign indebtedness and contemporary extraction?

Caught in a web of survival debts

'*I felt like I was in debt with the whole country!*' says Isabella, a migrant mother with NRPF charged for maternity care (Feldman 2018). For families with NRPF, demands to repay the cost of school meals are only one small part of a web of debts incurred as they try to survive in the UK's 'hostile' migration regime. Those who are undocumented have no legal right to work and often end up trapped in exploitative under-the-table work in order to survive. Others are forced to rely on friends or strangers, often in exchange for domestic labour, transactional sex or long-term personal indebtedness. In some cases, parents take out credit cards to cover the cost of basic necessities such as food. Survival debts have no borders. Some people will be trying to repay those who helped them to enter the UK, while others struggle to send remittances to children and other family members whom they have left behind. '*They are counting on us. "What are you doing? We expect you to send something to us, you know the situation, you know what was on ground before you left." You owe it to them. You have to.*'

However you manage to get by, you will be owing. By denying migrant families very basic essentials such as food, NRPF represents a denial of humanity. At the same time, it produces deepening webs of debt and pressures to repay or service debts. Here, one debt pays back another, all leading to growing debt. The UK's complex and draconian migration regime imposes limited or no rights to work, with NRPF excluding families from social support and programmes, even for those rendered 'legitimate' residents. This leaves credit card loans, state-negotiated repayment schedules, private loan companies and personal obligations as *a*, or even *the*, means to ensure sustenance and survival. NRPF produces and enforces destitution and therefore debt.

In the absence of formal access to welfare provision, destitute families with NRPF may be supported with accommodation and low-level financial support by local authorities under section 17 of the Children Act 1989. An estimated 5,900 children from families with NRPF across England and Wales received this support in 2012–13 (Price and Spencer 2015). However, the number of destitute families with NRPF is likely much higher. High numbers of families who try to access section 17 support are erroneously turned away. Some are told by social workers to 'max out' their credit cards on hotels before accommodation will be provided. Others are subject to invasive and discriminatory treatment, their Facebook pages and bank statements trolled for income generation that has not been reported. Anything from handmade bracelets sold for £3 each to a dormant bank account becomes a reason for exclusion from support. Determinations of 'deservingness' required by the legislation are often characterized by suspicion and racialized conceptions of who deserves support (Shilliam 2018).

'*I was saving that for a long five years. I didn't touch it. Everywhere I go, I take that box with me. Everywhere I go, I didn't touch it. I kept it. Even if I'm starving, I didn't touch that money. Even if I was in desperate need, I didn't touch that money. Because I was really desperate. This is the money that is going to save me out of this condition.*' While destitute families are often forced into hyper-exploitative working conditions, yet still have to borrow and go into debt to make payments, the Home Office charges migrants far more than it costs to process their applications. In 2018, the department made a £500 million surplus on immigration and citizenship fees.

'*We have to cough up £10,000 to pay the Home Office this year. For NHS alone you have to pay £1,000 per person. If you can't, you lose your leave and then you have to start all over again. You know how long it took you before, what you went through. All the years. We have to do it or else we lose it. We just have to look for the money. You don't want to start all over again.*' An application for 'limited leave to remain' costs £1,033 per person and must be accompanied by the fee for the immigration health surcharge. This needs to be paid every two and a half years for ten years before someone can even apply to settle indefinitely in the UK. The immigration health surcharge, which exempts the applicant from healthcare charging, has been increased over the years. As of January 2022, it was £624 per year per person. For an application for 'limited leave to remain' (thirty months), the surcharge is £1,560 on top of the £1,033 visa fee. Before the most recent increase it was £1,000 per application. In the chapter by Medien (Chapter 7), the entanglements between healthcare provision in the NHS, the enforcement of the hostile environment for racialized migrants and new forms of indebtedness and debt collection are explored in further detail.

The UK immigration rules make it almost impossible for those who cannot meet the requirements for financial self-sufficiency or who have spent periods undocumented to achieve formal settlement. While migrants may not be considered 'desirable' by the state for long-term residence in the UK, they may nonetheless be viewed as 'desirable' as high fee-paying students, short-term labourers with limited legal rights and so forth. But with no legal pathways to reside beyond the short term, staying in the UK in the long term often means becoming undocumented and subject to destitution and debt. The entanglements of racialized border control and subjection to new instruments of indebtedness are taken up in relation to the US by Rossipal (Chapter 9).

Punitive debts and the production of illegality

But if the debt cannot be paid, how will the creditor respond? The letter from the school reads: 'Please be aware that if the debt is not cleared further action will be taken to recover the debt.'

'*They said he couldn't go to prom … It was a threat, yes. They said he couldn't go to prom because of the money being owed. It was a once in a lifetime thing, why would you want to deny a child that opportunity, to miss that experience with his friends?*' Such responses do not just single people out, marking their destitution as a misdemeanour and their bodies as criminal or 'irresponsible'.

They are also a form of punishment. Children, made the carriers of the brown envelope of debt to their mothers, are shamed publicly, which is a punitive and emotive form of debt collection (Federici 2014). Children have been threatened with missing important school activities, and some have been subject to discriminatory abuse and taunting from other children as a result of their public display of debt. Others are sent to detention for failing to wear the proper uniform, school kit that remains unaffordable in the context of NRPF. Children become collateral, used to exert pressure on their mothers to service and repay debt. It is not at all uncommon, as shown by Nir (Chapter 16) in relation to Israel/Palestine and Stork (Chapter 17) in relation to Black access to education in the US, for childhood to become entangled with the creation of racialized, indebted subjects.

An indebted subject is thus produced at the interface of an immigration policy of state-enforced destitution and the global ubiquity of debt in financialized capitalism. Designed to deter migration and settlement, NRPF simultaneously entangles working-class migrant families in a web of bureaucratic and financial structures in the UK tied to the servicing of debts. The debt produced by the UK's migration regime is also used to sustain 'illegality' and thwart the efforts of undocumented individuals to 'regularize' their status at the point of immigration decision making. Charging some migrants for NHS healthcare, introduced by regulations in the UK in 1982 and ramped up under Theresa May's 'hostile environment', produces yet another source of debt for undocumented families and is often accompanied by aggressive debt collection outsourced to private companies. Under the immigration rules, applications for 'leave to remain' can be refused on grounds of suitability if an individual has an outstanding NHS debt of £500 or more and is not paying it back.

Colonial legacies and neocolonial debt

Many families with NRPF who experience destitution come from countries colonized as part of Britain's erstwhile empire. As with others who may move between being undocumented and having regularized status, it is impossible to precisely determine the number of destitute families with NRPF. However, Jamaican and Nigerian nationals with NRPF make up 51% of those who have sought local authority support, with a significant number of others coming from Ghana and Pakistan (Price and Spencer 2015). Thus, NRPF is highly racialized in effect, enforcing destitution and debt on working-class Black and Brown people from postcolonial states.

'There's no benefit system in Nigeria. There's nothing like that. Most of the state schools, the teachers are not being paid so they're not teaching the children well. You have graduates who at the end of school have to do transportation business. Driving tricycles. They've studied and they're doing that kind of job ... You want to find a way out of the system. You want to give your children a better life so they don't think it's all poverty, poverty around them. Everyone wants a better life. Who doesn't want a better life?' As part of the 'breadbasket' of the British empire, Nigeria's incorporation into the global capitalist economy was simultaneously marked by the colonial production of dependence on imported manufactured goods. British economic interests in the country continue to shape Nigeria's national borders, governance and social systems, despite the country's formal independence in 1960 (Uche 2008). In the postcolonial era, underdevelopment continues as Nigeria's rich petroleum resources provide a source of capital extraction for European and North American-based multinationals and the local wealthy elite through infrastructures set in place by these colonial legacies and neocolonial relations (Ovadia 2013).

Chocolate is another lucrative neocolonial industry, with extractive infrastructures established in the period of empire and, more recently, through trade liberalization (Fold and Neilson 2016). Cocoa is grown on smallholder farms in Nigeria, one of the world's leading producers; profits accrue to shareholders who bet on cocoa's future fortunes on speculative financial markets and to the multinational corporations headquartered in Europe and North America who manufacture it into chocolate and sell it at prices out of reach of most growers. As Nadine El-Enany (2020: 2) argues, Britain's migration regime is an 'attempt to control access to the spoils of empire [...] immigration law is the tool that ensures that dispossessed peoples have no claim to what was stolen from them'.

Much of the profit is extracted from the country through joint ownership arrangements with foreign companies like BP and Shell who pay limited royalties and benefit from opaque operations and tax shelters exposed by the Panama Papers.[1] This has left Nigeria with staggering sovereign debt: US$87 billion at September 2021, according to the Debt Management Office (DMO). High interest on these loans has meant that two-thirds of the federal government's reserves are directed towards external debt servicing. Combined with imposition of privatization and other forms of structural adjustment as conditionalities for International Monetary Fund assistance – conditionalities which appear to be returning in exchange for post-COVID support – little is left for healthcare, education and other social infrastructure. It is not surprising, then, that Oxfam's 2018 report on inequality ranks Nigeria at the bottom of 157 countries for the second year in a row, citing low social spending, ineffective taxation (a legacy of the Britain's colonial withdrawal arrangements), and increasing labour rights violations. Migration represents hope and survival.

If other migrants have been 'successful', or present as such, then the only explanation for destitution seems to be one of personal failing. '*Nobody knows how you are living. Nobody knows that you are living in one room. How many people are you going to tell? You don't tell. You just keep it to yourself. People will feel, "oh, she's doing well over there. She's doing well over there." That's the impression they have. That's what people see on Facebook. You see them on Facebook, they post a lot. Giving people the impression back home that they are doing good. You pretend that everything is going well for you, smooth, rosy. Because you know, Facebook, it's whatever they see. You don't want to tell people this is what you are going through. People are looking at you high-up there.*' As Villarreal (2014: S32) points out, the need to appear to have 'made it' in the 'big migration enterprise' means that stories of struggle and hardship often cannot be told.

More deeply and insidiously, then, NRPF can be understood as a policy set on deterring migration by making life in the UK 'hostile' for negatively racialized postcolonial subjects. It works alongside the deportability regime in efforts to remake Britain in its nativist image. At the same time, NRPF entangles postcolonial, working-class migrants in a cycle of debt, debt servicing and more debt tied to both public and private institutions and individuals in the UK and beyond. Such forms of differential inclusion produce racialized forms of debt and destitution and are little more than a neocolonial 're-drawing of the global colour line' (De Genova 2017: 1766).

What we are suggesting is that Britain's second empire resides not only in its overseas free ports and tax havens but within its local borders. Working-class migrant families with NRPF are rendered super-exploitable labour, revenue for a profit-making migration regime (from applications and legal fees to agents and smugglers), and sources of surplus generated through steady repayments of debt interest in their determination to regularize their status. Yet they are also rendered easily expendable by the second British empire. Profits in the migration regime are produced through the hardship and hard labour of these same dispossessed people and other workers.

The brown envelopes with which we began this chapter mark the debt owed by migrant families with NRPF. But we end by asking, once histories of colonial extraction and contemporary profit making in the migration-industrial complex are taken into account: who is in debt to whom?

Further resources

Chalabi, N. (2020) 'Children with No Recourse to Public Funds: The need for free school meals'. London: Hackney Migrant Centre. https://hackneymigrantcentre.org.uk/wp-content/uploads/2020/04/Children-with-NRPF-The-need-for-FSM.pdf (accessed 1 February 2020).

Dickson, E. (2019) 'Not seen, not heard: Children's experiences of the hostile environment'. London: Project 17. www.project17.org.uk/media/70571/Not-seen-not-heard-1-.pdf (accessed 1 February 2020).

Dickson, E. and Rosen, R. (2020) 'Postponing migrant destitution? Why we need to call for more than a suspension of no recourse to public funds'. https://archive.discoversociety.org/2020/08/19/postponing-migrant-destitution-why-we-need-to-call-for-more-than-a-suspension-of-no-right-to-public-funds/ (accessed 15 September 2022).

Dickson E and Rosen R (2021) '"Punishing those who do the wrong thing": Enforcing destitution and debt through the UK's family migration rules'. *Critical Social Policy* 41: 545–565. https://journals.sagepub.com/doi/10.1177/0261018320980634 (accessed 10 January 2021).

North East London Migrant Action (NELMA). https://nelmacampaigns.wordpress.com/ (accessed 1 February 2020).

Works cited

De Genova, N. (2017) 'The "migrant crisis" as racial crisis: Do Black Lives Matter in Europe?' *Ethnic and Racial Studies* 41(10): 1765–82.

El-Enany, N. (2020) *(B)ordering Britain: Law, Race and Empire.* Manchester: Manchester University Press.

Federici, S. (2014) 'From commoning to debt: Financialization, microcredit, and the changing architecture of capital accumulation'. *South Atlantic Quarterly* 113(2): 231–244.

Feldman, R. (2018) 'What price safe motherhood? Charging for NHS maternity care in England and its impact on migrant women'. London: Maternity Action. https://maternityaction.org.uk/wp-content/uploads/WhatPriceSafeMotherhoodFINAL.October.pdf (accessed 1 February 2020).

Fold, N. and Neilson, J. (2016) 'Sustaining supplies in smallholder dominated value chains: Corporate governance of the global cocoa sector'. In M. P. Squicciarini and J. Swinnen (eds), *Economics of Chocolate.* Oxford: Oxford University Press, pp. 195–212.

Ovadia, J. S. (2013) 'The Nigerian "one percent" and the management of national oil wealth through Nigerian content'. *Science & Society* 77(3): 315–341.

Price, J. and Spencer, S. (2015) *Safeguarding Children from Destitution: Local Authority Responses to Families with 'No Recourse to Public Funds'.* Oxford: Compas.

Shilliam, R. (2018) *Race and the Undeserving Poor: From Abolition to Brexit.* Newcastle upon Tyne: Agenda Publishing.

Uche, C. (2008) 'Oil, British interests and the Nigerian civil war'. *The Journal of African History* 49(1): 111–135.

Villarreal, M. (2014) 'Regimes of value in Mexican household financial practices'. *Current Anthropology* 55(S9): S30–S39. DOI: 10.1086/676665

Note

1 The Panama Papers were 11.5 million leaked files containing evidence of financial crime and political corruption enabled by the offshore financial system. Reports, which highlighted the global scale of the problem, first began to be released in April 2016 by the International Consortium of Investigative Journalists and its media partners. www.icij.org/investigations/panama-papers/five-years-later-panama-papers-still-having-a-big-impact/ (accessed 15 September 2022).

9

Libre: debt, discipline and humanitarian pretension

Christian Rossipal

Since 2013, immigration bonds set by the US Immigration and Customs Enforcement (ICE) have seen a steep increase – with a yearly median amount well above the prior $5,000 – making them an unaffordable alternative for the vast majority of asylum seekers who want to get out of detention. Already in 2013 the company Libre by Nexus saw a way to profit from this, and now acts as a middleman to secure bonds. Forced to sign contracts in English, and desperate to get out of detention, migrants are lured into a debt trap: Libre by Nexus helps migrants to get out, but it requires electronic monitoring by ankle bracelets that track GPS data – and the wearer pays a $420 monthly fee for this device.[1] With additional initial fees and the average immigration proceeding taking more than twenty-one months, the final amount to be paid often exceeds the bail bond itself. As Libre by Nexus's advertisement puts it, 'Not being able to pay for immigration bail costs more than your freedom.'

In liberal-leaning news outlets Libre by Nexus has been portrayed as an exceptional example of a company preying on precarious migrants, operating in a grey zone opened up by public policy.[2] Indeed, the company has been the target of multiple lawsuits. It was forced to pay millions in debt relief, and it faces cease-and-desist orders sought by state regulators in Virginia and California. The company was the target of a class action lawsuit which was eventually settled for $2.7 million after a 2019 ruling in Washington state that found it had knowingly utilized English contracts with Spanish-speaking clients. Thus far, however, this has not stopped the company's daily operations.

NOT BEING ABLE TO PAY FOR IMMIGRATION BAIL
COSTS MORE THAN YOUR OWN FREEDOM

WHEN A LOVED ONE IS IN JAIL, THE WHOLE FAMILY SUFFERS.
This is why, if you or a loved one is in immigration detention and can't post bail, at Libre we can help reunite your family. Sometimes the same day. Call today at (888) 997-7646 or visit www.librebynexus.com

Figure 9.1 An advertisement produced for Libre by Nexus depicting a family portrait 'behind bars' and reading 'Not being able to pay for immigration bail costs more than your own freedom' (2017).

In a March 2021 press release, Libre by Nexus referred to a lawsuit filed by Attorneys General of New York, Massachusetts, Virginia and the Consumer Financial Protection Bureau as 'baseless' and 'egregiously false'. Presenting themselves as 'a company dedicated to freeing immigrants from excessive, inhuman detention', Libre by Nexus shifts blame to abusive police, prison guards and state authorities. Regardless of still uncertain legal outcomes, Libre by Nexus seems to reveal something more than the story of a rogue company exploiting a legal loophole. It is not merely an exception. What can Libre by Nexus tell us about the intersections between state policy, postcolonial empire and the ghostly presence of financial capital? Where the chapters by Medien (Chapter 7) and Dickson et al. (Chapter 8) explored these themes in relation to healthcare, schooling, debt and racialized borders in the contemporary UK, this chapter takes up these questions in relation to the US and its specific carceral history. If situated historically – within the normalized system it is part of – the company sheds light on the important intersections mentioned above. In particular, it highlights the interrelation between debt and discipline.

Humanitarian gestures and racialized dispossession

Tropes of the non-tax-paying dependent 'illegal' and non-responsible racialized minorities appear constantly in the wake of financial crises such as the 2008 subprime mortgage crisis in the US. Those who found themselves in the subprime category during the 2008 crisis – borrowers who had low credit scores – were not only charged an interest rate far exceeding that of those in the 'prime' category, but were often blamed as the *cause* of the crisis induced by the financial system that dispossessed them in the first place.

Libre by Nexus echoes the subprime crisis and its vilification of Latinx immigrants, but the mode of operation is even more insidious. By actively embracing what could be described as humanitarian aesthetics, progressive buzzwords and an anti-Trump stance during his 2016–20 presidency, Libre by Nexus fashions itself as an agent in the struggle for social justice. This can be seen in the image in Figure 9.1, which drew on the national discourse and affect generated around Trump's 'zero tolerance' and family separations in 2018.

To avoid any ambiguous reading, this is reinforced by the caption 'When a loved one is in jail, the whole family suffers'. Another ad in the same print campaign further tells us that 'Your family shouldn't suffer detention for not being able to pay immigration bail'.

While this could be seen as a kind of 'humanitarian' gesture in its focus on family reunification,[3] the official Libre by Nexus website features a video that complicates things. A 13-year-old boy directly addresses the viewer:

> I like soccer and rap music. I love school and one day I want to grow up to be a lawyer. I want to help people. I was ten when I came to the United States. When I arrived, President Trump ordered that I be separated from my mom. I was locked in a concentration camp for migrant kids in Chicago. I was beaten there, bruised, beaten, and scared. The scars of that abuse run deep for thousands of kids like me who were abused at the order of President Trump. Thank god there is a company called Libre by Nexus. They got me and my mom out of jail and helped us sue the people who hurt us. If you have a loved one in immigration jail you need to call Libre by Nexus today. They are not afraid of Trump or his white supremacists. They fight for our people. They can save you like they saved me.

What makes this different from an ordinary and depoliticized humanitarian message is the reference to policy and the use of the term 'white supremacists'. At a first glance, this goes against the grain not only of most non-governmental organizations but also of critical scholarship on race – which would typically find that a naive colour-blindness attends multiculturalism in the neoliberal 'management of difference'. In other words, the position of Libre by Nexus might seem to contradict the idea that global capitalism construes itself as 'post-racial'. In the case of Libre by Nexus we see something ostensibly different and novel happening: the for-profit company is not 'unseeing race', but appropriating a critical discourse on white supremacy in its very dispossession of the racialized other.

The liberal paradox: borders and the flow of capital

While this rhetorical move is unique in its slyness, there is no real contradiction if we consider Libre by Nexus beyond a rhetorical level. The material consequences of their business model are perfectly aligned with the post-racial logic of differential inclusion, which operates through a 'predatory incorporation of previously excluded populations' (Chakravartty and Ferreira da Silva 2012). As a lawsuit from a group of affected migrants states, the company has been 'embracing immigrants only to feed off of them like a parasite'. This dynamic is of course not new; in fact, the very first privately owned prison in the US was an immigration-related prison (Jefferis 2019). The unique thing is, rather, how Libre by Nexus makes the dynamic visible – in an inverted kind of way – and by virtue of this the company is something of an exception.

While new borders are erected and militarized around the world it is not uncommon to hear commentators declare that this is merely the death rattle of a dying nation-state system; a desperate attempt from politicians to show their electorates that something is being done to 'put the national interest first' while business is offshored by global capital and anti-immigrant sentiment is on the rise. The conclusion drawn from this line of thinking might be that the 'death rattle' is ultimately a sign of waning sovereignty and the decline of the nation-state. At the same time, however, there is ample evidence to suggest that the neoliberal nation-state is an indispensable tool – if not a structural necessity – to facilitate the flow of global capital, ensure public dispossession and bail out capital interests during ever-occurring moments of crisis (Harvey 2004). This creates an inherent tension, or a 'liberal paradox' (Hollifield et al. 2008) between the free flow of capital and intensified border control – which has bearing on the nexus in which Nexus is situated.

Global capital not only shapes the economic landscape that indirectly affects migration drivers but also thrives in a complex symbiosis with state regulation and border authority. The detention of immigrants in the US is one of the most high-stakes examples you could possibly find of this deep interplay: with nearly 200 detention centres across the country, the US has the largest migrant detention system in the world. This is also the most privatized carceral system in the world – significantly more so than the US punitive prison system – with roughly two-thirds of all centres managed by for-profit firms, controlled by government agencies under the Department of Homeland Security.

Accumulation through migrant detention

With over 52,000 immigrants daily who were in 'civil' immigration detention (non-criminal incarceration), in 2019 the final annual count came to nearly 400,000 incarcerated people. In its current form, this mass-scale confinement of immigrants first occurred in the US during the 1980s (Jefferis 2020). Of those immigrants who were eligible to be released on bond, the government still held more than 60,000 persons in pre-trial detention.

After an ICE agent decides on whether a person can be released or held (in so-called mandatory or discretionary detention), the immigrant can request a 'bond redetermination hearing in immigration court' (Pepper 2019). This custody determination process has, however, been heavily criticized for resulting in automatic detention rather than individual consideration. The system is 'constitutionally unaccountable' (Jefferis 2020), and arguably breaks international human rights law, which stipulates that governments cannot arbitrarily detain migrants: detention can be used as a non-punitive last resort only after the individual case in question has been considered (Gilman 2016). The move to rely on monetary bond in the immigration detention system has, moreover, 'taken place relatively recently, after monetary bonds had already been discredited in the criminal pretrial justice system' (Gilman 2016: 197). Even if the immigrant is in fact given the opportunity to pay bond for release – despite these obstacles – the monetary amount is itself arbitrarily set and 'often not just arbitrary, but arbitrarily high' (Gilman 2016: 212). And this is precisely what Libre by Nexus exploits.

In the US detention system, state authority is an integral part of a neoliberal 'accumulation by dispossession', which is to say a general privatization and commodification of public assets and entities (Harvey 2004). Non-state actors hold and handle bodies for profit, paid for by the taxpayer and the migrants themselves – who often work inside the centres, to keep them running, for very low pay (typically one to three dollars *per day* for cleaning, laundry, kitchen work and maintenance). Detained immigrants pay for telephone services and often need to buy things like nutrition supplements – because of the inadequate food they are served – and are forced into the role of both 'captive consumers and laborers' (Conlon and Hiemstra 2014). Profit is ultimately ensured by something known as 'the bed mandate', or 'bodies in bed', which is a quota set by law that guarantees a certain minimum number of migrants to be detained at any given moment.

Debt and self-discipline

The US detention system merges an older form of discipline with a newer, highly technologized kind of control that has more in common with Amazon logistics than the traditional prison. As Stephen Ramos has shown, migrant detention directly mirrors 'systems of international supply chain coordination, assembly, transport, and sale' (Ramos 2018). More than a reflection of market logics, the detention system is itself a billion-dollar industry – and the two leading companies in detention centre management, CoreCivic and GEO Group, are publicly traded on the stock exchange. In other words, the detention system should not be seen as separate from the national prison-industrial complex, nor from the global neoliberal economy.

This entanglement between immigrant detention, the state and the market is related to debt in multiple ways. After the mortgage crisis of 2008 it became more widely known that speculation on consumer debt has been central to intensified financialization in the neoliberal era. What is less often pointed out is the way that debt is deeply intertwined with discipline. While we might associate the neoliberal paradigm with a general deregulation – or some kind of laissez-faire attitude – discipline continues to play a critical role. The notion that power can operate through disciplinary practices (rather than just absolute acts of physical force) is an insight often associated with Michel Foucault. Tayyab Mahmud (2012) has drawn on Foucault's work on discipline to argue that neoliberal states operate through an entanglement of debt and discipline whereby neoliberal subjects are obliged to manage themselves and their welfare in relation to ever-expanding forms of indebtedness.

The intertwinement of debt and discipline is of course nothing new. We should not forget that enslaved people were used as collateral in the US bond market (Martin 2010), nor that colonial powers forced debt contracts onto colonies (Mahmud 2012: 482). We also should not forget that international credit institutions in more recent times have imposed harsh austerity measures on postcolonial nation-states – a practice of 'structural adjustment' that is making a comeback as countries hit hard by the COVID-19 pandemic once again seek relief from the International Monetary Fund. In such cases, the relation between debt and discipline is rather obvious. In the neoliberal era, however, discipline is not necessarily imposed as a force from the outside. On the contrary, what is distinctive about discipline under neoliberalism is how the indebted are made to discipline themselves. This creates a mechanism of power that can be hard to recognize; a spectre of authority and financial capital which appears as if it comes from the individual herself (and in some ways it does).

Invisible carceral infrastructures

Forced to practise financial self-discipline, immigrants indebted to Libre by Nexus are doubly trapped: on the one hand, they are positioned as consumers of a financial product, and on the other hand, they are 'acted on as a product, a body that fills a bed in a system of incarceration and captivity' (Cuevas 2012). Even when migrants are released from detention and are supposedly free, their every step is monitored by GPS tracking. Beyond this they are, like any indebted consumer, subject to another kind of capture. Once indebted, people must practise self-control to fulfil the model of 'the entrepreneurial self' and are 'less likely to claim nonconformist views or indulge in nonconforming conduct' (Mahmud 2012). Through debt, neoliberalism creates compliant and docile subjects 'disciplined to conform to the logic of the financialized market' (Mahmud 2012: 470). Arguably, this also functions according to a carceral kind of logic. As Dawn Burton would put it, debtors are caught in a 'credit panopticon' (Burton 2008: 53). That is to say, as debtors we are internalizing a surveillant gaze. Our transactions are observed and recorded, and we could potentially be subject to control or audit at any given moment. This shapes the contours of how we behave.

Even if these dynamics are, to a large degree, structured by way of indirect market logics, the field they are part of is ultimately demarcated by law. Although the jurisdiction in question might vary, state authority has an important role to play: the 'hidden hand of the market and the iron fist of the law' still work in concert during the neoliberal era. At this juncture, the entrapment of racial minorities in a circuit of debt and incarceration could be seen as the epitome of contemporary capitalism and postcolonial empire. By extension, Libre by Nexus could be seen as fully congruent with the logic of neoliberalism rather than constituting an exception.

The advert reproduced in Figure 8.1 offers an unsettling visual representation of a detention system that is otherwise largely invisible to the public. This is not just the case of the immaterial financial networks discussed above, but also of the material infrastructure of detention. As Ramos puts it, the US detention centre is a 'black box, and its exact spatial contours are a mystery' (Ramos 2018: 58). Photography is prohibited inside and there is little insight into the day-to-day workings, with the exception of occasional leaks to journalists. Given the horrific conditions, systematic abuses and even deaths that have been reported on during the last years, it is incumbent upon us to not look away, despite these difficulties. As the advert makes perfectly clear, however, we cannot just take what is made visible at face value. In the chapter by Kushinski (Chapter 3) we were cautioned against taking performances of transparency by extractive industry corporations at face value, when the implications of 'business as usual' are potentially so grave. Here too, because the human stakes are immense, we have to critically trace and trace again the ghostly presence of this vast but largely opaque system.

Further resources

Cuevas, O. (2012) 'Welcome to my cell: Housing and race in the mirror of American democracy'. *American Quarterly* 64(3): 605–624.

Jonathan, J. S. (1998) 'Refugees in a carceral age: The rebirth of the immigration prison in the United States'. *Public Culture* 10: 577–607.

Libre (2019) Directed by Anna Barsan [Documentary]. https://fieldofvision.org/libre.

Ryo, E. and Peacock, I. (2018) 'A national study of immigration detention in the United States'. *Southern California Law Review* 92(1): 1–68.

Srikantiah, J. (2018) 'Reconsidering money bail in immigration detention'. *UC Davis Law Review* 52(1): 521–548.

Works cited

Burton, D. (2008) *Credit and Consumer Society*. London: Routledge.

Chakravartty, P. and Ferreira da Silva, D. (2012) 'Accumulation, disposses-sion, and debt: The racial logic of global capitalism – an introduction'. *American Quarterly* 64(3): 361–385.

Conlon, D. B. and Hiemstra, N. (2014) 'Examining the everyday micro-economies of migrant detention in the United States'. *Geographica Helvetica* 69: 335–344.

Cuevas, O. (2012) 'Welcome to my cell: Housing and race in the mirror of American democracy'. *American Quarterly* 64(3): 605–624.

Gilman, D. L. (2016) 'To loose the bonds: The deceptive promise of freedom from pretrial immigration detention'. *Indiana Law Journal* 92(1): 157–225.

Harvey, D. (2004) 'The "new" imperialism: Accumulation by dispossession'. *Socialist Register* 40: 63–87.

Hollifield, J. F., Hunt, V. F. and Tichenor, D. J. (2008) 'The liberal paradox: Immigrants, markets and rights in the United States'. *SMU Law Review* 61: 67–98.

Jefferis, D. C. (2019) 'Private prisons, private governance: Essay on develop-ments in private-sector resistance to privatized immigration detention'. *Northwestern Journal of Law and Social Policy* 15(1): 82–97.

Jefferis, D. C. (2020) 'Constitutionally unaccountable: Privatized immigration detention'. *Indiana Law Review* 95: 145–182.

Mahmud, T. (2012) 'Debt and discipline'. *American Quarterly* 64(3): 469–494.

Martin, B. (2010) 'Slavery's invisible engine: Mortgaging human property'. *The Journal of Southern History* 76(4): 817–866.

Pepper, J. (2019) 'Pay up or else: Immigration bond and how a small procedural change could liberate immigrant detainees'. *60 B.C.L. Review* 951:951–988.

Ramos, S. (2018) 'ICEBOX: The logistics of detention'. *Footprint* 12(23): 52–68.

Notes

1 Libre by Nexus has announced that they will stop using body-affixed GPS devices and transition to using dedicated cell phones with a preinstalled GPS tracking app. There is, however, nothing to indicate that this will be the end to invasive surveillance, nor to the company's profiteering, since the released migrant still needs to pay for the phone and Libre's own mandatory wireless plan.

2 See Miller, M. (2021) 'Virginia joins federal lawsuit against company accused of preying on immigrants' *Washington Post*, 22 February; Hauser, M. (2019) 'The high price of freedom for migrants in detention', *The New Yorker*, 12 March.

3 See Kish (Chapter 15) for more on humanitarian gestures in relation to new forms of discipline and indebtedness, and Stork (Chapter 17) on the extension of predatory lending into managing aspirations for children and their education.

Part IV

Emergence

The language of 'emergence', of emerging and frontier markets, is now so commonplace in print and news media that it has almost become an unremarkable term. But the ease with which commentators and analysts speak of 'emerging' markets (and their counterpoint, 'mature' economies in the Global North) reflects the successful relaunching of doctrines of linear progress that used to be organized under the language of 'modernization'. Mid-twentieth-century development was oriented around 'modernization': a form of industrial catch-up whereby the colonized world would become just like (an imagined version of) mid-century America's mass consumer society. The (white) Global North was the civilizational end point towards which former colonies should aspire. The fact that modernization theory is based on a fallacy – former colonies are merely 'undeveloped' because they have failed to 'take off' like America, and no attention is given to past and present forms of colonial extraction – has done little to soften its appeal in some quarters. But as 'modernization' and the end goal of 1950s America lost some of its sheen and relevance, 'emergence' took its ideological place. Emergence implies excitement, speed, growth and, in particular, the powerhouses of the Global South (including India, Mexico, Indonesia) where 'world-class' glass-and-steel financial districts are found in close proximity to underserved slums. But emergence also implies a form of catching up, of being late, of being *behind*, and has done little to shed the ideas of racial and civilizational hierarchy which previously lurked behind the language of modernization.

What – or rather, where – are 'emerging markets'? Are they the same territories as those that might previously have been termed the 'Global South', the 'Third World' or 'developing countries'? Each of these terms carries a significant amount of baggage, and many of us are socialized into using one while deliberately rejecting the others. The term 'Third World' entered the English language in the 1950s as a way to differentiate (former) colonies from the capitalist 'First' and communist 'Second' worlds in the context of the Cold War. Some may be reluctant to use the term 'Third World', because it is so often used in a derogatory and racist way about supposedly 'backward' places that it has come to carry understandably uncomfortable connotations. But, as Vijay Prashad (2007) reminds us, the 'Third World' can also be understood as a *project* rather than a place; a project in which formerly colonized people came together in an attempt to chart a more just, postcolonial international economic order. Coalescing around the Asian-African Conference in Bandung (1955) and the First Summit of the Non-Aligned Movement in Belgrade (1961) this 'Third World project' also incubated demands for a 'New International Economic Order' (NIEO).

The United Nations General Assembly adopted the Declaration on the Establishment of a New International Order in 1974, calling for, among other reforms of the international, 'The right of every country to adopt the economic and social system that it deems the most appropriate for its own development and not to be subjected to discrimination of any kind as a result'. The debt crises of the 1980s, and the imposition of Structural Adjustment Programmes through which governments were forced to privatize, liberalize and remove subsidies in exchange for International Monetary Fund/ World Bank support put paid to the momentum behind calls for a NIEO. The 'Global South' too can be considered a 'project', as Prashad (2012) argues. Tanzanian independence leader Julius Nyerere formed The South Centre in 1995 to continue the struggle for an equitable international economic order that emerged at Bandung and Belgrade. At the time of writing, The South Centre has been active in fostering dialogue and putting forward policy proposals to counter the 'Vaccine Nationalism' adopted by states in the Global North, and seeking out reform to international intellectual property regimes that would facilitate global vaccine access (Sklair and Gilbert 2022).

The shift to a language of 'emerging' and 'frontier' markets came during the 1990s too, as employees of the International Finance

Corporation (IFC), the private sector wing of the World Bank, sought to 're-brand' the 'Third World' away from the image of backwardness, corruption and poverty that they felt repelled the private capital needed for development. Yet, in seeking to 're-brand' the Third World/Global South in this way, those IFC officials were betraying their own ignorance of the various projects oriented towards a just postcolonial international order which their organization had helped to undermine (Tilley 2018). The gradual displacement of the language of the Third World/Global South as memories of the Bandung moment and its spirit fade has left the financial media in control of our geographical imaginaries. The language and imagery of emergence ('Asian tigers', 'African lions', 'The Next 11', 'The Frontier Five') 'capture and perpetuate the intensely competitive nature of international capital mobilization in the new pecking order of emergent nation states engaged in the race to *outperform* within the asset class of emerging markets, reminiscent of the analogous race for survival in the wilderness' (Lakshminarayan 2017: 854).

African nations are subjected to a particular kind of othering through this financial discourse: Africa is either 'rising' or 'in crisis', most often 'a combination of the two: Africa has the *potential* to rise if it can ever get itself out of crisis' (Pierre 2018: 12). Images of African otherness circulate alongside a denial of African agency: what matters is the investment decisions made by *external* financiers, and their 'risk appetites'. Ilias Alami (Chapter 10) explores the particular ways in which financiers investing in South Africa discount Black African rule and cast Black African workers as unruly and threatening to capital. At issue here is not merely the notion that racist representations *repel* much-needed investment. The power of finance is not merely in providing credit to those in need of it. Rather, what matters is that racist images shape the perception and calculation of risks by investors, and lead them to demand higher returns, given the 'risk' they allegedly face. The result is often a squeeze on labour and the state, while investors continue to paint themselves as the beneficent providers of capital that were imagined by the IFC when they rebranded the 'Third World' into a basket of 'emerging markets'.

The rise of the 'BRICs' (Brazil, Russia, India, China – and sometimes South Africa) as economic powerhouses has added complexity to any map of the former 'Third World' or 'Global

South'. Brazil has won several victories over the US and EU at the World Trade Organization, requiring powerful Northern nations to remove subsidies which made Brazilian sugar 'uncompetitive', and these rulings have been portrayed as victories for 'the South'. But the extractive practices in which Brazilian mining firms like Vale are engaged in Africa seem to echo older forms of colonial extraction. The Brazilian sociologist Gilberto Freyre coined the term 'lusotropicalism' to reflect an assumption that there was something common about the mixing of Portuguese and African people in the tropics – whether Brazil, Angola or Mozambique. The quasi-privatized Brazilian mining giant Vale has attempted to invoke lusotropicalist solidarity despite significant opposition to its extractive operations in Mozambique. Chinese investment is also a significant presence in lusophone Africa, as Jon Schubert (Chapter 11) shows. Railways built by the Portuguese to facilitate extraction of ore to the South African coast have been revitalized for an ore-hungry China, but the promise of economic diversification that would come with the updated railway lines has yet to materialize. As Schubert reminds us, though, Chinese investment should not merely be misread as another stage of imperial extraction. Chinese investment in southern African rail infrastructure dates back to the TAZARA railway. Both the UK and the US declined to finance this railway designed to provide coastal access to Zambia, cut off by the apartheid and white minority regimes of South Africa and Rhodesia, and a peripheral Bandung spirit (or perhaps Cold War posturing) was leveraged to secure relatively condition-free finance from China in the early 1970s.

Linsey Ly (Chapter 12) takes us to China's internal colonization of Inner Mongolia and the successive speculative visions for Han Chinese modernization of Mongolia that have resulted in a landscape littered with ghost cities and scarred by rare earth extraction. The rare earths extracted in China enable the functioning of magnets in wind turbines, photovoltaic cells and batteries in electric vehicles. The geological accident of rare earth concentration in China has led both the US Geological Survey and the European Commission to designate certain rare earths 'strategic' or 'critical' minerals: militarized energy security agendas are married to hopes for a 'green capitalist' future. Critical or strategic minerals are designated based on a calculation of their importance to US/European economic futures (if we are to decarbonize transport, how much battery metal will we require?), combined with a measure of 'supply risk'. Supply risk is determined by the geographical concentration of these 'green' minerals and the supposed level of risk for companies doing business in those territories, which turns out to be a measure of how likely mineral-rich countries are to set royalty and taxation rates that can fund public spending on infrastructure and social welfare (Gilbert 2020). Here we find ourselves looping back into Alami's concern with racialized imaginaries informing measures of 'risk' in emerging markets. What would it take to empower a former colony to 'adopt the economic and social system that it deems the most appropriate for its own development and not to be subjected to discrimination of any kind as a result', as envisioned by the NIEO? Perhaps it would require disrupting the stranglehold that financial media have on defining our geographical imaginaries, as well as a careful engagement with what it means to seek out minerals that are 'critical' to greening the Global North.

Works cited

Gilbert, P. R. (2020) 'Making critical materials valuable: Decarbonization, investment and "political risk"'. In: A. Bleicher and A. Pehlken (eds), *The Material Basis of Energy Transitions: Interdisciplinary Perspectives on Renewable Energy and Critical Materials*. Elsevier, pp. 91–10.

Lakshminarayan, S. (2017) 'Market fundamentalism in the age of "haute finance": The enclosing of policy space in "emerging India"'. *Ephemera* 17(4): 849–865.

Pierre, J. (2018) 'Africa/African'. In G. Desai and A. Masquelier (eds), *Critical Terms for the Study of Africa*. Chicago: University of Chicago Press, pp. 12–26.

Prashad, V. (2007) *The Darker Nations: A People's History of the Third World*. New York: The New Press.

Prashad, V. (2012) *The Poorer Nations: A Possible History of the Global South*. London: Verso Books.

Sklair, J. and Gilbert, P. R. (2022) 'Giving as "de-risking": Philanthropy, impact investment and the pandemic response'. *Public Anthropologist*. Published online 31 March. https://brill.com/view/journals/puan/4/1/article-p51_003.xml (accessed 18 August 2022).

Tilley, L. (2018) 'Recasting and re-racializing the "third world" in "emerging market" terms: Understanding market emergence in historical colonial perspective'. *Discover Society* 60. https://archive.discoversociety.org/2018/09/04/recasting-and-re-racialising-the-third-world-in-emerging-market-terms-understanding-market-emergence-in-historical-colonial-perspective/ (accessed 15 September 2022).

10

'Afro-pessimism' and emerging markets finance

Ilias Alami

In October 2012 the prestigious business magazine *The Economist* ran a cover story on crisis in South Africa. *The Economist*'s editors and writers undoubtedly knew that the situation in South Africa at the time (a deep socio-political and financial crisis, credit rating downgrades, foreign investment drying up and so on) was due to a complex entanglement of social, economic and political factors.[1] As such, they could have chosen many other visuals to illustrate the crisis. But with this sensational depiction of a mob of angry Black men armed with pikes, the cover seems to attribute the responsibility for 'South Africa's sad decline' to uncontrollable and aggressive (if not violent) masses of Black people. Note that the picture is completely decontextualized. There is no caption or other form of explanation. Nowhere is there any mention that these men were miners protesting the shooting by the police of thirty-four of their fellow workers at Lonmin's Marikana platinum mine in August 2012, in the context of wildcat strikes against extreme forms of economic exploitation and over-indebtedness. Shouldn't these contextual elements matter? How do images like this contribute to the discursive construction of South Africa as a particular type of investment destination? How do South African officials and investors respond to these kinds of images and discourses? In this chapter I bring *The Economist*'s cover into dialogue with key informants from my fieldwork in Pretoria-Tshwane, and explore what those actors call 'Afro-pessimism'. I show that relations of race and coloniality are reproduced through the production of financial knowledges and patterns of financial capital flows, with material consequences for the people living in the spaces construed as African emerging markets.

Figure 10.1 October 2012 cover of *The Economist* depicting protest in response to the shooting of 34 mineworkers at Marikana in August 2012, labelled 'South Africa's sad decline'.

(Mis)representing the crisis in South Africa

In late 2016, as I was conducting fieldwork on policymaking and emerging market investment in Pretoria-Tshwane, South Africa, a Treasury official told me at interview:

> We [South African state managers] have to demonstrate to the world ... that an *African* country is capable of running its own macroeconomic policy ... It's all about perception and confidence, which is why *race matters* ... This is also linked to the *decolonial element* of our transition [to democracy] ... we became independent very recently [referring to the end of apartheid in the early 1990s] ... so [to] people in London and the US [international investors] ... we are still unknown [in the sense that] people don't know whether South Africa will become like Zimbabwe or the Congo ... these are *real factors*. So there has been a very strong desire to demonstrate that we are credible [...]. [All emphases added]

Another key informant made a similar point:

> *Capital is pretty racist* in the way it deals with *a Black government* ... that relationship is always extremely difficult ... hence the cautiousness of the government *not to do anything wrong* because the reaction to whatever happens in South Africa is always very strong, more than what would happen in other [emerging] countries ... The *sensitivity of international investors* to whatever happens is extreme, and therefore the consequences for South Africa would be different than for another country in the same conditions [referring to non-African emerging markets]. [All emphases added]

These statements establish a direct connection between histories of (post)colonialism, empire, race and the operations of global capitalist finance in South Africa. They do so in several ways. First, they suggest that the remarkable timorousness of international investors in South Africa (meaning both a certain reluctance to invest and a tendency to move their money out of the country at the first sign of perceived trouble) is due to a number of racist worldviews, namely, a visceral distrust in Black state managers and the perception of South Africa as an 'immature' (because recently decolonized) country that may lapse at any moment into chaos, just like some of its unfortunate African neighbours did. Put differently, the historical specificities of South Africa do not seem to matter so much as the generic image to which it is associated, that of a weak (if not failed) Black African state in the making.

Second, both informants hinted at the difficulty of building market confidence in that context, even when the most business-friendly policies, institutions and regulations are set up. They suggested that policy making in South Africa is subjected to intense scrutiny by international investors, more than it is in non-African emerging markets (EMs). Any deviation from what investors consider an orthodox policy framework, such as a laxer fiscal stance, tends to be interpreted as proof of governmental incompetence, which is likely to be severely punished by large-scale capital flight. I confess to having been quite surprised at the time by the directness of these statements. After all, their authors were policy makers in government, not critical scholars or leftist activists! Yet they clearly articulated how global relations of race and histories of (post)colonialism are implicated in the *disciplining* of the South African state by global capitalist finance. I was also startled by how much this phenomenon was internalized by policy makers, that is, it seemed to be completely accepted – albeit with a sense of resignation – and factored into policy decisions. This means that, whether real or imagined, it had *material effects*.

Both informants, as well as several others, referred to this phe-nomenon as 'Afro-pessimism'. It was the first time I had heard this expression in the context of investing in EMs. The term 'Afro-pessimism' as used in this chapter should not be confused with US-centred theoretical Afro-pessimism, which argues that modern civil society is structured by anti-Black violence (Douglass et al. 2018). Afro-pessimism here refers to 'the perception that "Africa" has always been and will continue to be a scary, backward and poverty-ridden place' (Schorr 2011: 23), and therefore will forever be unable 'to overcome pressing challenges related to poverty, health, development or governance' (Nothias 2012: 54). Such negative representations of the continent pervade the Western and international media (Bunce et al. 2017). They consist in highly sim-plistic and essentialist discourses about the whole African continent, which is associated with notions of hopeless 'Africanness' (Nothias 2014).

The political role of Afro-pessimism

Media studies scholars have highlighted that the origins of Afro-pessimist scripts lie in colonial imaginaries of civilization and race, as well as how they contribute to the extremely poor understanding of the political-economic realities of the African continent among both Western elites and the general public (de B'Béri and Louw 2011). Furthermore, critiques of Afro-pessimism have shown that it plays a political role: it attributes the causes of underdevelopment, poverty, political instability and economic volatility to an essentially (Black) 'African' problem, thereby *depoliticizing* these structural issues. By portraying 'Africa as being to blame for its own ills and its lack of agency' (de B'Béri and Louw 2011: 342) and propagating 'the idea that "Africa" is hopeless and cannot rule "itself"' (Schorr 2011: 34), Afro-pessimism not only justifies the presence of an army of development practitioners and consultants on the continent, it also draws attention away from more structural questions of power and inequality, and the responsibilities that these might have in the plight of many African countries.

For instance, the infamous Marikana massacre was the outcome of an explosive cocktail of deeply intertwined local and global financial relations, involving local loan sharks delivering predatory forms of finance, the failure of microfinance as a national development strategy, the exploitative practices of extremely powerful platinum-mining companies deeply integrated into the globalized circuits of capitalist finance and the powerful role of credit rating agencies (see Bond 2013). These entanglements of mining finance, colonial imaginaries, extractive practices and racialized exploitation at Marikana are explored in more detail by Styve (Chapter 21). None of this is remotely hinted at by the sensationalist cover of *The Economist*. To be clear, I am not suggesting here that *The Economist* is intentionally propagating racist imaginaries. Rather, I want to ask: what does it mean that this bestselling news weekly, this 'confidante to the powerful' and highly influential 'emissary for the financial sector' (Zevin 2019), is reproducing such hackneyed Afro-pessimist tropes? Could this be symptomatic of how relations of race and coloniality structure EM finance in Africa, as my interviewees contended?

An Afro-pessimist bias in global finance?

Although there is remarkably little research on the topic, there are reasons to believe that Afro-pessimism is implicated in the operations of capitalist finance in African EMs. For instance, an influential collection of essays, *Investment and Risk in Africa*, tells us that 'Africa is perceived as being atypically risky', and that this is 'not a reflection of normal investor caution about foreign environments' (Collier and Patillo 2000: 3). A number of (mainstream) economic studies have found empirical evidence that sub-Saharan African countries' credit ratings tend to be lower than is warranted by their economic fundamentals and by the 'quality' of their institutions (e.g. ul Haque et al. 2000; Schorr 2011).

This bias concerns not only credit rating agencies but also market-assessed sovereign risk premiums.[2] In their work on financial capitalism in South Africa, Koelble and LiPuma argue that currency markets tend to assign to South Africa 'an abstract risk premium' because of the particular racial complexion of the country and the alleged risk 'posed by a Black African government on a continent where government failure is endemic' (Koelble and LiPuma 2006: 621). According to recent studies, Black African economies pay 'higher-than-normal' interest rates on private sovereign bond markets in comparison to other regions (Olabisi and Stein 2015). Borrowing costs are 'unjustifiably high', after controlling for factors such as the credit ratings of issuers and their macroeconomic fundamentals. In other words, Black African countries are forced to pay 'an unexplained "Africa Premium"' for participating in international bond markets, 'which may only be described as a penalty on African governments due to investor bias' (Olabisi and Stein 2015: 88, 99). These findings are significant: remember that processes of risk valuation and investment decision making are supposedly driven by the rational processing of allegedly objective investment criteria such as historical volatility and financial returns, macroeconomic fundamentals, an investor-friendly policy framework, strong institutions, political stability and so on (at least according to mainstream economists and financial investors). Yet, these studies indicate the existence of a bias against Africa in global finance, which affects the pricing, amount and quality of the financial capital that African countries receive.

This bias, though, is rarely explained. To the best of my knowledge, only one study tackles the question head on, and attributes this bias to 'the constructivism of Afro-pessimism' (Schorr 2011). Schorr argues that negative stereotypes of Africa in Western media and society shape the decisions of investors, and overall hamper the continent's ability to attract investment. This argument, importantly, sheds light on how Afro-pessimism shapes global (dis)investment to African markets, but it is ultimately unsatisfying. It essentially tells us that all that is needed to rectify this bias is to change unfairly negative perceptions, presumably by educating investors about the realities of the continent and by propagating more positive views of Africa. This argument tends to portray finance as a benevolent force which is merely impaired by 'bad' (racialized) representations, neglecting the role that finance has played in the brutal histories of extraction, exploitation and dispossession in Africa, from slavery to modern colonialism, high imperialism, the Third World debt crisis and so on (see Alami 2019a). If Afro-pessimism indeed contributes to the harsh disciplining of African states and to the extraction of wealth (under the form of an interest rate premium), then attributing these power-laden processes to a simple matter of (mis)representations seems unconvincing at best.

Towards a critical theory of Afro-pessimism in EM finance

In the remainder of this chapter, I want to gesture towards a radically different type of explanation, one that draws an explicit link between Afro-pessimism in EM finance and the deeply racialized power relations that structure global finance. The concept of racial capitalism is particularly relevant here. Several chapters in this volume engage with racial capitalism, including those by Medien (Chapter 7) on the entanglement of postcolonial migration, predatory lending and racialized borders, by Randell-Moon (Chapter 14) on racial imaginaries that animated settler colonists' exploitation of land and country in Australia and by Bhattacharyya (Chapter 22) on visualizing (alternatives to) racial capitalism. Here, I engage with racial capitalism in relation to the entanglement of colonial histories, racialized imaginaries and the processes underpinning cross-border capital flows. Let me explain: investment in EMs requires a process of discursive social construction whereby territorial objects – in this case, Black African countries – are transformed 'into specifically geographically bound investment categories' (Bassens 2012: 342). Afro-pessimist (and Afro-euphoric) myths and fantasies play a key role in this process. In particular, they operate as a specific 'mode of constructing investibility' for private financial capital (Tilley 2018). These imaginaries help to firmly locate African EMs at the bottom of the hierarchy of global financial relations, maintaining a sharp distinction with the 'superior' advanced West/North (considered the apex of financial modernity). Importantly, this process relies upon the production of *racialized difference* and, in particular, the construction of sub-Saharan African countries as the geographical embodiment of unruly Black populations and exotic wilderness. This fiction of embodied otherness creates a particular regime of desires and affects scripted for a (largely white) audience of international investors. On the one hand, African EMs are represented as a seductive and wild geographical frontier available for conquest, exploration and handsome financial profit opportunities for the courageous 'investor/ explorer' (Sidaway and Pryke 2000). On the other hand, they are portrayed as a source of unpredictability and continued anxieties, given the immutable threat that potential investment earnings may be disrupted by rebellious populaces (Gilbert 2018).

This particular regime of desires and affects influences how financial prospects are assessed in African EMs, which is reflected in how financial actors, often located in world financial centres such as the City of London, evaluate the riskiness and desirability of their assets (Alami 2019b). Indeed, the assets of African EMs, such as sovereign bonds, tend to be attributed remarkably high risk/reward ratios. Afro-pessimist representations of EMs as highly risky provide some justification for demanding high financial returns. Put differently, they contribute to sustained processes of value extraction from African countries.

The attribution of high risk/reward ratios to African assets has several implications. African EMs are acutely subordinated to 'push' factors, such as global liquidity and market sentiment (Bonizzi et al. 2019). Growing levels of risk aversion may result in a dramatic reversal of financial capital flows, which are extremely volatile and pro-cyclical, perhaps even more than in non-African EMs. Policy making in African EMs is also subjected to intense scrutiny by international investors (as mentioned by my interviewees). Moreover, African EMs suffer from a 'neighbourhood effect', where risk perception in one country may largely be influenced by market assessments of other Black African economies, potentially contributing to crisis transmission. Under this configuration, the scope for implementing progressive and/or developmental policies is extremely constrained, because the social pressure and discipline that international investors are able to exert on African EMs states is remarkable.

In other words, risk valuation of African EM assets is not an unproblematic process whereby economic data is revealed, rationally processed and disseminated. It is certainly not a value-neutral technique which is somehow impaired by distorted visions of Africa. Rather, it is eminently political: the production and mobilization of racialized difference is implicated in specific constructions of risk that allow the harsh disciplining of Black African states, their continuous financial subordination and the reproduction of opportunities for wealth extraction. Afro-pessimist and -euphoric fantasies in EM finance are firmly embedded in these broader structured relations.

This tentative theoretical formulation, then, might speak to the variegated processes in which racism 'enables key moments of capitalist development ... and operates both through the exercise of coercive power and through the mobilisation of desire', or what scholars in the Black radical tradition have called racial capitalism (Bhattacharyya 2018: ix; see Robinson 1983/2000). In this case, it is about the constitutive role that sedimented imaginaries of colonialism and empire continue to play as a means of enforcing discipline and continuous subordination, and as a means of profiting in and through capitalist finance. *The Economist*'s October 2012 cover strips the scene of its contextual specificities. Who these men are, where they are from and what motivates their rage and indignation does not matter. What matters is that they look angry and threatening. Their existence is diluted in a generic image of a homogeneous mass of poor and unruly Black people. But we should be concerned with Afro-pessimism not simply to deliver a superficial critique of the 'bad' stereotypes that may influence investment decisions, but as *a practice* of racial capitalism, and as an entry point to articulate a systematic critique of the racialized violence that underpins the operations of financial capital. At a time when African countries are fast becoming the newest investment frontier for EM finance, the task is urgent.

Further resources

Brown, S. and Zevin, A. (2020) 'In theory: Simon Brown interviews Alexander Zevin about the World according to *The Economics*'. https://jhiblog.org/2020/03/23/in-theory-simon-brown-interviews-alexander-zevin-about-the-world-according-to-the-economist/ (accessed 8 September 2022).

Gilbert, P. (2018) 'The risks of others: Imperial nostalgia and technologies of the financial imagination'. *Public Seminar*. www.publicseminar.org/2018/06/the-risks-of-others/ (accessed 6 August 2019).

Hudson, P. J. (2018) 'Racial capitalism and the dark proletariat'. *Boston Review*, 20 February. 2018. http://bostonreview.net/forum/remake-world-slavery-racial-capitalism-and-justice/peter-james-hudson-racial-capitalism-and (accessed 8 September 2022).

Schorr, V. (2011) 'Economics of Afro-pessimism'. *Nokoko*, 2: 23–62.

Tilley, L. (2018) 'Recasting and re-racialising the "third world" in "emerging market" terms: Understanding market emergence in historical colonial perspective'. *Discover Society* 60. https://discoversociety.org/2018/09/04/recasting-and-re-racialising-the-third-world-in-emerging-market-terms-understanding- market-emergence-in-historical-colonial-perspective/ (accessed 29 August 2019).

Works cited

Alami, I. (2019a) 'Global finance capital and Third World debt'. In I. Ness and Z. Cope (eds), *The Palgrave Encyclopedia of Imperialism and Anti-imperialism*. Houndmills and Basingstoke: Palgrave Macmillan. https://doi.org/10.1007/978-3-319-91206-6_123-1 (accessed 15 September 2022).

Alami, I. (2019b) *Money Power and Financial Capital in Emerging Markets: Facing the Liquidity Tsunami*. London: Routledge.

Bassens, D. (2012) 'Emerging markets in a shifting global financial architecture: The case of Islamic securitization in the Gulf region'. *Geography Compass* 6(6): 340–350.

Bhattacharyya, G. (2018) *Rethinking Racial Capitalism: Questions of Reproduction and Survival*. London: Rowman & Littlefield International.

Bond, P. (2013) 'Debt, uneven development and capitalist crisis in South Africa: From Moody's macroeconomic monitoring to Marikana micro-finance mashonisas'. *Third World Quarterly* 34(4): 569–592.

Bonizzi, B., Laskaridis, C. and Toporowski, J. (2019) 'Global liquidity, the private sector and debt sustainability in sub-Saharan Africa'. *Development and Change* 50(5): 1430–1454.

Boy, N. (2014) 'The backstory of the risk-free asset: How government debt became "safe"'. In C. Goodhart, D. Gabor, I. Erturk and J. Vestergaard (eds), *Central Banking at a Crossroads*. London: Anthem, pp. 177–187.

Bunce, M., Franks, S. and Paterson, C. (2017) *Africa's Media Image in the 21st Century*. London: Routledge.

Collier, P. and Pattillo, C. (eds) (2000) *Investment and Risk in Africa*. London: Palgrave Macmillan.

de B'béri, B. E. and Louw, P. E. (2011) 'Afropessimism: A genealogy of discourse'. *Critical Arts* 25(3): 335–346.

Douglass, P., Terrefe, S. D. and Wilderson, F. B. (2018) 'Afro-Pessimism'. In *Oxford Bibliographies*. www.oxfordbibliographies.com/view/document/ obo-9780190280024/obo-9780190280024-0056.xml (accessed 10 February 2020).

Gilbert, P. (2018) 'The risks of others: Imperial nostalgia and technologies of the financial imagination'. *Public Seminar*. www.publicseminar.org/2018/06/ the-risks-of-others/ (accessed 6 August 2019).

Koelble, T. A. and LiPuma, E. (2006) 'The effects of circulatory capital-ism on democratization: Observations from South Africa and Brazil', *Democratization* 13(4): 605–631.

Nothias, T. (2012) 'Definition and scope of Afro-pessimism: Mapping the concept and its usefulness for analysing news media coverage of Africa'. *Leeds African Studies Bulletin* 74: 54–62.

Nothias, T. (2014) '"Rising", "hopeful", "new": Visualizing Africa in the age of globalization'. *Visual Communication* 13(3): 323–339.

Olabisi, M. and Stein, H. (2015) 'Sovereign bond issues: Do African countries pay more to borrow?' *Journal of African Trade* 2(1–2): 87–109.

Robinson, C. J. (1983/2000) *Black Marxism: The Making of the Black Radical Tradition*. Chapel Hill and London: University of North Carolina Press.

Schorr, V. (2011) 'Economics of Afro-pessimism'. *Nokoko* 2: 23–62.

Sidaway, J. D. and Pryke, M. (2000) 'The strange geographies of "emerging markets"'. *Transactions of the Institute of British Geographers* 25(2): 187–201.

Tilley, L. (2018) 'Recasting and re-racialising the "third world" in "emerging market" terms: Understanding market emergence in historical colonial perspective'. *Discover Society* 60. https://archive.discoversociety.org/ 2018/09/04/recasting-and-re-racialising-the-third-world-in-emerging-market-terms-understanding-market-emergence-in-historical-colonial-perspective/ (accessed 8 September 2022).

ul Haque, N., Mark, N. and Mathieson, D. J. (2000) 'Rating Africa: The economic and political content of risk indicators'. In P. Collier and C.

Pattillo (eds), *Investment and Risk in Africa*. London: Palgrave Macmillan, pp. 33–70.

Zevin, A. (2019) *Liberalism at Large: The World According to The Economist*, London: Verso.

Notes

1 During the COVID-19 pandemic these entanglements once again asserted themselves as international rating agencies threatened to downgrade South Africa's credit rating, placing pressure on the state to adopt austere fiscal policies and raising the cost of borrowing.

2 This refers to the difference between the interest rate on an African sovereign bond and the interest rate on a US Treasury security of comparable maturity (the latter are considered the safest assets in the world). See Boy (2014) on how certain government debts came to be treated as 'risk-free'.

11

Dreams of extractive development: reviving the Benguela Railway in central Angola

Jon Schubert

A shiny, new, red-and-yellow train of the Benguela Railway pulls into the sleepy station of Catumbela, a small town of largely defunct small industries on the Catumbela River, halfway along the 30 km-rail line between the port city of Lobito and the provincial capital of Benguela on the central Atlantic coast of Angola. The pastel colours of the station building echo colonial-era aesthetics, and two rusty steam engines on the station plaza allude to the railway's glorious past, but the building is brand new. Like the railway tracks, it has been built by a Chinese civil engineering company. A few people board the train, mainly high school and university students as well as some female ambulant traders; in the waiting hall, a handful of passengers are dozing under a Chinese-built display that lists the next departures and arrivals, including a long-distance train to Huambo in the central highlands. The train is running on time, but nothing much is happening. We have seen in the chapters by Szeman (Chapter 1), Lassiter (Chapter 2) and Kushinski (Chapter 3) how oil extraction infrastructures come to be entangled with forms of settler colonialism and settler aspirations for an 'ordinary' life. This chapter moves on to the question: What dreams of development motivated the construction, decay and rehabilitation of this railway line? What stories can the railway line and its passengers today tell us about the legacies of colonial extraction, independence struggles and their entanglements with oil booms and indebtedness?

Figure 11.1 The CFB train pulls into Catumbela station.

Lines on the rose-coloured map

The Portuguese colonial empire in Africa was always, despite its brutality and totalizing ambitions, a much more precarious affair than its proponents would have it. Until today, Angolans and Mozambicans will gleefully tell you, 'our tragedy was that we were colonized by the Africa of Europe', reproducing in one pithy sentence racialized hierarchies of civilizedness. When, after the 1884/85 Berlin conference, the European colonial powers had to demonstrate effective control of the territory they claimed, the Portuguese (much like the Belgians in neighbouring Congo) relied on commercial concessions to expand their reach and increase the profitability of the colony. Though the Portuguese, after British encroachment, had to give up their Berlin dream of a continuous territory from Angola on the Atlantic coast and along the Zambezi valley through to Mozambique on the Indian Ocean – the famous 'rose-coloured map' (*mapa cor-de-rosa*) – the plan to eventually create a coast-to-coast railway link remained a core ambition.

At the turn of the twentieth century, the Scottish mining engineer Robert Williams – an associate of Cecil Rhodes – flew along the Central Atlantic coast of Angola to locate the best spot to build the end point for the planned Benguela Railway (Caminho de Ferro de Benguela, or CFB), to connect the mineral-rich heartlands of Katanga in the Belgian Congo (today the Democratic Republic of Congo, DRC) and the (then Northern Rhodesian) Zambian Copperbelt with the Atlantic coast. He found the perfect place in the natural deep-water bay of Lobito, sheltered from the ocean by a natural sand-spit, some thirty kilometres north of the provincial capital, Benguela (itself a slave trading port since the 1600s). In 1902, the Portuguese granted Williams a ninety-nine-year concession to build and operate the railway. Construction on the port started in 1903, with quays gradually being expanded until the Second World War. The CFB itself, built in large part through forced labour, was a marvel of British engineering.[1] By 1929 a 1,544-kilometre rail link connected Lobito to the country's eastern border, and in 1931 the rail link to the Congo and Zambia was established.

From its earliest days, the CFB and connected port were geared towards the need of colonial extractive capitalism, to provide a reliable, fast and cost-effective way of transporting African raw minerals to the industrial heartlands of Europe. Angola's two other colonial-era railway lines replicate this logic: the Luanda Railway (CFM) links the capital, Luanda, on the Atlantic coast north of Benguela to Malanje and the diamond-producing Lunda-provinces; the Moçâmedes Railway (CFM) connects the fishing town of Namibe, on the southern coast, to the granite quarries and cattle-ranching highlands of Huíla. Neither the colonial power nor the current government, however, ever had much interest in creating a north–south connection between these three lines. Mozambique's rail network, on the eastern coast of Africa, presents a mirror image, with three coast-to-hinterland lines but no north–south connection between them. This pattern is also evident in other ex-colonies across Africa, -where all railway lines were built for export and lead down to the sea (Rodney 2018 [1972]: 251). As a corollary, the CFB drew communities situated along the line into new, respaced social and economic relations. Sisal, maize, wheat, bananas and coffee were moved down from the Angolan highlands (Vos 2018), while imported consumer goods moved in the opposite direction (including, after the Belgian Congo's independence, luxury cars for newly independent

Zaïre's leader, Mobutu). Forests of eucalyptus trees were planted to provide fuel for the CFB's locomotives. And both port and railway attracted a considerable workforce – 44,000 staff for the CFB at independence.

Towards independence

Despite its claims of benign, multiracial harmony captured in the concept of lusotropicalism (see the introduction to Part IV, 'Emergence'), Portuguese colonialism also relied on racialized social hierarchies, much like the neighbouring settler republics. These were entrenched in law during the Estado Novo, the corporatist (fascist) dictatorship of António Salazar, from 1933 on. Only very few Black Angolans reached the status of 'assimilated', which would in principle have accorded them the rights of citizens. Accordingly, the colonial state trained only a limited number of skilled 'indigenous' workers, though at the port and railway Angolans were apprenticed in great numbers into technical professions – electricians, locksmiths, stationmasters, mechanics and train drivers. As both companies in typical, paternalistic mode also provided housing and in-kind subsidies for their employees, as well as preferential access to employment for employees' children, the CFB and port were effective motors for the gradual formation of a real working class – Angolans who did experience social mobility for themselves and their families through formal work. The CFB also served to promote a sense of shared identity, with migrant workers from the highlands moving down to the Benguela coast, spreading the use of the Ovimbundu language and of their respective Christian denominations to areas where they had not been dominant historically.

But while former CFB employees recall these as good times, and with great professional pride, their relative well-being was predicated on Portugal's continued hold on and economic exploitation of its colonies. While after the Second World War most African colonies started a process of (largely) negotiated independence, the Estado Novo regime doubled down by designating its African colonies as 'overseas provinces' and starting, belatedly, to develop the territories in order to bring the 'benefits of colonialism' to broader sections of their inhabitants.

Too little, too late – as the neighbouring French and Belgian Congos gained independence (in 1960), Angolan nationalists in different parts of the country in early 1961 took up arms against the colonizer. A fiercely fought liberation struggle and brutal Portuguese counter-insurgency war ensued (1961–74), which ended when left-leaning Portuguese military officers overthrew the dictatorship to put an end to the costly colonial wars. A period of transition to independence was negotiated in Angola, Guinea-Bissau and Mozambique. In Angola, however, there had been three competing liberation movements, and while the transition foresaw elections to constitute the first independent government of Angola, mistrust and rivalry, exacerbated by Cold War tensions, won the day. Immediately after independence (on 11 November 1975) Angola was plunged into a deadly civil war, which pitted against each other two of the three former liberation movements – the Marxist MPLA (Popular Liberation Movement of Angola) as the recognized government of Angola, and the 'rebel', nominally pro-Western UNITA (National Union for the Total Independence of Angola). The oldest of the three movements, FNLA (National Front for the Liberation of Angola), which had Western and Zairean support, was militarily defeated by the MPLA in 1975 and ended its armed struggle. As the MPLA managed to hold the capital at independence, and because UNITA received support from apartheid South Africa, the MPLA was quickly recognized as the government of Angola, while UNITA retreated into the bush, waging war from the hinterland against the cities. A peace agreement and multiparty elections in 1991–92 were derailed, and the civil war fiercely resumed, with some brief periods of lull, until the government's military victory in 2002.

The fortunes of the port and railway changed accordingly, as the combination of socialist planned economy and civil war soon led to a steep decline in agricultural production. UNITA regularly blew up the railway lines, although the CFB tried to uphold its service throughout, even if it meant that its train drivers were regularly killed or kidnapped while on duty. By 1989, the train was running only as far as Cubal, an inland municipality of Benguela, and rails, stations and rolling stock were in serious disrepair. The port of Lobito became the lifeline of the southern part of the country, where basic foodstuffs and military equipment were imported.

Oil money after conflict: an oil-fuelled reconstruction boom

It was only in 2002 that Angola's civil war ended, when government troops killed UNITA leader Jonas Savimbi in battle in the remote province of Moxico. Weeks later, what remained of UNITA's military leadership signed a memorandum of understanding to end the war. The MPLA's military victory coincided with the onset of a new 'commodity supercycle', as oil prices, driven by new demand from Asian countries, reached new heights. With Angola now offering perspectives of stability and new technological advances in offshore drilling, oil majors redoubled their investments. For the better part of the following decade, Angola vied with Nigeria for the top spot of sub-Saharan Africa's largest oil producer. And with the price of a barrel of crude oil at between US$70 and US$110, the MPLA government was flush with oil money, and thus able to rebuild the country after the conflict very much on its own terms (Schubert 2017), without any of the usual donor conditionalities that other countries faced in similar situations.[2]

Much of that reconstruction effort went into prestige projects like gleaming new skyscrapers and a revamped waterfront for the capital, Luanda, or football stadiums and roller hockey pavilions of dubious usefulness for the population. But the government also invested in kilometres of new roads. And at the heart of its ambitious infrastructure plans stood the rehabilitation of the Lobito corridor: the modernization and upgrading of the port of Lobito, and the restoration of the rail link to the DRC and Zambia.

This work was largely funded through oil-backed credit lines from China, and carried out from 2006 to 2014 by Chinese civil engineering companies, at an estimated cost of US$2 billion. China's investment in Angola is inscribed in China's larger reinvestment into partnerships with African countries as part of its global strategic expansion. China's renewed international engagement has often been viewed with scepticism bordering on hysteria by Western media and policy makers as proof of China's hegemonic global ambitions and, in the case of Africa, as a purely resource-driven new 'scramble for Africa'.

The Chinese presence in Africa

There are a number of issues with this picture. First, China's engagement with Africa predates the commodity boom of the 2000s, as the People's Republic of China offered military training to African independence movements and concrete development assistance in the 1960s and 1970s – with the TAZARA (Tanzania–Zambia) Railway as one of the most famous examples. China's more recent turn to Africa successfully built on this longer history, speaking a language of equitable partnership and respect that often stands in marked contrast to many African societies' experiences with European former colonial powers. Second, while there has indeed been a growing visibility of Chinese presence in Africa in the past two decades, we should be careful to ascribe this to one monolithic 'China' as a supposedly unitary actor. In fact, a multitude of actors are active across the African continent, ranging from official government and Communist Party contacts to state-owned and state-affiliated companies, to private enterprise ranging from petty trade to heavy industries, to precarious menial workers, especially in the agriculture and construction sectors. Third, the language of 'new colonialism' obscures African agency in these exchanges (again at all levels) – especially in the case of Angola, members of the ruling party elite have been particularly adroit at mobilizing Chinese economic interest and investment for their own personal gains (Power and Alves 2012).

Rehabilitation of the CFB was officially completed in 2014, and the line now runs to Luau in Moxico province, on the border with the DRC. But while the rehabilitated line has proven a boon for commuters between Lobito and Benguela, and for female small-scale traders, especially in the east of the country where road links were almost nonexistent, the Angolan government's ambitious schemes to revive large-scale mineral exports through the port of Lobito have not yet materialized. On the one hand, as former railway workers told me during fieldwork in 2018 and 2019, the rehabilitation was poorly planned and executed, from a lack of spares for the new Chinese and US locomotives to the design of the line: according to them, the Chinese built the curves too tight and the railway beds too high, and the new concrete sleepers cannot absorb the vibrations in the rails as well as did the old wooden crossbeams, leading to frequent derailments and speed limitations. On the other hand, the DRC has not modernized its rail line yet. The state of the rails and the rolling stock in the DRC is so poor that the new, heavy-duty, wide-gauge locomotives that Angola acquired cannot reach the Katangan manganese mines. And so, the few little mineral cargos that have been exported so far have been transported by container rather than in bulk. This cargo has to be transloaded from the Congolese trains to the Angolan trains at the border train station, and is then exported in Lobito through the container terminal rather than the brand-new minerals terminal.

Legacies of colonial extraction

The promise offered by the Benguela Railway is tangled up with the legacies of colonial administration. More generally, the limitations of the Benguela Railway point to the failings of an idea of development based on colonial models of extractive capitalism: the economic rationale for the line has always been that the distance from Katanga and the Copperbelt to Lobito is about two-thirds shorter than the current export route, via road cargo, to Durban (on South Africa's Indian Ocean coast). This made sense in the 1950s and 1960s, when most minerals were still sent to Portugal, which sold them on to the heavy-industry centres of West Germany and Sweden. Yet, nowadays, most mineral exports are destined for Asia, imported by China, Korea, Japan, India and Vietnam. So, even if the route to Lobito might be shorter than the route to Durban, the shorter sea travel to the minerals' end destination from Durban more than offsets potential savings from the shorter rail route on the Lobito Corridor.

Beyond such practical considerations, the development model pursued in dreams of the CFB's past glories does nothing to diversify Angola's economy (nor that of the DRC and Zambia, for that matter) away from the extraction of raw minerals and hydrocarbons, and reproduces Africa's dependency on global markets as a primary commodity exporter (Khisa 2019). Just wishing agro-industries and small businesses along the Corridor into existence will do little to tap the rail link's full potential, or transform the livelihoods of populations largely excluded from national development schemes. Following a downturn in world oil prices in late 2014, and having financed the reconstruction of the CFB with oil-backed loans from China, Angola has effectively mortgaged its future oil revenues for debt repayment. China holds 70% of Angola's foreign debt, and debt servicing made up more than 56% of total government expenditure for 2020, resulting in cuts to social spending and economically orthodox austerity measures that hit the poorer parts of the population hardest.

Predicating Africa's 'rise' on intensifying resource extraction undermines any potential for sustainable, less ecologically and socially exploitative economic activity. It will instead only intensify local, regional and global asymmetries, and entrench existing inequalities. Sure, the commuting students boarding the train at Catumbela are grateful for the cheap and safe transport the train provides; so are vegetable growers and petty traders from the east, who are now able to sell their produce in Huambo and Benguela markets (Duarte 2013). The dreams of diversified national economic development that underpinned and justified the reconstruction of the line, however, seem further off than ever.

Further resources

Grobler, J. (2014) 'Chinese infrastructure lubricates outflow of Angolan and DRC resources'. *Pambazuka News*, 10 April.

King Cobra and the Dragon (2012) Directed by Solange Guo Chatelard and Scott Corben. [Documentary Series] Al Jazeera. www.aljazeera.com/programmes/peopleandpower/2012/01/20121484624797945.html (accessed 2 September 2022).

Marchal, J. (2017) *Lord Leverhulme's Ghosts: Colonial Exploitation in the Congo*, trans. M. Thom. Reprint edition. London: Verso.

Niang, A. (2019) 'The colonial origins of extractivism in Africa'. *Al Jazeera*, 17 August. www.aljazeera.com/indepth/opinion/colonial-roots-africa-corruption-problem-190806084604839.html (accessed 2 September 2022).

Park, Y. G. (2016) 'One million Chinese in Africa'. *SAIS Perspectives*. 12 May. www.saisperspectives.com/2016issue/2016/5/12/n947s9csa0ik6km km0bzb0hy584sfo (accessed 2 September 2022).

Schubert, J. (2020) 'Colonial resonances: Extractive capitalism in urban design in Lobito, Angola'. *Roadsides* 004 Architecture and/as Infrastructure. https://roadsides.net/schubert-004/ (accessed 2 September 2022).

Works cited

Duarte, A. (2013) 'The ambivalent character of reconstruction: Winners and losers of the Lobito transport development corridor'. *Journal of US-China Public Administration* 10(9): 914–926.

Khisa, M. (2019) 'Whose Africa is rising?' *Review of African Political Economy* 46(160): 304–316.

Power, M. and Alves, A. (2012) *China and Angola: A Marriage of Convenience?* Cape Town, Dakar, Nairobi and Oxford: Pambazuka Press.

Rodney, W. (2018) *How Europe Underdeveloped Africa*. 2nd edn. London and Brooklyn NY: Verso.

Schubert, J. (2017) *Working the System: A Political Ethnography of the New Angola*. Ithaca NY and London: Cornell University Press.

Vos, J. (2018) 'Coffee, cash, and consumption: Rethinking commodity production in the Global South'. *Radical History Review* 131 (May): 183–188.

Notes

1 For further discussions of the entanglements between British colonialism, forced labour and working-class formation, see Styve (Chapter 21).

2 See also the discussions of debt and discipline, donor conditionalities and their entanglement with migrant lives and racialized, postcolonial borders in chapters by Medien (Chapter 7), Dickson et al. (Chapter 8) and Rossipal (Chapter 9).

12

Spectral cities and rare earth mining in the North China Plain

Linsey Ly

Resource imaginaries and rare earth frontiers

I am inside the Kangbashi New District Urban Planning and Exhibition Hall. Before me, there is a full-scale architectural model of the very city we are standing in, precise to a startling degree of accuracy. In the miniaturized version of the museum on the 3D map that houses this microcosmic rendering of the city, I half expect to see a replication of myself taking notes, a simulacrum world within another world. Built in the mid-1980s at the height of Deng-era economic reform and the pursuit of a 'socialist market economy', Kangbashi is among China's first prototypes in an experimental urban planning strategy of prefabricating futurist metropolises. These would eventually accumulate to produce the phenomenon of modern ghost cities: fully realized modernist cosmopolises, profoundly absent of inhabitants. Under the conditions of what I call spectral urbanism, these new cities provide a large-scale stage for the Communist Party of China's (CPC) repeated campaigns to modernize the nation by rendering the future into being. In each modern ghost city, an urban exhibition hall houses these reformulations of past, present and future, broadcasting to audiences how the new city is a blueprint of the nation's 'prosperous and harmonious future'.

During the revolutionary years of Maoist politics between 1949 and 1976, urbanism became the expression of a goal to transform society through centralized planning, a science of social design and organization that would link Marxian theory with practice, where cities became the stage for actual enactments of socialist modernity and the measure of its progress. An array of survey materials with

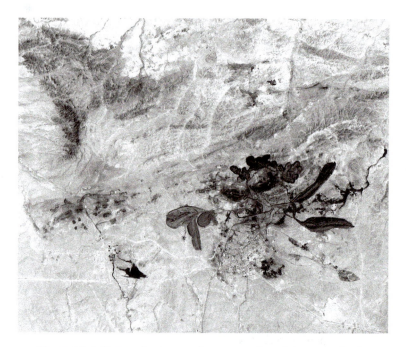

Figure 12.1 Composite image of a rare earths mining complex in
Baotou, Inner Mongolia.

population projections, land-density statistics and GDP graphs
suggests that the future is not only knowable but quantifiable.

Maps, photos and satellite images are similarly used as forms of
empirical visual evidence because they can be said to provide a kind
of visual testimony that attests to the facticity of a thing, its actually
existing reality in the world. As evidentiary artefacts, visual texts
often record, document or capture what is visibly present within
the frame of perception. But 'evidence' does more than just tell it
like it is, as the chapter by Kushinski (Chapter 3) on the livestreaming
of efforts to cap the *Deepwater Horizon* blowout makes clear. The
technologies that produce these kinds of objects and anchor attendant
claims about what can be known about the world have long been
used as tools for the deployment of imperial imaginaries and empire
building, particularly when in service of military campaigns, claims
to territorial sovereignty and nation-state consolidation. In the case

of this composite image (Figure 12.1) of a rare earth mining complex in Baotou, Inner Mongolia, rare earths are also fundamental to almost every aspect of the commodity chain involved in the recording, production and circulation of this satellite image. What Ferry and Limbert (2019) call 'resource imaginaries' are caught up in particular temporalities: ways of imagining the past, present and future that shape the ways we use, produce, name, allocate and manage resources and the affective states they often invoke, whether it is hope, despondency, resignation or competition. In this sense, substances as abundant as rare earth minerals that are framed as scarce are not just found or discovered, but in fact emerge through practices of making and imagining resources. The role of photographic evidence and visual surveillance in staking these claims has far-reaching implications for how social actors understand the relationship between territory, state sovereignty and resource commodities.

Rare earths are not only implicated in every step of producing this satellite image of a large-scale mining complex; they are fundamental to the 'green' technologies at the heart of liberal environmental justice narratives that ultimately centre on the reproduction of mineral capital. Rare earths are essential for the permanent magnets that allow wind turbines to operate. Royal Dutch Shell has taken considerable stakes in wind energy providers, describing itself to investors in 2018 as an 'energy transition company'. Since 2020, BP has signed contracts worth hundreds of millions of dollars for the supply of wind turbine technology to emerge from General Electric. The production of these green technology commodities forms the most developed and comprehensive response to the call to reduce reliance on fossil fuels and curb carbon emissions in an effort to address climate change. Yet, in their reliance on rare earth extraction and processing, such 'green' technologies are sustained by the very pollution and environmental degradation that they seek to address, whereby a global division of toxic labour has emerged that relegates the devastating cost of manufacturing rare earth commodities to China's industrial heartland. These frontier zones are caught up in the confrontation of urban development and rare earths mining.

Even as they are essential to technologies such as the engineering and manufacture of wind turbines associated with the pursuit of sustainable futures in line with the 2015 Paris climate targets, the extraction, production and surplus waste of rare earth commodities drive us ever closer to ecological disaster and life-systems collapse in the areas where they are mined and processed.

Viewed in the national imaginary as China's cultural and geographic periphery, Inner Mongolia is a provincial-level autonomous region that has long been viewed as a frontier zone for the extraction of natural resources. The high environmental cost of mineral ore, processing rare earth metals and storing the toxic waste produced by these extractive industries is often positioned in public discourse as a strategic necessity legitimized by the benefits of modernization, securing China's position in the global economic order. Turning Inner Mongolia into a frontier zone that can be mined for rare earths, despite the certainty of long-term life-systems collapse, is linked to the 'politics of sacrifice' essential to settler-colonial imaginaries. These optics demonstrate how states must view land as 'empty' territories 'absent of life' so that the extraction of resources can take place, often at the expense of already existing human, animal and plant life. Territories that are largely considered 'wasteland' do not exist outside of these optics. As Anna Tsing has observed, 'frontiers are created so they can be blasted away'. Inner Mongolia must be positioned as a sacrifice zone, in order to be subjected to policies of constant political, material and economic revision by the state's latest notion of the national future. This push to modernize, urbanize, develop and 'catch up' with other developed nations was throughout the twentieth century anchored to a future-oriented imaginary. This deferred vision or ideal of what Chinese society can be is always located in another temporal field, the yet-to-be, that legitimizes the costs and sacrifices of the present.

From the period of Sino-Soviet collaboration to high Maoist socialism, the practice of realizing these visions of progress at the margins of the collective imaginary has shaped the landscape, peoples and body politic of Inner Mongolia into different versions of state futures, not relegated to history. Here, at the so-called edges of the nation, the state often concentrates its most stringent economic development plans, placing this 'frontier zone' at the centre of national policy and planning. These long-term modernization programmes have lately resurrected elements of a Sino-imperial colonialist imaginary, sustaining forms of territorial and temporal displacement that draw on the views of previous imperial governance. These fundamental contradictions of contemporary life in China in the aftermath of neoliberal economic reform make visible the violence of global circuits of capital as they are routed through racial fault lines previously inscribed through settler colonialism.[1] Racialized antagonisms are exacerbated by state-funded resettlement in the autonomous region, resurrecting notions of sociocultural and biological difference between Han Chinese, ethnic Mongol and other Indigenous groups, in struggles over primordial claims to the use-value of broken earth.

The satellite image in Figure 12.1 depicts mining operations in an outlying border province in China's contested northern territories. Throughout the twentieth century, this region was continuously remade in successive stages of governance, from imperial Japan to the period of Sino-Soviet collaboration. As Julie Klinger (2017) notes in her work, frontiers are not found but made. Subject to constant revision, the land here and its peoples have provided a stage for the deployment of state futures, from the imperial aspirations of the Japanese puppet state Manchukuo to the promissory optimism of agrarian collectivization under Mao, mass famine following the Great Leap Forward and environmental degradation in the wake of industrialization that secured China's economic rise after the period of market liberalization. The material remains of these imaginaries, traces of which sediment in the land and in collective memory, in abandoned infrastructures and repurposed cities, form stratigraphic layers that variously submerge, settle and now rupture forth, unearthed through the extractive regimes and mining practices driving the People's Republic of China's economic policies. While the satellite image makes the mine and its topographical features visible, it also makes present the processes of displacement, violence and profound absence that have been central to the development of contemporary China. Now, as the CPC looks to pull its unruly margins within the centrifugal influence of the state once again, there is a temporal uncertainty that threatens to unsettle these futural orientations.

The use of racial ordering that builds upon these hierarchies of difference is thus indelibly linked to the violence of buried mineral capital. Mineral capital names the subterranean pursuit, discovery and extraction of value in the Earth's subsoils, the way these socio-material entanglements shape and are shaped by the emergent landscapes they finance – in this case urban, ecological and temporal.

In this way, entire subterranean and urban life-worlds are simultane-ously made possible by the opening of rare earths mines, which are in turn bound to the surface environments of which they are a part. Beliefs about the use-value of increasingly compromised land from the perspective of the various governmental orders that have laid claim to this contest draw on the unsettled pasts of colonial violence, national identity and extractive regimes that resurrect frontier nar-ratives as the basis for claims to sovereignty.

Ghost cities and mineral capital in China's frontier zones

Here, at the end of the world, frontiers are rendered figuratively absent and literally rended of life. Mythologized as the birthplace of Han civilization, Inner Mongolia's environments are now officially recognized as potent sites of extraction, a strategic resource frontier where mineral capital's potentiality and value are laced through the soil in mineral deposits now claimed by the state as a form of national patrimony. Under a neoliberal capitalist reordering of space, ethnic Mongols and other Indigenous minorities with a priori claims to the land are dehumanized through a settler-colonial imaginary, operating vis-à-vis racializing discourses, that transforms them from sovereign to colonial subjects. The subterranean obliteration of the Earth through large-scale mining practices cannot take place without also annihilating surface landscapes and livelihoods, disjoining toponyms from the places they named just decades before. I argue that the spectacular scale – the spectacle – of this form of destruction, the immense expenditure of productive violence necessary to the circulation and accumulation of mineral capital, is always already haunted by its own spectral precondition: an economy of death and excess.

The metonymy between the present absence of a *tabula rasa* frontier, the blasted landscapes of mining zones and the empty high-rises of the modern ghost city makes visible what is there and not there. What is distinctive about the project of internal neocolonialism of China's modernity is the way urban development patterns and mining industries both work in tandem and yet produce contradictory futures.

Chinese capitalism and imperial ruins

The relationship between imperialism and ruination that is expressed in the concept of 'modern ruins' has been taken up by scholars such as Laura Ann Stoler and Anna Tsing to show the persistence of the colonial past in the present, that the project of colonialism which modernity had relegated to the confines of history is alive and thrives in the forms of global capital and the profound inequalities of life and resources that it produces. This notion of the afterlife of empire refuses linear narratives of progressivist history, yet remains embedded in notions of a temporal past. Visual artists have also grappled with how to make sense of an imperial past that will not stay in the past but impresses itself on the present through scarred landscapes and the persistence of racialized forms of exploitation, as discussed by Styve (Chapter 21). Part of what makes this satellite image of Baotou compelling is that it is constituted by so many visions, versions and attempts to project futures, to effect transformation in society, to enact modernity: from the grand social engineering endeavours of Sino-Soviet collaboration, the Japanese Imperial Army's puppet state, failed revolutionary promises of high Maoist socialism and, more recently, the disfiguring force of market socialism. To varying degrees, the materiality of the Earth and the mineral ore mined here has played a part in each instantiation of these regimes and forms of governance.

This rendering of the Earth's topographical features can be read as both a representational image and a text. Even in their claims to objective empiricism, in the use of photographs as a form of evidence seeking to substantiate, record or document, as representational and evidentiary artefacts, there is always a particular narrative being constructed, even if that narrative is about a self-referential claim to authority. Political domination and public dissent are premised on speculation about the afterlife and futures of the image. How is the Chinese state both regressive and experimental in its use of the image to enact the real? How are sight, the image and the privileged status of the visual anchored to forms of positivist thinking?

Even as the optic frames of the state which look to large-scale infrastructural projects to produce and reproduce their own monumental modernism, these structures in their grandness can also tend towards a betraying of their contradictions. Surveillance can be thwarted, pressure resisted. Mineral wounds laid bare, veins of toxic water captured in their brilliance. Mineral mines are homes and abodes of accumulation. They connect surface and below-ground, provide an entry point, an articulated joint of metabolism, passage and transference. The injunction to dig, uncover and unearth is always already accompanied by the particular violence of exploration's imperative to know. The role of the state and the use of the God's-eye view to naturalize manufactured landscapes flattens history/sociality/life to a feature of the land, rather than highlighting the vibrations of their vitality, their co-constitution, our interconnectedness.

The history of geological exploration and its role in the deployment of colonial visions of world order has been well documented from the perspective of the British empire, as well as in relation to European adventurers in China (Shen 2014), but it is as critical to understanding the lens through which the CPC views its own colonial subjects. Inner Mongolia is today the centre and origin of the trade in rare earths, commodities considered to be a crucial resource material by the US Geological Survey and European Commission and for the complex of capital interests they represent. This discourse of resource necessity, in tandem with the idea of resource scarcity, legitimizes efforts to repossess large swaths of Inner Mongolia, displacing existing populations of ethnically Indigenous minorities and other subaltern citizens. Inner Mongolia and, in particular, the area surrounding the Bayan Obo Steel and Rare Earths Mining Complex are considered to be frontier spaces in the cultural imaginary of the nation-state, but borderlands do not simply exist, they must be made. Satellite images are so often inculcated in establishing the presumed emptiness of a landscape where the absence of people enables the violent expulsions of settler colonialism and the rending of environments.

As a mineralogical punctuation event in geological processes, the Anthropocene is the name of an empire not yet at its end. Any accounting of the force and trajectory by which the world is continuously fashioned in this necessarily reorganizes ongoing geosocial processes. Geology is a transactional zone in which ideas about 'Origins', subjectivity and mattering become entwined with histories of dispossession, displacement and violence. In this thinking about geology as an intensive, extractive praxis and cosmology there is a constant need to question what Tuck and Yang (2012) refer to as settler 'moves to innocence'; a newly found consciousness that permeates scientific and public discourses buttressed by a wilful unknowing: a conscientious failure to acknowledge the violent repercussions of colonialism, industrialization and capitalist modes of production. Domesticating extraction, and rendering the artefacts of extractive industries as playful features of an 'everyday' landscape, as Szeman (Chapter 1) describes, encapsulates the entanglement of extraction, settler colonialism and just such moves to innocence. Naming these forms of violence and their excess is to refuse their status as epiphenomenal events in liberalism's origin narratives wherein the positioning of politics answers the need to justify or explain away the centrality/embeddedness in the taking of life. In the eclipse of modernity, the misguided history lesson of histories is to place the repressive dimensions of coloniality and racialization firmly in the past, while continuing to perpetuate a settler-colonial present. The injunction to settle Western colonial knowledge production and extractive practices while simultaneously domesticating and resettling them into new territories and frontiers – armed with eco-optimism and geoengineering – overcomes coloniality without relinquishing its power continuously generated in the ability to make and imagine the good life: to formulate, implement and speak to/ of/from the future.

Further resources

Klinger, J. M. (2017) *Rare Earth Frontiers: From Terrestrial Subsoils to Lunar Landscapes*. Ithaca NY: Cornell University Press.

'Lithium Worlds'. https://lithiumworlds.com/ (accessed 14 September 2022).

Tsing, A. (2003) 'Natural resources and capitalist frontiers'. *Economic and Political Weekly* 38(48): 5100–5106.

Works cited

Ferry, E. and Limbert, F. (2019) *Timely Assets: The Politics of Resources and Their Temporalities*. Santa Fe: SAR Press.

Klinger, J. M. (2017) *Rare Earth Frontiers: From Terrestrial Subsoils to Lunar Landscapes*. Ithaca NY: Cornell University Press.

Shen, G. Y. (2014) *Unearthing the Nation: Modern Geology and Nationalism in Republican China*. Chicago: University of Chicago Press.

Tuck, E. and Yang, K. (2012) 'Decolonization is not a metaphor'. *Decolonization: Indigeneity, Education & Society* 1(1): 1–40.

Note

1 On the racial fault lines inscribed by settler colonialism see also Szeman (Chapter 1), Lassiter (Chapter 2), Comyn (Chapter 4), Cordes (Chapter 5), Randell-Moon (Chapter 14) and Nir (Chapter 16).

Part V

Gestures

Have you ever gazed into the eyes of a relative or historical figure you've never met, trying to get a sense from a photograph of what they might have thought or felt? Perhaps, delving deeper into the mystery, you've focused on the way they hold themselves in relation to the people around them, the way they have clothed themselves. Perhaps you've wondered at the subtle of meaning in a captured gesture: a nervous handshake, a sideways glance, two people standing unusually close? As the obsessive combing-over of visual 'evidence' by those in thrall to conspiracy fantasies demonstrates, there is something profoundly seductive about the photograph which purports to be a picture of 'how things really were' and give us a glimpse into a crucial moment in the past, yet which also hides so much.

The lure of the image or the object as 'evidence' is perhaps both more compelling and more unsatisfying when the 'crime' or set of relationships we are seeking to understand is related to financialization and neoliberalism amid their entanglements with colonialism and imperialism. As we later explore in Part VIII, 'Imaginaries', these systems are too large, complex and multifaceted to be captured in a single moment or image.[1] Yet the trained eye can see their imprint in many photographs and objects. The chapters in Part V each take otherwise innocuous images or things and help us to realize that the gesture or transaction they represent contains worlds.

Holly Randell-Moon (Chapter 14) presents the 1975 image of two men passing one another sand, a gesture marking the symbolic 'return' of land by the then Australian Prime Minister Gough Whitlam to Indigenous Gurindji elder and activist Vincent Lingiari. The ritual was intended to reverse the extortion of that land from Lingiari's ancestors by the British, and to represent an apology for the decades of settler-colonial violence and oppression perpetuated by that and the later Australian governments. Randell-Moon unpacks how this image is framed by the processes whereby early colonial myths that held that the land currently known as 'Australia' was *terra nullius* or free for the taking transformed into a system of racial capitalism where non-Indigenous people used the land as a source of wealth, investment and speculation connected to global markets. But Randell-Moon also takes us *behind* the camera to explore the life and career of Mervyn Bishop, the first Aboriginal photographer employed by major newspapers and by the Australian Department of Aboriginal Affairs. His own biography reveals how control over the production of official photographs had itself been a tool of colonialism and racial capitalism, allowing the dominating forces to shape the story again and again.

Randell-Moon's frame-within-a-frame is mirrored in the chapters by Alessandra Ferrini (Chapter 13) and Zenia Kish (Chapter 15), each of which presents images that speak to the power of images. Kish introduces us to the popularity of the American writer, motivational speaker and 'venture philanthropy' celebrity Jaqueline Novogratz, whose bestselling 2009 book *The Blue Sweater* links the titular article of clothing to her company, Acumen, and its goal of mobilizing modern financial techniques to provide charitable programmes to poor people in 'developing countries'. When still a fresh-faced charity worker in Rwanda in 1987, Novogratz saw a boy in the street wearing her unique beloved blue knitted sweater which she had treasured as a child growing up in the US but later thrown in a local clothing donation box. In the decades since then, the image of the sweater has been a key prop for Novogratz as she travels the world to promote the work of Acumen as the best way to recognize the profound ways in which we are all connected by globalization and to remedy the gap between rich and poor. Yet, as Kish notes, this charismatic image hides a problematic story: Acumen and other companies present a feel-good 'ethical imaginary' to rich investors, but the policies of microfinancing, which offers small loans to the poorest individuals to start a business, often do little to alleviate the 'gap' between rich and poor. They seek to use the 'masters' tools' of global finance to solve problems which global finance itself has created, and they end up perpetuating the entangled legacies of finance and colonialism in a new, more charismatic form.

In a similar fashion Ferrini (Chapter 13) presents us with another imagine-within-an-image, this one of a 2009 encounter at a Rome airport when media tycoon and Prime Minister Silvio Berlusconi (soon to be deposed by scandal) greeted autocratic Libyan ruler Colonel Muammar Gaddafi (soon to be deposed by NATO-backed militias in a civil war) on the latter's first and only visit to the country. At that meeting, which was intended to usher in a new age of economic cooperation, especially concerning Libya's rich oil deposits, Gaddafi wore pinned to his chest an image of Omar al-Mukhtar, iconic leader of the Libyan resistance to Italian colonial occupation in the first half of the twentieth century who was tortured and killed by Italian forces in 1931. Taken by many Italian diplomats as an intentionally offensive gesture, Ferrini explains that Gaddafi's mobilization of the image signalled the deeper histories of colonialism and realities of neocolonialism that simmered underneath the early twenty-first-century meeting, in particular the hidden worlds of finance, oil and military threat that define postcolonial relationships.

These three chapters, then, help us see that, even though no photograph can capture the complexities of the entanglement of finance, debt, colonialism, empire and history, a keen eye can find the traces of these relationships in what might at first appear to be the most innocuous photograph or most innocent gesture. Images like these are never innocent: they emerge from and reflect the world. These images reach us through the eye of the photographer and how they frame and select their image; through the hands of the editor and archivist who chooses which images will be preserved and catalogued; through the choices of the user of the photograph who determines how it will be described and what story it will illustrate. Collectively, we speak of the way that those who have power express it through their power to look, to frame and to define the visual field as 'the gaze'. Under the gaze, subordinated groups (colonized nations, racialized people, women and non-binary people, etc.) come to judge themselves by the measure set by dominant groups, internalizing the sense that they are constantly being observed and never measuring up.

Each of these moments and more are bound up in a world shaped by finance, colonialism, empire and race and so can reveal that world, even if that world is, itself, not pictured in the image.

Note

1 And, as Kushinski (Chapter 3) on the live-streaming of *Deepwater Horizon* shows, initiatives that purport to render the operations of financialized extraction visible and transparent often have the effect of obscuring power relations and restoring the 'normality' of capitalism as usual.

13

Italy, Libya and the EU: co-dependent systems and interweaving imperial interests at the Mediterranean border

Alessandra Ferrini

The image featured in this chapter portrays former Italian Prime Minister Silvio Berlusconi greeting former Libyan president Colonel Muammar Gaddafi at Rome's Ciampino airport, on 10 June 2009. It documents Gaddafi's first visit to Italy, occurring exactly four decades after he seized power in Libya. Gaddafi's visit to Rome was intended as a celebration of the signing of the Treaty on Friendship, Partnership and Cooperation between Italy and Libya that took place a year earlier in Benghazi. A total of seven events took place between 2008 and 2010 in both countries, to publicly perform this new-found friendship as well as to define the different terms of the treaty, specifically, on issues like migration, oil and gas trade, as well as infrastructural development and financial investment. Moreover, these bilateral agreements addressed historical contentions while prompting a series of policies that shape the EU's relation to its Mediterranean border. This image incarnates the warming of relations between the two countries after a century of stormy dealings, but it also gained iconic status because it records an act of diplomatic defiance that sparked great controversy. What does this image and the context in which it was received tell us about Italy's relationship with its colonial past? How is this colonial past being replayed through contemporary diplomatic initiatives which open up financial opportunities in exchange for the securitization of refugees? Do Italy and Libya's postcolonial relations replay formal colonialism, or represent a new form of co-dependency?

Figure 13.1 Italian Prime Minister Silvio Berlusconi greeting former Libyan president Colonel Muammar Gaddafi at Rome's Ciampino airport on 10 June 2009.

Imperial Italy

The animosity between Italy and Libya dates back to the Italo-Turkish War that resulted in the Italian occupation of the regions of Cyrenaica, Tripolitania and Fezzan between 1911 and 1913, which were previously part of the (then crumbling) Ottoman empire. These distinct provinces were eventually merged by the Italians into one country, which they called Libya after the name given to this territory by the ancient Romans. Two issues are of notice here, concerning the legacies of empire: firstly, the fact that Libya as we know it today is a colonial creation, and secondly, that Italian colonial expansion was fuelled by an appeal to so-called 'romanità', that is, the conceiving of the Italian nation-state (unified only in 1861) as a continuation of the Roman empire. As such, Italianness was defined through imperial aspirations, a project for the re-establishment of the glory of ancient Rome – a notion that would be at the core of Benito

Mussolini's Fascist ideology, used to instil a sense of national pride and collective pursuit.

The Italian colonial occupation was especially brutal during what is known as the 'pacification of Libya' (1922–32) under Mussolini's rule. The atrocities committed in this period include the use of chemical weapons and concentration camps, which resulted in the genocide of the Senussi population in Cyrenaica that was fighting against the colonial regime. The capture and execution of their leader, Omar al-Mukhtar, brought this period to an end. The following decade was marked by progressive ethnic segregation as racial laws were passed by the Fascist regime in 1937 (mainly concerning the African territories) and 1938 (concerning the metropole and extending to the Jewish community). Having become a crucial battleground during the Second World War, at the dawn of Italian occupation in 1943 Libya was split in two: Cyrenaica and Tripolitania were administered by the British, and Fezzan by the French. In 1951 all provinces gained independence through the constitution of the Libyan monarchy, headed by King Idris I, which, nonetheless, retained strong ties with the British empire. In 1969, by positing himself as the heir to the Senussi and Bedouin anticolonial resistance, Gaddafi's so-called 'bloodless revolution' allowed him to reclaim Libya's sovereignty, away from European control.

Meanwhile, in 1955 – right after independence – oil reserves were discovered, a find that led to the establishment of several oil-extraction companies, mostly in the hands of colonial powers. As Lassiter (Chapter 2) reminds us, since the establishment of the first commercial oil well in 1859, oil extraction has found seemingly endless ways to entangle itself with empire, conflict and profit making. A year later, in 1956, the first bilateral agreement between Libya and Italy was signed. King Idris I demanded reparations for the colonial occupation, financial compensation and the repatriation of several items. No formal apologies were issued, yet Italy agreed to invest in the development of Libyan infrastructure. This ambiguous move – granting financial investment while refusing to take responsibility for colonial violence – left Italy open to further demands, which were made in 1969 by Gaddafi. As these were again not met, Gaddafi proceeded with the expropriation and nationalization of all possessions owned by the remaining Italian settlers, followed by their expulsion – a population amounting to around 20,000 people.

Anti-Italian rhetoric was a building block of Gaddafi's regime and it included the institution of the Day of Revenge in 1970, to commemorate the day when Italian settlers were expelled and to keep alive the memory of Italian colonial violence – a tradition that was abolished in 2008 as a result of the Treaty on Friendship.

Treaties of friendship

Yet, despite these reciprocal hostilities, Italy's National Hydrocarbon Corporation (Ente Nazionale Idrocarburi, ENI) was granted privileged access during Gaddafi's rule, while, for example, British Petroleum's extraction sites were nationalized. Indeed, Gaddafi struck out several deals with Italy (especially in regard to oil and gas supply) and sternly requested and negotiated various forms of compensation and investment in Libya. These dealings were carried out even during the 1980s, when Gaddafi's regime entered into open opposition to several Western powers, including President Reagan's US government. Italy was caught in the middle of these frictions and was attacked in retaliation for the US-led 1986 bombing of Tripoli. Gaddafi accused Italy of having supported the US by allowing the US army to make use of the transmission station on the island of Lampedusa. As a result, he discharged two missiles towards the island that, however, landed in the sea and missed their target. This situation exposed Italy's pull between different poles and aspirations: its commitment to NATO and the EU, on the one hand, and, on the other, its interest in maintaining a strong presence in the Mediterranean, a legacy of Fascist imperial politics encapsulated in the idea of *Mare Nostrum* ('Our Sea'), the ancient Roman name for the Mediterranean Sea that was revamped and appropriated by Mussolini. Since the loss of its colonies in the mid-1940s, Italy has indeed attempted to maintain its hegemony in this area, in order to establish itself as a regional power (Abbondanza 2016). As a result, even when sanctions were imposed on Libya, first by the EU in 1986 and then by the UN Security Council between 1992 and 2003, Italy still retained its bilateral economic relations with Libya.

The Treaty on Friendship was part of a more generalized change of attitude towards Gaddafi in the Global North that began in the early 2000s as he declared support for the US Bush administration's

War on Terror and subsequently promised to dismantle his chemical weapons programme. Having become an ally, Gaddafi took off for a series of state visits, signing various bilateral agreements with most Western powers. Nonetheless, Italy's diplomatic negotiations with Libya started earlier, as the first draft agreement between the two countries was signed in 1998, during the first Romano Prodi government. Known as the Joint Communiqué, it comprises a series of commitments on the part of the Italian government and, through a joint venture, the implementation of some projects in Libya. As Gaddafi disagreed with what Italy was prepared to offer, the negotiations fell through. It was Silvio Berlusconi who restarted these talks in 2002 and, by 2008, managed to sign the Treaty on Friendship. As his government took on an aggressive and repressive approach to the soaring number of migrants entering Italy from Mediterranean waters, Berlusconi was now ready to make a more appealing offer to Gaddafi: a higher investment ($5 billion over twenty-five years), including the building of a motorway stretching across the country, the repatriation of key artefacts and a formal apology for the colonial occupation. Libya, for its part, would guarantee to Italy a privileged position on the import of fuel and a crackdown on migration. This latter point gave way to the so-called 'push back' policy – funded by Italy and later backed by the EU after initial opposition – that is, the right to send migrants arriving by sea back to Libya, where they are incarcerated in detention camps that severely violate human rights.

As a result of these negotiations, in March 2009 Berlusconi gave a short speech to the Libyan Parliament in Sirte, in which he officially apologized for the colonial past. His speech, however, was rather brief and convoluted, and avoided using the word 'colonialism' or any of its derivatives. Similarly, within the Treaty's text, the violence that was perpetrated by the Italians in Libya, or Italy's accountability in this matter, are not clearly mentioned (Labanca 2008; Kashiem 2010). Rather, colonial history is mostly addressed as 'a painful chapter', in order to deflect responsibility. As a result, several scholars have argued that the Treaty's texts and Berlusconi's 'performance of guilt' during his address to the Libyan Parliament were part of a strategy of deception (Bentley 2016; De Cesari 2012; Gazzini 2009). The apologies were also characterized as a 'parody' (De Cesari 2012) and, in the Italian press, as a 'theatre of hypocrisy'

(Romano 2008). The notion of having 'closed a chapter' was then also at the core of the frenzied media reporting of Gaddafi's first visit to Rome, which was greatly opposed by Italian public opinion and the ruling class. These considerations, thus, bring us back to the image of Berlusconi and Gaddafi at Ciampino airport and to the controversy that Gaddafi sparked. The focal point of this image is the handshake between the two premiers. In keeping with most depictions of political ceremonials, this gesture and pose represents due regard, amity and agreement: the intended pose to celebrate the Treaty on Friendship. Yet, an incongruous element threatens this display of reciprocity: a black-and-white image pinned to Gaddafi's chest, in place of military decorations.

Acts of defiance

This is the act of defiance that provoked outrage: a photograph portraying Omar al-Mukhtar, in chains, surrounded by Italian officers, taken just a couple of days before he was executed. Even though Berlusconi's apologies had taken place only three months earlier, Gaddafi's use of al-Mukhtar's image acts as a reminder and proof of the indelibility of colonial trauma, even in the face of international diplomacy and economic deals. The vagueness of the apologies and absence of direct references to colonial history and crimes, is thus addressed by the Libyan leader through the 'wearing' of this photograph. The gesture was perceived as mockery by the Italian political class. Accordingly, public opinion was also quick to interpret it as a symbol of Gaddafi's untrustworthiness, highlighting the deeply rooted denial of accountability with regard to the colonial past that is widespread within Italian society.

During the three days across which the meeting unfolded, while the debates were largely dominated by protests, several agreements were ratified. For instance, the deal on migration had been creating various contentions since its inception in 2008. Gaddafi was often accused of controlling the number of migrants' crossings in the Mediterranean in order to secure higher Italian investments. On the other hand, Italy was under pressure from the EU to coerce Libya to adhere to the 1951 Refugee Convention. Regardless, in order to stop the flow of migrants landing on Italian shores, Italy was financing the operation of surveillance, containment and incarceration, despite the copious accounts of human rights violations that were reported in the detention camps administered by Libya. Gaddafi's disregard for the Convention was actually very clear: throughout the meeting in Rome, he voiced his disbelief with regard to the necessity of providing asylum to African migrants. This, however, did not deter Italy from making payments to Libya.

On 12 June 2009, on his last day in Rome, Gaddafi also held meetings with Emma Marcegaglia, the president of the General Confederation of Italian Industry (Confindustria), in the presence of the chief executives of numerous Italian companies already present in Libya, such as: Enel, a multinational energy company (formerly state owned); the Italian global banking and financial services UniCredit; and Ferrovie dello Stato Italiane, the state-owned holding company that manages infrastructure and services on the Italian rail network. Marcegaglia defined Libya as a free zone for Italian companies, noting, among others, Finmeccanica, the Italian multi-national company specializing in aerospace, defence and security that, as a result of the Treaty, had received a €541 million commission to develop telecommunications across the entire rail system in Libya. Finmeccanica was already heavily involved in the country through the joint venture Liatec (Lybian–Italian Advanced Technology Company), and, among other deals, more recently it has been favoured for the development of an electronic system for the control of the Saharan frontiers in Libya. At the end of these dealings, Gaddafi announced priority for Italian companies in Libya, the creation of a free market economy and five years' tax exemption for Italian companies investing in Libya, including low rates on energy provision. It is also important to note how, as a result of the Treaty, ENI, which had already been enjoying privileged access to oil and gas reserves in Libya, was able to increase its presence.

On the other hand, in 2008 – right after the signing of the Treaty – the Libyan Central Bank bought €50 million of ENI's corporate bonds, while a month later the Libya National Oil Corporation (NOC) announced that it was prepared to acquire up to 10% of ENI (with the aim of joining its administration board) – a percentage which was then fixed at 8% by the Italian Parliament amid general concerns about Libya's growing stakes within the Italian economy. Moreover, the Libyan Investment Authority (LIA) had invested substantially in Italy, even during the embargo, because its legal constitution made it exempt – even if this ultimately directly benefited Gaddafi's financial empire. Where Schubert (Chapter 11) describes the entanglement of old British and Portuguese imperial infrastructure with new patterns of Chinese investment and oil-backed loans, here it is the former colony that seeks a stake in the former colonizers' extractive operations. Due to the instability generated by the 2008 financial crisis, and to the Treaty's acceleration of trade, LIA was able to invest in UniCredit, Italy's largest bank by assets, which had been impacted by the recession. Since as early as 2002, when Berlusconi restarted diplomatic ties with Libya, investments had also been made in FIAT, Mediobanca and the football team Juventus, to name a few.

'Good neighbourliness'

With the Libyan popular uprising in 2011, however, Italy was quick to uphold the Treaty, even though it should have been legally suspended through a mutual agreement between the two parties. Moreover, Italy disregarded its commitment, stated in the Treaty, 'not resort to the threat or use of force against the territorial integrity or political independence of the other Party or any other form incompatible with the United Nations Charter' (*Trattato di Amicizia* 2008). By allowing use of its air bases to bomb Gaddafi's troops, Italy thus failed to refrain 'from any form of direct or indirect interference in internal or external affairs that fall within the jurisdiction of the other Party, adhering to the spirit of good neighbourliness' (*Trattato di Amicizia* 2008).

At the same time, however, as the US and the EU were applying sanctions to Libya, Italy was not keen to interrupt its bilateral economic deals. For instance, although ENI's activities were affected by the conflict, they subsequently improved steadily, with a production peak in 2016. Moreover, Italy's eagerness to stop the migration flux and fully reinstate its economic deals led the following governments to strike similar deals with the UN-backed Government of National Accord in Libya, headed by Fayez al-Sarraj. To facilitate the rehabilitation of the Treaty after its infringement, Italy demonstrated its support for this new government by reopening its embassy in Tripoli in

January 2017, thus becoming the first Western power to do so. This move was followed by the signing of the Memorandum of Understanding that year (subsequently ratified again in 2020), which ensures that Libya acts as the container of the migratory flux to Europe, a practice that violates human rights according to the 1951 Refugee Convention. What is most remarkable about this memorandum is that the focus is on the securitization of the Libyan border in order to prevent departures of migrants (through heavy investment from Italy and the EU), while little effort is made to clarify Italy's investments in Libya, beyond the policing of borders. Such unbalanced relations are further reinforced by the approval and support given to Italy in this operation by the EU, as evidenced by the negotiations with Tunisia led by Italian and EU representatives in May 2021 in an attempt to strike a similar deal over the control of migration. These talks coincided with Italian Prime Minister Mario Draghi's first visit to Libya, where he professed his willingness to reinstate the Treaty of Friendship, Partnership and Cooperation. Where the chapters in Part III, 'Borders', by Medien (Chapter 7), Dickson et al. (Chapter 8) and Rossipal (Chapter 9) all speak to the entanglement of racialized borders and new forms of predatory micro-lending, here we find hostile border regimes entangled with postcolonial forms of financialized oil extraction.

In conclusion, referring back to the image at the centre of this chapter, it can be argued that Italy's reparations for the colonial occupation have been performed primarily to secure neocolonial deals. On the other hand, it is also worth noting how these relations are not completely one sided and that Libya was also able – given the wealth and negotiating power afforded to its government by the control of abundant natural resources – to reciprocate investment and become deeply enmeshed within the Italian economy. Thus, what has followed is that the past colonial domination has created a co-dependency between the former colony and the metropole that is deeply rooted within their political and economic systems. As financial capitalism renders this process less tangible and visible, it creates the optimal system for neocolonialism, perpetrating imperialist politics through what postcolonial and subaltern studies scholar Gayatri Chakravorty Spivak (Spivak and Young 1991) defines as a 'radiation': something that you cannot feel as much as colonialism but that, nonetheless, exists just as much. As argued by Bentley, moreover, Italy's main form of financial reparation – the building of basic infrastructure such as roads and a hospital, led by Italian companies, as well as university scholarships for Libyan students – in return for privileged access to natural resources and control over internal policy in relation to people's movement, 'reproduces a recognisable colonial script' (Bentley 2016: 166). As a result, it can be argued that Gaddafi's use of Omar al-Mukhtar's image while in Rome did create outrage precisely because it manifests and makes visible these very intangible and invisible relations, as well as pointing to the deceptive nature of the language of political diplomacy and of its public performance.

Further resources

Bialasiewicz, L. (2012) 'Off-shoring and out-sourcing the borders of Europe: Libya and EU border work in the Mediterranean'. *Geopolitics* 17(4): 843–866.

De Cesari, C. (2012) 'One photograph: Colonialism contained', *Photography & Culture* 5(3): 343–345.

Giuffré, M. (2012) 'State responsibility beyond borders: What legal basis for Italy's push backs to Libya?' *International Journal of Refugee Law* 24(4): 692–734.

Joffé, G. and Paoletti, E. (2011) 'The foreign policy process in Libya'. *The Journal of North African Studies* 16(2): 183–213.

Ronzitti, N. (2009) 'The Treaty on Friendship, Partnership and Coopera-tion between Italy and Libya: New prospects for cooperation in the Mediterranean?' *Bulletin of Italian Politics* 1: 125–133.

Vari, E. (2020) 'Italy–Libya Memorandum of Understanding: Italy's international obligations', *Hastings Int'l & Comp. L. Rev.* 43(1): 105.

Varvelli, A. (2019) 'Libya–EU relations: Prospects and challenges', in A. A. Ghafar (ed.), *The European Union and North Africa: Prospects and Challenges*. Washington DC: Brookings Institution Press, pp. 121–148.

Works cited

Abbondanza, G. (2016) *Italy as a Regional Power: The African Context from National Unification to the Present Day*. Rome: Aracne.

Bentley, T. (2016) *Empires of Remorse. Narrative, Postcolonialism and Apologies for Colonial Atrocity*. London and New York: Routledge.

De Cesari, C. (2012) 'The paradoxes of colonial reparation: Foreclosing memory and the 2008 Italy–Libya Friendship Treaty'. *Memory Studies* 5(3): 316–326.

Gazzini, C. (2009) 'Assessing Italy's Grande Gesto to Libya'. *Middle East online*, 16 March. https://merip.org/2009/03/assessing-italys-grande-gesto-to-libya/ (accessed 15 September 2022).

Kashiem, M. A. (2010) 'The Treaty of Friendship, Partnership and Cooperation between Libya and Italy: From an awkward past to a promising equal partnership'. *Journal of California Italian Studies* 1(1). http://dx.doi.org/10.5070/C311008884. Retrieved from https://escholarship.org/uc/item/4f28h7wg (accessed 19 May 2020).

Labanca, N. (2008) 'Compensazioni, passato coloniale, crimini italiani. Il generale e il particolare'. *Italia contemporanea* 251: 227–250.

Romano, S. (2008) 'Scuse italiane alla Libia e teatrino delle ipocrisie', *Corriere della Sera* 4 October.

Spivak, G. C. and Young, R. (1991) Interview: 'Neocolonialism and the secret agent of knowledge'. *Oxford Literary Review* 13(1/2): 220–251.

Trattato di Amicizia, Partenariato, e Cooperazione (Bengazi, 30 August 2008), ratified by Italy with Law No. 2009/7 (TFPC).

14

Racial capitalism and settler colonization in Australia: Australian debts to Gurindji economies

Holly Eva Katherine Randell-Moon

Aboriginal and Torres Strait Islander readers are advised that the following chapter contains images and names of people who have died.

A gesture foregrounds two figures who stand against a cobalt blue sky and rust coloured landscape. They are both focused intently on the product of that gesture: sand being poured from one hand to another. The figures are Gurindji leader Vincent Lingiari and Australian Prime Minister E. Gough Whitlam. The photograph was taken by Murri photographer Mervyn Bishop, one of the first Aboriginal photographers to work for a news organization in Australia. It records Lingiari accepting a symbolic gesture of the return of First Nations land after many years of resilience and resistance to the pastoral industry's encroachment onto their land. It is an iconic image of First Nations self-determination. Bishop's aesthetic choices for the photograph are central to public understandings of this self-determination.

Lingiari was a spokesperson and one of the many leaders of the Gurindji Walk-Off, which involved Gurindji, Mudburra and Warlpiri workers and their families protesting conditions on a Northern Territory cattle station. Lasting for ten years, their Walk-Off significantly included the demand for land. The implementation of the Aboriginal Land Rights (Northern Territory) Act 1976 and the eventuation of land title claims and holdings by First Nations of almost 50% of the Northern Territory are attributed to the Walk-Off. As Lingiari later explained, 'This my place. It musta been one time. It was my place before you [Lord Vestey, cattle station owner] come over on top of me' (Lingiari 2016: 181).

The image tells a story of the financial traces of racial capitalism and its deposits in Australian nation building. Racial capitalism refers to the role of race and racism in generating profit (see Bhattacharyya 2018), and an extended reflection on how we might 'map' racial capitalism is the focus of Bhattacharyya (Chapter 22). This chapter explains how racial ideas influenced the settler colonial treatment of First Nations peoples and devalued their contributions to the land and their work on it. By devaluing the First Nations economies and land management that existed prior to British settlement, colonial authorities and the later Australian government were able to profit from First Nations' unacknowledged labour. When First Nations peoples did participate in settler colonial and state economic activity such as the pastoral industry, they were racially discriminated against and received lower or no wages. Organized resistance to this racial discrimination and theft of land, exemplified in the Gurindji Walk-Off, represents a challenge to some of the fundamental ideas of wealth generation in Australia.

Race, pastoralism and dispossession

When British settlers invaded Australia at the end of the eighteenth century, they were able to profit from First Nations lands which had been sustainably managed for thousands of years. In his book *Dark Emu* (Pascoe, Bunurong, Tasmanian and Yuin 2014), historian Bruce Pascoe outlines how First Nations peoples used complex agricultural and aquacultural techniques to extract food from the land while reducing the effort to do so. He quotes a settler account of an automatic fishing machine made of reeds and a special kind of wood (Pascoe 2014: 6–7) and landscape engineering designed to automatically sort fish into a series of pools for harvesting (Pascoe 2014: 72–73). These practices were carefully managed so that natural resources were not depleted. British settlers ignored First Nations' land management and their sustainable economies. Settlers simply saw an uncultivated land prime for large-scale farming and resource extraction. Racial ideas and their story of human hierarchies influenced the economies of settler colonialism in Australia. Settler colonization is premised on land possession as a long-term practice (Wolfe 2006: 402). That is, settlers colonize territory for the purpose

Figure 14.1 Prime Minister Gough Whitlam pours soil into the hands of traditional landowner Vincent Lingiari, Northern Territory.

of remaining there. Settler colonization, as with colonization, is justified by the idea that land which is 'uncultivated' and not used for economic profit can be appropriated.

In the lands now known as 'Australia', the principle of *terra nullius*, Latin for land belonging to 'no one', was used by British settlers to claim possession of Indigenous lands. As Eualeyai/Kamillaroi scholar Larissa Behrendt points out:

> Aboriginal people in Australia claim to have the world's oldest living culture. There is evidence that Aboriginal people lived in Australia up to 100,000 years ago ... In this context, it is extraordinary that the doctrine of *terra nullius* would be used to assert Britain's claims

to 'discovery' and to attempt to legitimize the assertion of British sovereignty over Australia. (Behrendt 2010: 171)

The use of 'First Nations' in this chapter reaffirms that Indigenous peoples were sovereign Nations and peoples, despite British claims.[1] Emergent theories of race helped to justify the extraordinary possession of First Nations Country. Those responsible for colonization held that the 'stronger' races would inevitably extirpate 'weaker' ones, a view articulated by Charles Darwin after his visit to Van Diemen's Land in 1836 (Curthoys 2008: 233). Economic reasons for the settler colonization of Australia were mutually supportive of the racial science that constructed First Nations peoples as a 'dying race' who would ultimately vacate the land for British industry. Britain had an increasingly poor and criminalized urban population as a result of the economic inequalities of the Industrial Revolution. In order to generate profit, this population was exploited as cheap labour and then criminalized for vagrancy under the Poor Laws if they could not afford accommodation. As a result, Australia was settled through mass convict transportation as one means of relieving Britain of this population.

While First Nations peoples were ostensibly offered some rights as British subjects, British settlers constructed themselves as superior, based on their ability to transform natural resources into property and commodity items. First Nations presence on Country was therefore viewed as an impediment to the industries practised by settlers, and these racial ideas justified extensive violence. When the settlement from Sydney, in the Eora Nation's homelands, extended west into Wiradyuri Country (known as the Bathurst plains by settlers), martial law was declared, resulting in a number of killings and massacres (Banivanua Mar and Edmonds 2013: 345). My convict ancestors settled in this area and benefited from the cheap land. Landownership would never have been possible in their homeland, given that their poverty had resulted in a criminal status.

Expanding the settlement inland helped to 'develop a high-productivity export trade in primary goods' and 'Australia's relatively high incomes' during the middle to later parts of the nineteenth century 'were derived from resources that could be exploited cheaply and were abundant in relation to the supply of labour' (Frost 2013: 341).

Seeking greater profits, the pastoral industry expanded into the interior of the continent. Located in the middle of Australia, the Northern Territory's 'open' and less settled spaces were considered ideal for cattle husbandry in the middle of the nineteenth century. These assumptions were premised on the erasure of Indigenous presence, custodianship and sovereignty. In *Yijarni: True Stories from Gurindji Country*, Gurindji historians detail a number of massacres and violent punishments for being on Country and killing cattle. A map is provided which locates massacres across Gurindji and neighbouring Warlpiri Country (Brenda Thornley, First Nations knowledge 2014, as quoted in Charola and Meakins 2016a: 28–29). Often police were complicit in this violence. Gordon Buchanan, a pastoralist in the late nineteenth century, bluntly stated the economies of this violence: 'Imprisonment for cattle-killing was quite impracticable; and if no punishment were inflicted it would have been impossible to settle the country' (as cited in Charola and Meakins 2016b: 72).

The extent of settler violence indicates the significant resistance waged by First Nations in the area. Violence began to subside when more Aboriginal settlements were established at the stations at the end of the nineteenth century. As outlined in *Yijarni*, First Nations peoples lived in camps near the stations in poor-quality accommodation and were provided with basic food rations and clothing. Children were expected to work (Meakins 2016: 183) and were routinely subjected to kidnapping for this purpose and to force their guardians onto stations to work (Wadrill, Gurindji 2016: 127; Meakins and Charola 2016a: 98). Aboriginal peoples built much of the infrastructure for the stations which involved hard manual labour (Wavehill, Gurindji 2016, 97). This included roads, water bores (which were pumped by hand) (Lingiari, Gurindji 2016, 177) and the construction of the Wave Hill airstrip in 1929 (Danbayarri, Gurindji 2016).

Because the Crown claimed all First Nations country through settlement, they provided leases to pastoralists for a small fee in order to foster economic activity. Lord Vestey owned Wave Hill as well as Limbunya Stations, beginning in 1913 and until the 1990s. Gurindji peoples call this 'Vestey time' (Gurindji knowledge, as cited in Meakins and Charola 2016b: 3, 235). According to Michael Woods, 'the Vesteys were the largest landowners in the Northern

Territory' (Woods 2013: 125) and operated a global company that benefited from British imperial and colonial trading networks (Woods 2013: 124–125), with businesses extending to Latin America and Africa (125).

Protection, welfare and Walk-Offs

Protection policies were introduced in the early twentieth century. Under these policies, First Nations peoples were rendered wards of the state and subject to state control concerning where they lived, worked and who they married (see Foster 2000). Pastoralist responsibilities then shifted from treating First Nations peoples as criminal (because they were 'trespassing' on pastoralist land) to welfare populations (where they were dependent on pastoralists for food and shelter). Pastoralists benefited from Protection policies which enabled the exemption of wages for First Nations peoples in exchange for welfare provision (Anthony 2007: 46). At the time of the Wave Hill Walk-Off in 1966, Charlie Ward reports that white workers were paid approximately $33 a week, compared to $6 for Aboriginal workers (Ward 2016: 23). Mick Rangiari explained: 'We are good people and the Vesteys did not treat us the same as everybody else … They been get rich by the Gurindji people and nothing was given back to us' (Rangiari, Gurindji 1998: 5). Despite these harsh conditions, Thalia Anthony suggests that there were possibilities for 'transgression' because First Nations workers and their extended families and communities generally lived on their Country. As such, they were able to continue practising (albeit in limited ways) their languages, laws and ceremonies (Anthony 2007: 47; see also Jimmy and Biddy Wavehill, Gurindji 2014, as quoted in Charola and Meakins 2016a, 114).

Towards the middle of the twentieth century, there were a number of industrial strikes and Walk-Offs by First Nations workers, including the 1946 Pilbara Pastoral Workers' Strike in Western Australia (see Hess 1994). In 1966 the Commonwealth Conciliation and Arbitration Commission overturned a clause in the Cattle Industry (Northern Territory) Award which denied equal wages to Aboriginal workers. Due to industry fears that equal wages would cut into industry profits, the award was given a three-year transition (Ward 2016:

23). This prompted First Nations action. Under the direction of a Gurindji Elder, Sandy Moray Junganaiari, and with external assistance from Dexter Daniels, from Roper River and the North Australian Workers Union, workers at the Wave Hill Station vacated on the morning of 23 August 1966. As Minoru Hokari (2000) notes, calling the Walk-Off a 'strike', as it is sometimes known, interprets the resistance through an assumed white lens of economic bargaining. While wages were one concern, as outlined by Lingiari (Gurindji 2016) and Mick Rangiari (Gurindji 1997, 1998) among other leaders, land was their central demand. The Gurindji workers explained, 'One way walk-off, that's it!' (First Nations knowledge, as cited in Hokari 2000: 107). In 1967 they settled at Wattie Creek, known as Daguragu, which the Gurindji leaders explained is 'the main place of our dreaming [sic]' (Hokari 2000:110).

Freehold title and the handover

Publicizing their cause to unions, student associations and the media in the south and east coasts of Australia, the Gurindji community were able to convince the Federal Government under Gough Whitlam to release land from the Vesteys' lease. Aboriginal Freehold Title was made possible under the Aboriginal Land Rights (Northern Territory) Act 1976, initiated by the Whitlam government. This allowed First Nations peoples to own their land. The freehold deeds for the land at Daguragu were not awarded to the Gurindji community until 1986, owing to ongoing legal and bureaucratic processes (Ward 2016: 308). The community formed the Murramulla Gurindji Company, meaning 'traditional owner', in 1970, to operate their cattle business (Ward 2016: 63). The Gurindji Aboriginal Corporation was formed in 2014 as a result of Native Title over the township of Kalkaringi (which incorporated Daguragu). The handover photograph features prominently on their website (Gurindji Aboriginal Corporation 2018). I gave notice to this Corporation regarding the writing of this chapter. Native Title recognizes that First Nations peoples have rights to land derived from their traditional law and customs. This is significant, because Native Title recognizes that the Crown's right to possess land (stemming from *terra nullius*) does not override First Nations' law.

The famous handover occurred on 16 August 1975 at Wattie Creek. Charlie Ward reports that it was an improvised performance by the government entourage based on reversing an earlier attempted treaty between Wurundjeri Elders in Port Phillip in the nineteenth century (Ward 2016: 183). Ward notes that there is a medieval European equivalent called 'livery in deed' (Ward 2016: 185). This ritual is actually connected to the settlement of Australia through the livery of seisin, which encompasses the livery in deed where two parties meet on land to exchange soil to ratify transfer of ownership (Miller, Eastern Shawnee Tribe 2010: 22). Captain James Cook engaged in these and other practices by planting a flag in Sydney cove in 1770 to claim British possession *in absentia* of First Nations peoples through *terra nullius* (see Behrendt, Eualeyai/Kamillaroi 2010: 174).

Photography 'has played a part in the history of attempted genocide' of First Nations peoples by documenting their erasure (Dewdney 1994: 17). This is because the camera is often viewed as a 'truthful recording of nature' (Dewdney 1994:19), as if what is being photographed is simply being represented as it is. Andrew Dewdney explains how this ignores the staging and posing of subjects as well as lighting and framing used to record and represent the image in a certain way. There are also the cultural meanings through which we interpret images. Photographs of First Nations people in the nineteenth century circulated as part of a global visual economy where images of 'disappearing races' had value because they could be marketed as the only record of a community's existence. Although these images were supposed to reflect the exotic difference of First Nations peoples, they were often highly staged according to similar sets of ideas about so-called 'less civilized' peoples. Art historian Nicholas Mirzoeff describes how the anthropologist Herbert Lang travelled to Africa on behalf of the American Museum of Natural History to photograph 'traditional' people in Mangbetu. Based on the writings of other Europeans who had travelled to Africa, he expected to see a great hall for tribal meetings in one of the towns. When he did not find one, the residents built one, which he photographed as proof of 'native' culture (Mirzoeff 2000: 146).

Because the meaning of a photograph is constructed through the cultural and historical context in which it is viewed, colonial photography in Australia has in turn been appropriated by contemporary First

Nations communities to instead evidence 'the impact of colonisation upon their culture' (Dewdney 1994, 27). In this way, photography can be used by First Nations peoples to reverse the colonial gaze. In considering the photographic image in Australian history in relation to First Nations peoples, it is significant that the handover was photographed by Mervyn Bishop, from Brewarrina in Muruwari, Ngemba, Weilwan and Yualwarri Country, New South Wales. His life story also demonstrates how racial policies influence First Nations mobility and the development of another industry, news photography.

Protection policies, which dictated where Indigenous children could receive education, influenced Bishop's early schooling and he was fortunate to receive a 'bursary to attend Dubbo High School' (Bishop, Murri 1994: 80; Bishop, Murri and Randell 2019). Bishop has recounted that there 'weren't many Aboriginal kids' during his school years (Bishop, Murri 1994: 84). This was still true several decades later when I attended the same school. Bishop's academic achievements led him to Sydney, where he worked as a cadet photographer for the *Sydney Morning Herald*. This career path was conspicuous, as he was the only Aboriginal photographer working for a metropolitan news organization at the time. Despite winning the prestigious News Photographer of the Year award in 1971 for 'A Life and Death Dash', he was not promoted. He later concluded: 'I'd hit a barrier in what I had to remind myself was still a white world' (Bishop, Murri 1994: 84). He then worked for the Federal Government's Department of Aboriginal Affairs (Bishop, Murri 1994: 84), which is how he came to photograph the handover. One of Bishop's aims was to establish a photography unit in the Department, which would also 'train other Aboriginal people and establish an Aboriginal picture library' (Bishop, Murri 1994: 85). This would have been significant in enabling First Nations control over how Aboriginal Affairs were represented and understood by the public, in addition to securing further First Nations contribution to news photography. Although I received permission from Bishop to use and write about the handover image, the copyright lies with the Department of the Prime Minister and Cabinet.

As explained in an interview with my nephew Finn Randell, Bishop's position in the Department of Aboriginal Affairs gave him priority in photographing Lingiari and Whitlam before the other media. He had the subjects restage the handover, with Lingiari positioned at the front (Bishop, Murri and Randell 2019). Whitlam is significantly taller than Lingiari. This is muted by Bishop's framing and positioning of the latter, which works to subtly undermine the ordering of the subjects' names in the official government title for the photograph. Based on the subject arrangement in Bishop's work, a different visual caption is offered: 'Vincent Lingiari receives Gurindji soil from Gough Whitlam'. Or perhaps, given its centrality to the image: 'Gurindji land relates Gough Whitlam to Vincent Lingiari'.

The presumptive right of Crown possession saturates the racial economies of colonial trade and the later development of capitalism under Australian governments. In the chapters by Comyn (Chapter 4) on Aotearoa New Zealand and Cordes (Chapter 5) on the US, the connection between debt and racialized subordination in laying the groundwork for settler colonialism is clearly articulated. The economic development of Australia likewise is indebted to the First Nations labour that carefully sustained and supported arable farming land for British settlers at great profit. When First Nations peoples did contribute directly to economies such as the pastoral industry, their labour had no wage value. The extraordinary Gurindji and Murri peoples who feature in this story form part of a larger narrative of First Nations mobility and Australian economic activity. The Gurindji Walk-Off is a story about Country where economies of responsibility to land and peoples continue, despite the obstacles of Vestey and settler times, which are a brief (but violent) insertion into ongoing First Nations histories of Country.

Gurindji ≈ Country ≈ life

Acknowledgement

I would like to acknowledge the sovereignty of Wiradyuri peoples on whose lands this chapter was written and pay respects to Elders past, present, always.

Further resources

Bishop, M. Murri (1994) 'Looking back on thirty years'. In A. Dewdney (ed.), *Racism, Representation and Photography*. Sydney: Inner City Education Centre, pp. 79–88.

Bishop, M. Murri and Randell, F. Non-Indigenous (2019) 'Pieces of wisdom'. https://player.whooshkaa.com/pieces-of-wisdom?episode=403318 (accessed 31 August 2022).

Gurindji Aboriginal Corporation (2018) www.gurindjicorp.com.au/ (accessed 31 August 2022).

Works cited

Anthony, T. (2007) 'Criminal justice and transgression on northern Australian cattle stations'. In I. Macfarlane and M. Hannah (eds), *Transgressions: Critical Australian Indigenous Histories*, 35–61. Acton: ANU Press, pp. 35–61. https://press-files.anu.edu.au/downloads/press/p21521/pdf/book.pdf (accessed 31 August 2022).

Banivanua Mar, T. and Edmonds, P. (2013) 'Indigenous and settler relations'. In A. Bashford and S. Macintyre (eds), *The Cambridge History of Australia: Volume 1, Indigenous and Colonial Australia*. Port Melbourne: Cambridge University Press, pp. 342–366.

Behrendt, L. Eualeyai/Kamillaroi (2010) 'The doctrine of discovery in Australia'. In R. J. Miller, J. Ruru, L. Behrendt and T. Lindbert (eds), *Discovering Indigenous Lands: The Doctrine of Discovery in the English Colonies*. Oxford: Oxford University Press, pp. 171–186.

Bhattacharyya, G. (2018) *Rethinking Racial Capitalism: Questions of Reproduction and Survival*. London: Rowman & Littlefield.

Bishop, M. (1971) 'Life and death dash' (black and white photograph).

Bishop, M. Murri (1994) 'Looking back on thirty years'. In A. Dewdney (ed.), *Racism, Representation and Photography*. Sydney: Inner City Education Centre, pp. 79–88.

Department of the Prime Minister and Cabinet (Bishop, M. / 1975). 'Prime Minister Gough Whitlam pours soil into the hands of traditional land owner Vincent Lingiari, Northern Territory' (colour photograph).

Bishop, M., Murri and Randell, F. Non-Indigenous (2019) 'Pieces of wisdom'. https://player.whooshkaa.com/pieces-of-wisdom?episode=403318 (accessed 31 August 2022).

Charola, E. and Meakins, F. Non-Indigenous (eds) (2016a) *Yijarni: True Stories from Gurindji Country*. Canberra: Aboriginal Studies Press.

Charola, E. and Meakins, F. Non-Indigenous (2016b) 'Other reported accounts of conflict'. In E. Charola and F. Meakins (eds), *Yijarni: True Stories from Gurindji Country*. Canberra: Aboriginal Studies Press, pp. 67–72.

Curthoys, A. (2008) 'Genocide in Tasmania: The history of an idea'. In A. D. Moses (ed.), *Empire, Colony, Genocide: Conquest, Occupation and Subaltern Resistance in World History*. Oxford: Berghahn Books, pp. 229–252.

Danbayarri, D. Gurindji. (2016) 'The first aeroplanes at Wave Hill Station: 1929'. In E. Charola and F. Meakins (eds), *Yijarni: True Stories from Gurindji Country*. Canberra: Aboriginal Studies Press, pp. 137–143.

Dewdney, A. (1994) 'Racism, representation and photography'. In A. Dewdney (ed.), *Racism, Representation and Photography*. Sydney: Inner City Education Centre, pp. 15–39.

Foster, R. (2000) '"Endless trouble and agitation": Aboriginal activism in the protectionist era'. *Journal of the Historical Society of South Australia* 28: 15–27.

Frost, L. (2013) 'The economy'. In A. Bashford and S. Macintyre (eds), *The Cambridge History of Australia: Volume 1, Indigenous and Colonial Australia*. Port Melbourne: Cambridge University Press, pp. 315–341.

Gurindji Aboriginal Corporation (2018) www.gurindjicorp.com.au/ (accessed 31 August 2022).

Hess, M. (1994) 'Black and red: The Pilbara Pastoral Workers' strike, 1946'. *Aboriginal History* 18(1): 65–83.

Hokari, M. Non-Indigenous (2000) 'From Wattie Creek to Wattie Creek: An oral historical approach to the Gurindji walk-off'. *Aboriginal History* 24: 98–116.

Lingiari, V. Gurindji (2016) 'Events leading up to the walk-off'. In E. Charola and F. Meakins (eds), *Yijarni: True Stories from Gurindji Country*. Canberra: Aboriginal Studies Press, pp. 176–182.

Meakins, F. Non-Indigenous (2016) 'Conditions under the Vesteys'. In E. Charola and F. Meakins (eds), *Yijarni: True Stories from Gurindji Country*. Canberra: Aboriginal Studies Press, pp. 182–186.

Meakins, F. and Charola, E. Non-Indigenous (2016a) 'European accounts of Gurindji moving to cattle stations'. In E. Charola and F. Meakins (eds), *Yijarni: True Stories from Gurindji Country*. Canberra: Aboriginal Studies Press, pp. 98–100.

Meakins, F. and Charola, E. Non-Indigenous (2016b) 'Introduction'. In E. Charola and F. Meakins (eds), *Yijarni: True Stories from Gurindji Country*. Canberra: Aboriginal Studies Press, pp. 1–4.

Miller, R. J. Eastern Shawnee Tribe (2010) 'The Doctrine of Discovery'. In R. J. Miller, J. Ruru, L. Behrendt and T. Lindbert (eds), *Discovering Indigenous Lands: The Doctrine of Discovery in the English Colonies*. Oxford: Oxford University Press, pp. 1–25.

Mirzoeff, N. (2000) *An Introduction to Visual Culture*. London: Routledge.

Pascoe, B. Yuin, Bunurong, and Tasmanian (2014) *Dark Emu: Black Seeds, Agriculture or Accident?* Sydney: Magabala Books.

Rangiari, M. Gurindji (1997) 'Talking history'. In G. Yunupingu (ed.), *Our Land is Our Life: Land Rights – Past, Present and Future.* St Lucia: University of Queensland Press, pp. 33–38.

Rangiari, M. Gurindji (1998) 'They been get rich by the Gurindji people'. In A. Wright for the Central Land Council (ed.), *Take Power Like This Old Man Here: An Anthology of Writings Celebrating Twenty Years of Land Rights in Central Australia, 1977–1997.* Alice Springs: IAD Press, pp. 4–5.

Wadrill, V. Gurindji. (2016) 'They Took the Kids Away'. In E. Charola and F. Meakins (eds), *Yijarni: True Stories from Gurindji Country.* Canberra: Aboriginal Studies Press, pp. 127–128.

Ward, C. (2016) *A Handful of Sand: The Gurindji Struggle, After the Walk-Off.* Clayton: Monash University Press.

Wavehill, R. Gurindji (2016) 'How Gurindji Were Brought to Work on Wave Hill Station'. In E. Charola and F. Meakins (eds), *Yijarni: True Stories from Gurindji Country.* Canberra: Aboriginal Studies Press, pp. 84–97.

Wolfe, P. (2006) 'Settler colonialism and the elimination of the native'. *Journal of Genocide Research* 8(4): 387–409.

Woods, M. (2013) 'The elite countryside: Shifting rural geographies of the transnational super-rich'. In I. Hay (ed.), *Geographies of the Super-Rich.* Cheltenham: Edward Elgar, pp. 123–136.

Note

1   The chapters in this book concerned with various geographical locations make different decisions about the terminology used to describe pre-settler societies in settler colonies. While Indigenous is appropriate in some contexts, it can appear offensive, due to historic usage whereby First Nations or First Peoples were referred to in a dehumanizing manner, as part of the 'indigenous flora and fauna'. The choice of terminology throughout this chapter – as elsewhere in the book – thus reflects an attempt to use the most respectful language for each of the varied contexts under consideration.

15

Connected by a blue sweater: ethical narratives of philanthrocapitalist development

Zenia Kish

It all started with a strange coincidence, when American Jacqueline Novogratz was only twenty-five years old. It was 1987, and Novogratz was working in the Rwandan capital, Kigali, to establish the country's first microfinance institution for women. Jogging through the streets one day, she was stopped in her tracks by the appearance of a young boy 'wearing the sweater – *my sweater*'. She thought back to her childhood, growing up as the oldest of seven children in a working-class family in 1970s Virginia. Only receiving new clothing on special occasions, she came to treasure a blue wool sweater given to her by an uncle. With a pair of zebras and a snow-capped mountain on the front, she recalls, 'the sweater made me dream of places far away'. Writing her name on the tag, Novogratz claimed it as hers forever. Her childhood fashion sense, however, later gave way to teenage tastes, and she eventually deposited the sweater at a charity donation shop, happy to be rid of it.

Until Kigali, 1987. She greeted the boy wearing the blue sweater and, peering at the tag, saw her name written there. Over ten years after she had given it away in Virginia it had by chance ended up here, on her Kigali jogging route, somehow connecting these unlikely moments and places in her life. *The Blue Sweater* became the name and iconic cover image of her first book, the photograph of an anonymous young child restaging this implausible encounter with a material trace of her childhood halfway around the world. This chance meeting was not simply a reminder of the circumstances separating this boy's childhood from her own – the subtitle's 'Gap between Rich and Poor'. She interpreted it as evidence that 'we are all connected' to 'people we may never know and never meet across

Figure 15.1 Cover image of Jacqueline Novogratz's *The Blue Sweater.*

the globe', through both our actions and our inactions. This insight seeded a new moral imperative: it became her mission to 'understand better what stands between poverty and wealth' (Novogratz 2009: 3). Today, Novogratz is widely known as the founder of Acumen, a non-profit fund that invests in businesses seeking to alleviate poverty across the Global South. She is a leading example of an impact investor, a broad category of financiers who prioritize a triple – social, environmental and financial – bottom line in their investments with the goal of using market-based solutions to address far-reaching social and environmental problems. Her book, and the images associated with it, are popular among aspiring social entrepreneurs and development professionals, some of whom claim that reading it changed their lives and their career paths. The book's cover provokes questions about whom we identify as possessing agency to incite social change, what global connections 'between rich and poor' look like and why children continue to be used in popular develop-ment discourse as a prime icon of the Global South.[1]

In this chapter I use the example of Jacqueline Novogratz and her vision (and visualization) of global interconnection to explore how moral storytelling is used across the ethical finance sector to personalize solutions to structural, historically embedded inequalities. Such storytelling serves to centre typically Western entrepreneurs or investors and their notions of innovation as uniquely positioned to solve global problems; in doing so, they generally favour individualistic entrepreneurial solutions that minimize the ongoing effects of histories of colonial inequalities built into the international economy favouring wealthy nations, and other relevant socio-economic contexts. Further, these narratives privilege the perspectives of international financial actors as authoritative, marginalizing those whose problems are being 'solved'. To be sure, impact investors – who claim to be driven by social and environmental values as much as by financial returns – are working at the institutional level to build new markets, develop novel financial instruments and cultivate unconventional forms of entrepreneurship. However, my focus in this chapter will be on how such market-making also takes place at very intimate levels of self-fashioning and interpersonal connection to produce an ethical imaginary of poverty action. I use the notion of *ethical imaginary* to designate a cultural ethos produced and shared among a particular group of people, in this case financial actors like Novogratz who use emotion-laden claims to promote market-based values as the primary means to solve global poverty.

Drawing on ethnographic research with impact investors and analysis of storytelling practices within the sector, I use feminist postcolonial scholarship to argue that their performance of ethical subjectivity is integral to the reinscription of debt-based relations of global inequality. Storytelling is a tool, in these contexts, to assert moral legitimacy by positioning social entrepreneurship and impact investing as a *more ethical* approach to development than either existing institutions or alternative approaches, such as citizen-led strategies. This narrow ethical imaginary[2] deflects from the ways that such business models expand new forms of debt across the Global South, such as through microfinance and digital financial services, and serves to frame social change as a matter for markets rather than political and civic participation.

(Post)colonial intimacies

Mobilizing emotional attachments to faraway places and people is not a new strategy for either imperialism or international finance. As the chapter in this volume by Alami (Chapter 10), on racialized imaginaries and emerging markets finance, shows, mobilizing such attachments is fundamental to the operation of contemporary financial markets. Anthropologists and historians have long studied how colonialism depended on interpersonal, even intimate, encounters as much as it did on violence in the 'contact zones' where explorers and settlers confronted indigenous residents (Pratt 2008).[3] These 'intimate frontiers' of empire are spaces where hierarchies of race, gender, family, sexuality and labour are negotiated, both defining and contesting how power is distributed between colonizers and the colonized (Hurtado 1999; Stoler 2001). Laura Ann Stoler argues that to understand the intersections of race and empire, 'intimacies must matter', because political authority and economic power rely on strategically managing social relationships (Stoler 2001: 835). In this sense, it is important to approach intimate sites and practices *as political*, i.e. having to do with power relations. Lisa Lowe develops this idea further to explore how colonialism, and the modern liberal subject that developed in tandem with it, unfolds through a '"political economy" of intimacies' (Lowe 2015: 18). Intimacy here is not defined narrowly in terms of sexual or familial relationships. Rather, it offers a broader framework for identifying who and what are deemed valuable, and who is included and excluded, in a dominant economic order – in this case, global capitalism.

The intimacies that governed social difference and connection in supported colonial economies continue to have an afterlife in contemporary international development finance, which uses finance and debt in ways that are haunted by imperial histories of resource extraction, exploitation and impoverishment. This is partly because, as Jacqueline Novogratz's story of the blue sweater exemplifies, many actors who benefit from the inequitable distribution of global wealth established under colonialism demonstrate their benevolence through displays of intimate connection with global poverty.

The Blue Sweater is an exploration of these intimate connections. Novogratz uses vivid storytelling to illustrate how her ideas for addressing poverty are all rooted in the encounters and relationships she personally experienced in her early career, first as an international banker in Brazil and then working in development across Africa. The solutions become visible, she argues, when one makes space for personal connection: 'the story of the blue sweater is also my personal story: Seeing my sweater on that child renewed my sense of purpose in Africa' (Novogratz 2009: 3). Earlier, working in Brazil, she observes, 'The chasm between rich and poor was stunning. I'd never experienced such poverty alongside such wealth before, and I'd also never felt such a strong desire to make a difference or *felt so fully alive*' (2009: 7; emphasis added). For Novogratz, these encounters trigger a deeply personal calling to lead a mission-driven life as an investor. While such storytelling professes an ethical commitment toward helping those living in poverty, it centres Novogratz (and her feelings) as the protagonist of the story while othering those she meets along the way. Indeed, even after many years had passed since she gave it away, she still identified the blue pullover as '*my* sweater'. This impulse to turn everything of value in the sector into a personal story localizes larger ethical and political questions with appeals to individual entrepreneurial passion for change and self-knowledge. It also circumscribes the very possibility of recognizing – let alone narrating – structural histories of inequality and the complex approaches needed to respond to such issues as poverty and climate change.

The overarching solution to poverty that Novogratz proposes is to expand markets – including new debt relations like microfinance – into novel areas of social life across the diverse postcolonial landscape of the Global South. When she had her chance encounter with the Rwandan boy in the blue sweater, she was trying to establish a fledgling microfinance organization in Kigali focused on women. For her, the mid-1980s introduction of this new debt mechanism in Rwanda benefited women borrowers by providing them with loans, a new source of power; much the same logic is behind the educational lending initiatives discussed in this volume by Stork (Chapter 17). 'Money,' Novogratz writes, 'is freedom and confidence and choice. And choice is dignity' (Novogratz 2009: 87). Because the practice of micro-loans was so new at the time, others challenged the legitimacy of charging interest to women with extremely limited means and no collateral. Novogratz countered that this was a necessary form of disciplining the women to enter capitalist markets:

'Think of charging fair interest as practice for the women to interact with the formal economy' (Novogratz 2009: 45). Further, Novogratz asked the lending organization's participants to contribute some of their own money to the organization as a way of securing their stake in it, even though the women didn't have much.

While Novogratz asserts that this increased their self-determination and dignity, it also individualized poverty as a problem to be fixed through personal risk taking in still-forming markets. Extensive studies beginning in the mid-2000s have shown that microfinance institutions and their descendants, such as mobile financial services app M-Pesa in East Africa, have not lived up to promises to lift the poorest out of poverty. Indeed, in many contexts they are associated with various negative social and economic impacts, ranging from burdening families with unsustainable financial risk and predatory loans, to increasing domestic violence and debt-related suicide and exacerbating the very gender inequalities they are supposed to fix. Novogratz thus enacted intimate bonds of tutelage and trust that recall the paternalism of older imperial hierarchies, while neglecting the relevance of structural inequalities in the global economy that continue to enrich wealthy countries while reproducing gendered poverty on a wide scale.

Performing ethics in the philanthrocapitalist economy

After working in Rwanda, Brazil and elsewhere as a young development professional, Novogratz went on to found Acumen. The organization describes itself as an anti-poverty impact investment fund that operates across the Global South to 'solve the problems of poverty' (Acumen.org n.d.). Acumen describes itself as a non-profit venture philanthropy fund, reinvesting returns back into the organization. It distinguishes itself from charities by not 'giving philanthropy away', but by investing impact capital 'in companies and change makers' focused on global challenges (Acumen.org n.d.). Acumen therefore enters the world of poverty alleviation by reimagining earlier modes of international development aid and loans through a financial model that shifts risk from indebted nations to risk-taking individuals and small businesses in the Global South.

The fund's financial mission is embedded in Novogratz's ethical vision of deeper connection. Acumen's Manifesto, available on their website, suggests that poverty can be fixed by philanthropic investors who develop and perform the *right* character traits and feelings:

> It thrives on moral imagination: the humility to see the world as it is, and the audacity to imagine the world as it could be. It's having the ambition to learn at the edge, the wisdom to admit failure, and the courage to start again. It requires patience and kindness, resilience and grit: a hard-edged hope.

Although the Manifesto never defines 'it', the referent is implied. 'It' is the work required of the change maker to solve global inequality; much of this work, the Manifesto suggests, is internal to the individual. One must cultivate humility, audacity, courage, wisdom, ambition, hopefulness and leadership. In this rendering, the subject of global poverty is a relatively wealthy, educated and mobile individual in the West who must learn the right way to connect with the targets of their work: others who live in poverty, usually in unfamiliar locations. As a transnational economy predicated on particular forms of intimacy, the refinement of these sentiments into desirable poverty action is an important dimension of the ethical investing industry.

One of the important outputs of the impact investing sector, I argue, is *feeling ethical*. Cultivating this feeling is seen as central to fostering better financial subjects able to infuse market-friendly solutions into global challenges with ethical justifications. Similar registers of humanitarian ethicizing are at play in the immigration bond advertisements discussed by Rossipal (Chapter 9). Such ethical performances are also seen as crucial to raising real capital: one must communicate a sense of care about social impact in order to win over investors. In this way, the impact sector reflects Sara Ahmed's (2004) notion of an affective economy: affect (or emotion), she argues, assumes value by mediating exchanges between people (as well as texts and objects). Ahmed draws on Karl Marx to argue that 'emotions work as a form of capital', both of which accumulate value through circulation: as social forms of communication, emotions gain in intensity the more they circulate (Ahmed 2004: 120). By circulating and intensifying the feeling that they are acting ethically, impact investors are able to attract more capital from investors and foundations that seek to engineer social change so long as it is profitable.

This is done, in part, by training ethical investors and social entrepreneurs in storytelling skills that emphasize personal transformation and emotional investment in the work – like Novogratz's story of self-discovery – which is supported by a sub-industry of consultants, trainers, conferences and programmes devoted to developing participants' sense of morality, empathy and compassion. Following Acumen's lead, many similar programmes have emerged in the US alone, including fellowship programmes for budding social entrepreneurs by Echoing Green, Mulago Foundation, Aspen Institute, Ashoka, and Acceso. Storytelling becomes a tool for performing one's passion. As an impact communication strategist explained at an industry conference, social entrepreneurs 'understand that the business is going to be successful because of something connected to *you as the entrepreneur*: my background, my emotional connection to the issues, all of that becomes a part of your authenticity'. By centring investors and entrepreneurs as the most important ethical agents enacting development, these stories reproduce a much longer history of both colonial and development narratives that erase the subjectivity and actions of those ostensibly being 'saved' from poverty.

Under Novogratz's leadership, Acumen has become a significant cultural broker in this economy of intimacies. They run leadership training programmes around the world, coordinate Acumen+, a global network of volunteers who stage local events and fundraise, and offer an online curriculum through the Acumen Academy. Through the Academy, one can take courses on moral imagination, open-mindedness, living a meaningful life, 'Social Entrepreneurship 101: Discovering Your Passion and Path to Change the World', and 'Storytelling for Change'. Perhaps most significantly, in 2006 they launched an annual Acumen Fellowship programme for promising young leaders in the field that consists of three months of class study in New York City and a nine-month internship at one of Acumen's global investee companies. The programme's objective is to cultivate the 'architects', 'game changers' and 'visionaries' of the new social innovation sector.

During the initial workshop period in New York City, fellows are assigned Acumen's 'Good Society Reading List', which primarily comprises classics from the history of Western liberal thought, including Plato, Rousseau, de Tocqueville, Hobbes and the Universal Declaration of Human Rights. Fellows are guided to develop what Novogratz calls 'moral imagination', which she defines as a combination of humility, empathy and audacity. An applied workshop to test these values sends fellows out into New York City to attempt to survive for a full day and access social services without money or a cell phone. This lesson is intended to teach the fellows respect for the poor, but does so by suggesting that they can 'try on' a feeling of vulnerability for a day and thereby presume a deeper knowledge of the experience of living in poverty.

The impact imaginary

Through such activities, social entrepreneurs and the ethical investors who fund them are celebrated for their potential to shape new, more equitable futures. They do this by mobilizing hyper-individualized accounts of investor and entrepreneurial breakthroughs, typically represented by well-educated Western subjects who 'discover' the problems of those living in poverty and strive to fix them with grit and seemingly little outside help. For Ananya Roy (2012), this is a manifestation of 'poverty capitalism', through which the resources and cultural practices of the 'bottom of the pyramid' are mined by international capitalist interests. This takes many forms, from expanding 'bottom billion' consumer markets and financial services that increase indebtedness without necessarily improving livelihoods, to the expansion of value extraction from natural resources in the Global South, to new models of social value extraction such as data mining via increased digitization of banking, farming, healthcare, digital identities and other areas of previously untracked social life.

What is distinctive about our current moment of transnational capitalism is the extent to which 'the modern [Western] self' is increasingly 'crafted through encounters with such poverty', which take place in zones of intimacy between impact investors, philanthropists, social entrepreneurs, development workers and those who are identified as the global poor (Roy 2012: 148). While poverty is made more visible, individual micro-entrepreneurs are envisioned as the primary solution to complex problems, rather than structural changes to how regional and global economies are organized. The impact economy is invested in a privatizing, entrepreneurial vision but offers no compass, for instance, for fortifying the economic sovereignty of nations in the Global South against the extractivist predations of multinational corporations and inequitable international trade agreements, expanding the public sector and social services or developing alternative models to unsustainable, unlimited capitalist growth.

Novogratz opens her book by painting a vivid picture of a young boy who manifests a material trace of her personal history in an unexpected context. She wants the reader to imagine – indeed, to visualize – the importance of establishing intimate connection with others as a way of bridging inequality and misunderstanding through empathy. At the same time, her personalization of social change through encounters like this one depoliticizes poverty as an inefficient market problem, rather than a multidimensional and highly political problem rooted in older structures of colonial and postcolonial extraction. Understanding these new agents of finance, then, requires questioning how their frontier intimacies matter and how they mobilize ethical performances as a means of both cultural and economic value production.

Further resources

Elyachar, J. (2012) 'Next practices: Knowledge, infrastructure, and public goods at the bottom of the pyramid'. *Public Culture* 24(1): 109–129.

Karim, L. (2011) *Microfinance and Its Discontents: Women in Debt in Bangladesh*. Minneapolis: University of Minnesota Press.

Roy, A. (2010) *Poverty Capitalism: Microfinance and the Making of Development*. New York: Routledge.

Roy, A., Negrón-Gonzales, G., Opoku-Agyemang, K. and Talwalker, C. (2016) *Encountering Poverty: Thinking and Acting in an Unequal World*. Oakland: University of California Press.

Stoler, A. (2010 [2002]) *Carnal Knowledge and Imperial Power: Race and the Intimate in Colonial Rule*. Oakland: University of California Press.

Works cited

Acumen.org (n.d.) 'Our manifesto'. https://acumen.org/manifesto/ (accessed 18 August 2022).

Ahmed, S. (2004) 'Affective economies'. *Social Text* 22(2): 117–139.

Hurtado, A. L. (1999) *Intimate Frontiers: Sex, Gender, and Culture in Old California*. Albuquerque: University of New Mexico Press.

Lowe, L. (2015) *The Intimacy of Four Continents*. Durham NC: Duke University Press.

Novogratz, J. (2009) *The Blue Sweater: Bridging the Gap Between Rich and Poor in an Interconnected World*. New York: Rodale.

Pratt, M. L. (2008) *Imperial Eyes: Travel Writing and Transculturation*. London: Routledge, 2008.

Roy, A. (2012) 'Subjects of risk: Technologies of gender in the making of millennial modernity'. *Public Culture* 24(1): 131–156.

Stoler, A. (2001) 'Tense and tender ties: The politics of comparison in North American history and (post) colonial studies'. *The Journal of American History* 88(3): 829–865.

Notes

1 Stork (Chapter 17) also examines entanglements between childhood, racial capitalism and predatory forms of putatively 'humanitarian' lending in the US, while Nir (Chapter 16) examines the links between settler colonialism, financialization and experiences of childhood in the Occupied Territories.

2 Compare with the more expansive imaginary cultivated through the drawing produced by Bhattacharyya (Chapter 22), and with the anti-colonial imaginaries traced out by Styve (Chapter 21) in her discussion of Otobong Nkanga's artwork and by Samaniego and Mantz (Chapter 20) in their discussion of *Mesoamérica Resiste*.

3 See in particular the chapter by Randell-Moon (Chapter 14) on the Gurindji walk-off and relations between settler pastoralists and First Nations in Australian 'contact zones'.

Part VI

Play

Why are we so invested in imagining children as innocent? All of us, former children, surely remember moments of cruelty, greed and nastiness from ourselves and our peers. As cultural and educational theorist Henry Giroux has argued, the myth of the pure and innocent child serves to distract us from all the ways that our society shapes childhood and how, in turn, cultures of childhood and of play reflect the overarching power structures of our broader society.

Consider for a moment that even the idea of childhood (a period of life where one is competent to do manual labour but not expected to do so, where one is expected only to learn and play) is a fairly recent Western invention. In the Middle Ages, young working-class Europeans would have been expected to work from a very young age. And which bodies are allowed to even be a 'child' is a matter of power: in the Americas from the sixteenth to the nineteenth centuries, enslaved Africans were considered and treated as adults before puberty (including as targets of sexual exploitation). At the same time, the white children of plantation owners were held to be precious flowers of youth until well into their twenties. Since the mid-twentieth century the age range designating 'youth' has drastically expanded as labour markets have changed; 'youth' often now includes people well into their thirties (longer than the life expectancy of a nineteenth-century factory worker in London). So, even though, biologically speaking, humans naturally take a remarkably long time to reach sexual maturity and some degree of physical independence, the idea and importance of childhood, youth and human development is deeply shaped by culture, society and economic pressures.

Just as childhood is shaped by these forces, so too is play. As the anthropologist the late David Graeber (2014) argues, play may be the fundamental activity of not only humans and not only animals but also all forms of life: purposeless, usually social, generally enjoyable activity. The ground-breaking work of Jean Piaget confirmed what most of us observe: children play imaginative and social games as a way to learn about the world and their place in it. Today, 'serious games' (including simulations, role-plays and gamified learning platforms) are an important part of corporate, military and other forms of adult training around the world. Play is always political: consider ancient Rome, where enslaved gladiators were made to 'play' for the entertainment of the patricians ... to the death. Or consider what the popular game 'Monopoly' teaches children about capitalism and the economy: it's a ruthless fight to the finish (this, in spite of the fact that 'Monopoly' was originally designed as a critique of free-market capitalism's impacts on housing markets).

Today, although we imagine childhood as a period of life free from financial concerns, it is anything but. Beyond the ways that the stress of familial financial precarity might impact youngsters, the broader sociological and cultural force of financialization encourages parents and teachers to begin 'investing' in education, skills development and competitive competencies at an early age. 'Financial literacy' education is increasingly part of the curriculum in many schools. Many children's toys and games encourage the development of financial dispositions. On one level it is quite natural for children to learn and play in the shadow of, and in ways that reflect the dominant social institutions of, their era. But when this play is taken as neutral or natural (rather than shaped by a set of social institutions), what are the consequences?

The two chapters in Part VI both explore how youth and play are entangled with financialization, neoliberalism and the legacies of colonialism. They both seek to uncover the key hidden assumptions at work.

Oded Nir (Chapter 16) investigates a conventional indoor children's play area in the southern Israeli town of Sderot, close to the border with the Gaza Strip. It has been built underground in a bunker to protect its users from Palestinian rocket attacks, launched in reprisal for Israel's many devastating and deadly military incursions. The conflict between Israel and Palestine is often (unhelpfully) presented as an ancient and eternal struggle dating back to biblical times, conveniently (for some) inviting us to forget the political, economic and sociological dimensions. Nir details how, since the 1980s, the state of Israel has aggressively pursued neoliberal policies and financialization that are uniquely tailored to both sustain and benefit from its ongoing occupation of Palestinian territories and its access to cheapened Palestinian labour. Yet these policies have also had a dramatic negative effect on most Israelis, whose indebtedness and financial precarity encourage them to move into illegal Israeli settlements and otherwise participate in a conflict with which they might not otherwise agree. For Nir, the underground playground, which often evokes notions of the timeless joys of childhood, instead speaks to something else: the way that systems of financial oppression, inequality and exploitation become normalized. Financialization, because of the way it seeks to transform future potentials into present-day commodities, alters our sense of time and of the future. The playground can be seen as a monument to the way that a financialized Israel is culturally invested in narratives of an endless present over real and meaningful change.

Ben Stork (Chapter 17) focuses on an advertisement from the US's United Negro College Fund, which targets Black donors to contribute to the cause of offering financial assistance to Black youth seeking university education. Stork relates the long history of educational segregation and inequality in the US, from the days of slavery where reading and writing could mean a death sentence, to the post-Second World War era, when Black people were structurally denied access to universities. But in the last decades of the twentieth century these barriers have transformed and been accompanied by new forms of 'predatory inclusion', where Black people are targeted for highly exploitative loans for programmes that fail to help graduates close the staggering racial wealth and earnings gaps that plague that country. Stork notes that the advertisement in question has its seventeen-year-old Black female protagonist address the potential donors framing her success as 'your dividend': to donate is not merely to do good and give back to one's community, it is to 'invest' in the future of Black people. As laudable as that may seem, Stork notes that it signals the profound shift that has occurred under neoliberalism and financialization, where even the human development that education provides or the cause of equality for Black people in America must be reframed in financial terms.

Both chapters, then, mobilize themes of childhood, play and education to sensitize us to the profound economic as well as cultural power of financialization. In both cases, this power is freighted with the legacy of colonial and racial power regimes: in the case of Nir, the Zionist project that has sought to colonize Palestine for Jewish settlement; in the case of Stork, what Saidiya Hartman (2007) calls the 'afterlives of slavery' in a country built on that institution and the anti-Black structural racism it inaugurated.

A brief note that each chapter uses the term 'securitization' in a distinct but related way. For Nir, securitization refers to the military practice of building up security infrastructure to protect 'assets' and 'investments', a notion of securitization that binds together the military and financial spheres. Here, in contrast to security (an achievable goal), securitization justifies endless manoeuvring and an infinite horizon of risks to be managed. Stork (Chapter 17), uses securitization in a more technical sense: in the world of finance it refers to the way that many financial assets (say, a bunch of mortgages) can be bundled together and sold in different ways. This is done to counterbalance risks and to offer financial customers bespoke forms of exposure to very specific types of risk. In both cases, securitization is an ongoing, never-ending process.

Works cited

Graeber, D. (2014) 'What's the point if we can't have fun?' *The Baffler*, 24. https://thebaffler.com/salvos/whats-the-point-if-we-cant-have-fun (accessed 15 September 2022)

Hartman, S. (2007) *Lose Your Mother: A Journey along the Atlantic Slave Route*. New York: Farrar, Straus and Giroux.

16

Eternal conflict: Sderot's underground playground

Oded Nir

By now, the Israeli–Palestinian conflict is over a hundred years old. Its origins can be traced to the Zionist settlement in Palestine in the late nineteenth century, driven by the development of capitalism in Europe. Despite Zionism's revolutionary ambitions, it resulted in the gradual dispossession and immiseration of the local Palestinian population. In 1948, following British withdrawal from Palestine, a war broke out between the Zionists and the Arab militaries of the neighbouring countries. In Palestinian memory, this war is called the *Nakba*, or the disaster: around 800,000 Palestinians were displaced by the Zionist forces, becoming refugees in their own country, or in neighbouring ones. In 1967, another war resulted in further displacement of Palestinians. Those who stayed in the West Bank and Gaza Strip, conquered by Israel in 1967, are effectively still today under Israeli control. But they enjoy no citizenship rights, and are subjected to constant human rights violations. In 1987, the first *Intifada* (or armed resistance) of the Palestinian population erupted, against the prolonged Israeli occupation.

The *Intifada* had forced Israel to negotiate with the Palestinians. The purpose of the 1990s Israeli–Palestinian peace process aimed to end the conflict by creating a sovereign Palestinian state alongside Israel. But the talks failed, and today the oppression of the Palestinians by Israel continues, with ever-growing Israeli restriction on what enters or leaves the Palestinian territories, which increasingly resemble a huge open-air prison, in which Israel employs 'securitization' tactics to neutralize Palestinian resistance or even its mere possibility. Efforts to achieve a peaceful resolution to the conflict have all but died away since 2000. Indeed, peace has turned into Israeli violent pacification

Figure 16.1 'Inside the Big Blue bomb shelter'. An image of the underground playground in the southern Israeli town of Sderot.

during this time period. The conflict thus turns eternal or timeless: peace as a possible resolution for it has disappeared; and we can only hope that the complete annihilation of the Palestinians is not considered a possible outcome, either.

Neoliberalism in Israel

But why has this absence of time from the conflict become acceptable to Israelis (assuming, of course, that Palestinians get less of a choice in the matter)?[1] To understand why timelessness comes to be attached to the Israeli–Palestinian conflict, we would have to take a detour through the history of Israeli neoliberalization and financialization, and their relation to the conflict. As I hope to show, this relationship, which started as a contingent and accidental one, is today one of necessity: financialized Israeli capitalism necessarily entails the continuation of this conflict. The neoliberalization of Israel is usually traced back to the 1985 Economic Stabilization Plan. This latter programme, as many commentators note (Krampf 2018: 183–184;

Shalev 1998: 126), provided the foundation for all that we know as the hallmarks of neoliberalization: concerted attacks on organized labour, privatization of state-owned industries and the gradual receding of the state from providing social services, allowing capitalist market forces to govern these more or less directly.

It is important to mention that it is not only the right that spearheaded Israeli neoliberalization: the Israel Labour Party had abandoned any serious commitment to the cause of labour by the 1990s. One should understand this abandonment of welfare-state politics as a necessity rather than a mere ideological preference. In his analysis of Israeli neoliberalization, Arie Krampf (2018: 200) echoes a truth already articulated by David Harvey's (2005: 5–38) study of neoliberalism: that the adoption of neoliberal reforms takes place when welfare-state policies are no longer effective in securing profits and the domination of the bourgeoisie as a class. Israeli welfare-state capitalism was brought to the brink of economic collapse before the adoption of the 1985 plan. The choice, even if it was never articulated by Israeli policy makers in quite these terms, was either to follow the neoliberal path dictated by the US or to abandon capitalism altogether. Israel, unsurprisingly, chose to try the former.

The story is usually portrayed as a success story, in which neoliberalization saved the Israeli economy. But it is here that the Israeli oppression of Palestinians becomes important as more than an external condition of Israeli capitalism. As Daniel Gutwein (2004) argued, neoliberal reforms put pressure on poor Israelis: securing better jobs and particularly a place to live became increasingly difficult as privatization advanced. The Israeli settlements in the territory occupied in the 1967 war – the Occupied Territories, as they came to be called – provided a temporary solution to this contradiction. Cheap housing, and government jobs, made the settlements attractive to the Israeli poor, who flocked to them. Thus, a certain welfare state continues to exist today in the settlements, as Amtanes Shehada (2017) argues. The entanglement of welfarism with the violence of settler colonialism is also touched upon by Randell-Moon (Chapter 14).

The continuation of a kind of welfare state in the settlements is why, in the 1990s, the great majority of the Israeli settlers in the Occupied Territories were non-ideological, a fact that puzzled the Israeli Left but did not send it looking for the economic determinants. It is important to emphasize that this persistence of the old within the new – of welfare state within the greater neoliberal logic of Israel – is similar to what is usually called in Marxist criticism uneven and combined development (UCD) (Warwick Research Collective 2015). UCD is a useful concept to understand the ways in which capitalism develops outside its European centres. This development does not follow the same linear pattern in these new locales: older social orders or forms are preserved alongside the most advanced capitalist forms of production. The reasons for these confusing combinations are usually straightforward: the preservation of an older social form becomes a condition for the newer capitalist development. For instance, in some cases agricultural slave labour could be the only source of income for establishing a profitable, completely modernized factory – and so the result is the preservation of older forms alongside new ones. It is in this sense that the preservation of the welfare state in the Israeli settlements in the Occupied Territories was necessary, if Israel was to start playing according to neoliberal rules: the economic safety it provides to the poorer part of the Israeli population makes possible implementing neoliberal form on a greater scale.

It is precisely this argument about the way in which the Israeli occupation 'solves' temporarily the contradictions of capitalism in Israel that provides us with the real necessary connections between the conflict and capitalism. Other arguments, such as the one tying Israeli capitalism's arms trade, or profits from the occupation itself (if they can indeed be calculated) are much weaker. For the latter, in our liquidity-driven age, seem to imply that a different 'investment strategy' on the part of Israeli capitalism would make the conflict itself resolvable, without touching the very structure of the economic system. According to this line of argumentation, if Israeli capitalists would only invest in fair-trade coffee and Amsterdam real estate, instead of putting their money into guns and the occupation, Israeli–Palestinian peace would naturally follow. The problem with this argument is that it ignores the way in which cheap land in the territories temporarily resolves the pressures exerted by neoliberalism on poor Israelis. As such, the Israeli–Palestinian conflict cannot end without abandoning capitalism, or at least radically changing the way in which it is structured.

One must give this argument about the necessity of the Israeli occupation for the existence of capitalism its full political and historical weight. It means that the standard understanding of peaceful resolution in Israel–Palestine, the establishing of a Palestinian State alongside Israel, is no longer a realistic option after so many years of massive Israeli settlement in the West Bank. This situation makes a one-state solution – having Israelis and Palestinians share the same state with equal rights – a more realistic one, despite the fact that there is currently no political force that has made it its goal (although see Abunimah 2006). It is important to emphasize that as Israel annexes, formally or informally, more and more West Bank land, the existence of the single state is factually becoming a reality, despite how unpopular it is. That the one-state option is something that the bourgeoisie on both sides denounce also makes it a possible banner for the working class. It should be clear that supporting a one-state solution does not mean that one abandons anti-capitalism: the seemingly bourgeois demand for the equality of anyone living in the speculative single state becomes deeply anti-capitalist, since the existence of Israeli capitalism, as I have tried to show above, depends precisely on the ability of the Israeli state to violate the rights of Palestinians.

The Israeli occupation of Palestine, and continued oppression of Palestinians, becomes a condition for the existence of neoliberal Israel. This neoliberalization is usually associated with the 2003 reforms made to the financial market (Gottfried 2019: 104–5). One should see these reforms as a reminder that nationalization – the state taking ownership of assets and enterprises that it does not own – is not something neoliberals shy away from, when it serves their purposes. In 2003, the Israeli state nationalized the huge pension funds owned by the General Organization of Workers – which unites almost all labour unions in Israel – only later to sell them to Israeli banks. This proved to be the opening move for the increasingly more immediate and direct relation of Israeli citizens to the financial market: the movement of the stock exchange and financial indicators are now watched much more closely than anything else in trying to plan for the future.

Financialization and managing the future

It is here that time itself begins to emerge as something strongly influenced by this growing dependence on the market. The relation between privatizing pensions and the way time is imagined is not too difficult to find. As Hadas Weiss puts it, 'financialization ... links savings directly to the market. It therefore bypasses political negotiation of expensive guarantees. Workers' fortunes on retirement become a factor of market performance' (Weiss 2015: 512; Levi Faur and Mizrachy 2016). Thus, if pensions were once a matter of a nation's responsibility for its citizens' future, to be decided upon through public institutions and political intervention, it is precisely the national temporal imagination that is eroded as the financialization of pensions advances.

I have so far argued that, first, Israeli neoliberalism is necessarily dependent on the continuation of the Israeli oppression of the Palestinians (barring some radical reorganization). But the second point, about the growing dominance of finance in the Israeli economy, already has to do more concretely with issues of temporality and our sense of historicity. The latter term, borrowed from Fredric Jameson, designates our ability to map our individual everyday experience onto some larger historical movement.

Here the details of financialization in Israel become important: not only pensions (or their absence) and their obvious bearing on one's future are relevant, but also other forms of the penetration of finance into everyday life. Even if in comparison to other Organisation for Economic Cooperation and Development countries, household debt in Israel is not very high, the rise of indebtedness since the early 2000s is dramatic (Shami 2019). Israelis increasingly rely on loans to survive, with real wages stagnating in the last several decades, and real estate prices climbing steadily, despite small corrections here and there. The programmes devised to lower real estate prices, put forth by the Israeli government, have largely failed to produce the desired effect. Critical empirical research on the connection of finance in Israel to real estate does not exist. But it would not be too speculative to imagine that capital increasingly relies on rent extraction for financial profits in the Israeli case (Tz'ion 2020).

And so housing construction becomes increasingly driven by financial speculation: new construction is not about producing homes useful to citizens but, rather, about the construction process itself and its products as profit-generators. One should notice the contrast between this financialized housing market and a different Israel time, in which the construction of housing was a matter of national planning and goals, executed by government order. One can even remember the days when the military was in charge of paving roads and infrastructure projects (but also of cultural ones, like education!), when large segments of the system of production were relatively autonomous from market forces. This contrast is instructive, because it immediately brings out the sense of time that animates the previous era, in which one's everyday activity is related to some imagined social whole and its future. Being involved in government-planned construction projects, or voting for a government that builds houses that you could easily buy or rent, meant that one could imagine oneself participating in the realization of a collective project. This sense of one's own relationship to history in the making is of course completely absent from the current situation, in which new construction is dominated by the impulses of finance capital.[2]

To draw more directly the connection between capitalist financialization and a sense of timelessness: the increasing penetration of the market into every realm of life in Israel is precisely what generates this timelessness, which as I have argued, applies also to the current state of the Israeli–Palestinian conflict. It should be clear that the very attempt to imagine and create the future through economic activity is not in itself problematic. In capitalism, debt and credit make possible future-oriented projects that competition would otherwise make impossible (Dienst 2011). For example, a loan to build new infrastructure, like fibre optic cable, is needed long before the use of this infrastructure can generate any profit. It is the way in which such future making takes place within contemporary capitalist finance that becomes problematic. As Max Haiven (2011: 108) puts it,

> what is fundamentally new about today's financial markets is their sheer complexity and speed, which have produced the preponderance of streamlined 'investment vehicles' that broadly fall under the heading of 'derivatives': intricate commodifications of risk made up of 'securitized' fragments of potentially tens of thousands of separate speculative investments and bets. Unlike more straightforward securities (like stocks and bonds), derivative products do not represent ownership or debt obligations so much as promises to buy or sell the rights to other securities at some point in the future. As finance accelerates, promises pile atop promises and fragments are rebundled to such an extent that the original property they ostensibly represented is lost in the ether.

As such, the original use value of a thing is lost in the bundling and rebundling of commitments, predictions and intentions codified into the derivative. Derivatives are themselves attempts to think historically: a condensed grouping of predictions and commitments about the future. Or, as Haiven (2011) puts it, following LiPuma and Lee, derivatives are themselves 'strategies of representation', or so many attempts to generate a sense of historicity. Yet, as Jameson (2015: 121) argues, derivatives fail to do just that precisely because of how quickly these predictions change, each derivative projecting 'futures which are ephemeral, one-time effects much like postmodern texts; futures which are each one of them events rather than whole new dimensions or elements'. Thus, contemporary financialization becomes synonymous with an absence of historical imaginary and a sense of time that relates together individual experience to some larger, non-immediately accessible, past and future.

Endless war and the underground playground

My argument so far has interpreted the eternal present of the Israeli–Palestinian conflict – the fact that the possibility of its end has been removed – as originating in the growing financialization of Israeli capitalism. At this point, I can finally touch on the picture of the playground which opens this chapter. The playground is in the southern Israeli town of Sderot, which has been the target of Palestinian small missile attacks (in response to murderous Israeli operations in the neighbouring Gaza). This is not simply an indoor playground. It was built underground, so that the town's children can play without fear of being hurt. Thus, what is truly monstrous about the playground in the picture is that is treats the violent conflict as a natural phenomenon, one that has no beginning and no end, but that is, rather, a constant nuisance that must simply be tolerated. Outside, war might be going on, but playing can continue (unperturbed?) underground.

It is precisely in this sense that this underground playground can become a clear figure for the sense of timelessness and non-relation to history that is the result of financialization. Where Stork (Chapter 17) describes how children and young adults come to manage their educational futures in relation to a logic of investment, here children's experience of play is shaped by a derivative logic that detaches financial decision making from any particular imagined future. The playground is abstracted from its socio-spatial context, so that its existence is no longer a good index of social peace – much like the failure of the derivatives to project a stable future. It is easy to see how the playground-bunker contrasts with the way we usually imagine playgrounds: in our filmic imaginary, playgrounds are places in which social relations are negotiated. They bear the gaze of the watchful mother, but also of the creepy attacker, hidden in plain sight; the interaction between kids always standing in for the truth of adult interaction. And, after hours, it turns into the non-place of illicit interactions. It is crucial that playgrounds open up to the urban syntax that surrounds them. Constantly in the background, the city or town that surrounds a playground provides a 'totality effect', an 'everything else' or otherness that allows the represented subject matter in the playground to stand as a useful reduction of the unrepresentable social whole (Jameson 2016: 64–87). Sderot's bunker playground, in contrast, is abstracted from its social surrounding presents and ceases to function as the locus of diachronic social mapping.

Thus, here the reading of the playground itself as part of the 'text' that is a city once again encounters timelessness. The abstraction of the bunker-playground is an abstraction: a removal from some social time, from a historical trajectory. As I have tried to demonstrate, this absence of time and the possibility of resolution, or what Eric Cazdyn (2012) calls the time of the chronic, that one keeps encountering, is precisely the unseen results of the financialization of Israel.

Further resources

Gutwein, D. (2006) 'Some comments on the class foundations of the occupation'. *Monthly Review Online*, 16 June. https://mronline.org/2006/06/16/some-comments-on-the-class-foundations-of-the-occupation/ (accessed 2 September 2022).

Haiven, M. (2011) 'Finance as capital's imagination? Reimagining value and culture in an age of fictitious capital and crisis'. *Social Text* 29(3): 93–124.

Weiss, H. (2015) 'Financialization and its discontents: Israelis negotiating pensions'. *American Anthropologist* 117(3): 506–518.

Works cited

Abunimah, A. (2006) *One Country*. New York: Metropolitan Books, 2006.

Cazdyn, E. (2012) *The Already Dead: The New Time of Politics, Culture, and Illness*. Durham NC: Duke University Press.

Dienst, R. (2011) *The Bonds of Debt: Borrowing against the Common Good*. London: Verso.

Gottfried, S. (2019) *Contemporary Oligarchies in Developed Democracies*. Cham, Switzerland: Palgrave Macmillan.

Gutwein, D. (2004) 'Hearot al hayesodot hamaamadiyim shel hakibush' [Some comments on the class foundations of the occupation]. *Teoriya ubikoret* 24: 203–11.

Haiven, M. (2011) 'Finance as capital's imagination? Reimagining value and culture in an age of fictitious capital and crisis'. *Social Text* 29(3): 93–124.

Harvey, D. (2005) *A Brief History of Neoliberalism*. Oxford: Oxford University Press.

Jameson, F. (2015) 'The aesthetics of singularity'. *New Left Review* 92: 101–132.

Jameson, F. (2016) *Raymond Chandler: The Detections of Totality*. London; New York: Verso.

Krampf, A. (2018) *The Israeli Path to Neoliberalism*. New York: Routledge.

Levi Faur, D. and Mizrachy, I. (2016) 'The making and remaking of Israeli citizenship via credit ranking regime: With special emphasis on minority and dis-privileged groups'. Jerusalem: Barriers Towards EU Citizenship. https://zenodo.org/record/582901 (accessed 2 September 2022).

Shalev, M. (1998) 'Have globalization and liberalization normalized Israel's political economy?' *Israel Affairs* 5(2–3): 121–155.

Shami, L. (2019) 'Household debt in Israel'. Jerusalem: Taub Center for Social Policy Studies in Israel. http://taubcenter.org.il/wp-content/files_mf/householddebtinisrael2019eng16.pdf (accessed 2 September 2022).

Shehada, A. (2017) 'Dokh mekhkar: Medinat harevakha shel hamitnakhlim'. *Teoria Ubikoret* 47: 203–222.

Tzion, H. (2020) 'Hayavim luknot dira: Kah shavarnu si behekefei hamash-kantaot' [Must buy an apartment: This is how we broke the record in mortgage levels]. *Ynet.Co.Il*, 1 February. www.ynet.co.il/articles/0,7340,L-5669511,00.html (accessed 2 September 2022).

Warwick Research Collective (2015) *Combined and Uneven Development: Towards a New Theory of World Literature*. Liverpool: Liverpool University Press.

Weiss, H. (2015) 'Financialization and its discontents: Israelis negotiating pensions'. *American Anthropologist* 117(3): 506–518.

Notes

1 See chapters by Samaniego and Mantz (Chapter 20), Styve (Chapter 21) and Ly (Chapter 12) on non-linear experiences of time that arise out of the entanglement of colonialism and finance.
2 Compare this to the way debts were engineered in order to sever the relationship between Indigenous people and land, and to convert that land into private property, in other settler colonial contexts discussed by Comyn (Chapter 4) and Cordes (Chapter 5).

17

I am your dividend

Ben Stork

Flanked by trees, telephone poles and wires, a woman in silhouette walks toward the camera and away from the horizon. A voiceover intones: 'I'm only seventeen but I know about investing.' This image is from 'Sydni', one of five ads in the United Negro College Fund's (UNCF) 'I am your dividend' campaign. Each TV spot includes its long-standing slogan 'A mind is a terrible thing to waste ...' and adds '... but a wonderful thing to invest in', introducing a new financial product, the already defunct 'Better Futures Stock', as a means of contributing to the Fund. 'Sydni' is the longest and most compelling of the commercials.

While the UNCF and this advertisement are not literally offering a return on investment, the image of Black students and the purpose of higher education in 'Sydni' depicts education as fundamentally an economic value proposition, moving the commercial beyond earlier discourses of opportunity, community uplift and inclusion, into the picture of financialized capitalism. Instead, 'Sydni' and the UNCF's revised slogan represent education as a speculative transaction wherein present investment either pays out or is paid back, later, and entrepreneurial students pursue college as a hedge against declining labour market outcomes. What is learned in university classrooms, much as what is produced in financialized capitalism, is subsidiary to the paper value of the degree. This transition is especially significant with regard to Black students and their exposure to a predatory, extractive and constraining system of higher education funding. In what follows I put 'Sydni' in context of both the historical promise of education in the American Black community and the post-Second World War shifts in US higher education that lead to

Figure 17.1 Still from 'Syndi | #betterfutures Full Story 2013', part of the UNCF 'I am your dividend' campaign.

the ad's embrace of financialized higher education, which renders Blackness as a surplus value for 'investors' while exposing Black students to predatory finance capital.

Black American life and 'the education gospel'

Education, especially literacy, is historically central to Black life in the US. Criminalized as a fundamental threat to chattel slavery, reading and writing – skills associated with formal schooling – bore a significant promise of liberation for the enslaved. As Frederick Douglass (2010 [1845]) writes in his *Narrative*, literacy opened 'the pathway from slavery to freedom'. Following the Civil War and formal emancipation, education remained a site of significant contestation as literacy tests, combined with poll taxes and other repressive mechanisms, maintained the disenfranchisement of Black Americans, and the poor generally, throughout the post-Reconstruction US South.

In this context of repressive exclusion and disenfranchisement, Black thinkers Booker T. Washington and W. E. B. DuBois also debated the promising role of higher education in the Black community at the turn of the twentieth century, with each advancing a case for education in the name of racial uplift. Washington argued for mass practical education on the grounds of economic advancement and empowerment; DuBois, the first Black PhD to graduate from Harvard, advocated for a vanguard 'Talented Tenth' to lead Black Americans toward further liberation and equality. Despite their differences, both understood education as a social and economic good, prefiguring recent discussions of the value of higher education in the US, including for Black Americans.

Both visions of higher education and racial uplift align with what sociologist Tressie McMillan Cottom (2017) refers to as 'the education gospel'. Drawing on the work of earlier scholars, McMillan Cottom describes the education gospel as 'our faith in education as moral, personally edifying, collectively beneficial, and a worthwhile investment no matter the cost'. In *Lower Ed*, her devastating critique of for-profit colleges, McMillan Cottom argues that the role of this gospel must be understood in terms of the late twentieth-century redefinition of higher education as an 'individual good' rather than a collective venture. She further insists that in this updated context the gospel mutates from a theory of social change into a blanket answer to personal and systemic hardships. This change in both the conception of higher education and the function of the education gospel is intimately tied to the financialization of higher education. Unsurprisingly, this shift toward individually financed economic good occurs in the aftermath of higher education's limited opening up to Black and other excluded communities during the post-Second World War period.

'A mind is a terrible thing to waste': the United Negro College Fund and post-war US higher education

Founded in 1944, the same year the Serviceman's Readjustment Act of 1944 (or GI Bill) was signed into law, the UNCF began raising money to expand college access to Black Americans, especially at historically Black colleges and universities (HBCUs). While the GI Bill offered a range of benefits, including educational benefits, to returning veterans, it structurally, and intentionally, excluded most Black veterans. The UNCF provided an alternate source of funding for Black institutions and the students they serve, spreading the 'education gospel' in the face of the state's racist exclusion, while also contributing to the explosive growth in American higher education post-Second World War.

Fuelled by public investments in the warfare/welfare economy of the Cold War, US higher education grew by nearly every measure. Increases in the number and size of two-year, open-enrollment community or junior colleges, combined with pushes for tuition fee-free attendance, provided access to more, and more diverse, students, especially in the years following the 1954 *Brown v. Board of Education* Supreme Court Decision. Centred on accessible, comprehensive post-secondary education for all state residents, California's Master Plan for Higher Education in California, 1960–1975 exemplified this trend by calling for an enlarged and integrated, tuition fee-free, three-tiered system of research institutions, smaller state universities and a network of junior colleges. Following implementation of the plan, California also emerged as a bellwether for the American university as a site of intense struggle around race, class and imperialism as student movements developed at all levels of the state system. The founding of the Black Panther Party at Merrit Junior College and the Ethnic Studies movement at San Francisco State illustrate how post-war higher education expansion led to demands for change in the name of emancipation, peace and the radicalization of knowledge production. Unsurprisingly, these events prompted a backlash that played a key role in the financialization of higher education in the US.

Coincidentally, the UNCF introduced its famous slogan, 'A mind is a terrible thing to waste', in 1972, the same year that Congress expanded the federal student loan programme and created the Student Loan Marketing Association, or Sallie Mae. So, just as the slogan and accompanying advertisements rolled out, the American state shifted its approach to funding college education. The build-up of student borrowing that followed was not simply added on to the existing system. Rather, as Morgan Adamson (2009) writes, 'While the federal loan program expanded the number of students attending the university, it quickly became the largest source of federally funded aid for higher education.' The emergent dominance of student loans in paying for higher education not only changed the relationship between students and universities but also helped to restructure universities by moving them toward a 'cost-sharing' model. Student loans on the one hand tied higher education financing more tightly to the labour market as repayment pressures reshaped the educational experience for students, while, on the other hand, converting admissions into a central revenue source for university operations generally. Combined, these factors altered the experience of education, transforming it into a more directly economic activity, with students pushing for so-called employable fields with high 'wage premiums', while universities changed both their curriculums and physical infrastructures to attract students and federally guaranteed loans for tuition.

'I'm only seventeen but I know about investing ...': knowledge, investments and the racialized entrepreneur of the self

To return to the image we began with, by the time the UNCF introduced the 'I am your dividend' campaign in 2013, the changes to US higher education described above had expanded and intensified, affecting all students, but especially historically excluded students. Despite the loan burden and rising cost of tuition, college attendance remained, until around the time of the Great Recession of 2008, a 'good deal' for most students. However, the stress on degrees in an increasingly post-industrial economy produced intense pressure to pursue post-secondary education, especially for the US Black population already suffering from long-term structural unemployment. Ronald Reagan declared as a presidential candidate that the state should not 'subsidize intellectual curiosity'; by the end of his presidency in 1988, inclusion and opportunity were indexed to an economic calculation resting on the speculative value of degrees. With the education gospel fully turned toward economic returns, Black and other economically vulnerable students were exposed to a racialized, predatory credit system.

Though this period represented the subsumption of public goods into economic processes associated with neoliberalism, the holistic vision of education did not entirely recede. Now individual student borrowers invested in themselves to secure private gains in the name of community advancements. Seeming to speak to Booker T. Washington's emphasis on a practical education benefiting individual and community alike, while allowing for DuBois's rhetoric of a talented tenth to perpetuate the dream of meritocracy, the new regime of education financing appeared consistent with the UNCF's mission. This logic is on full display in 'Sydni', where higher education and the Black student are simultaneously presented as investment vehicles and the moral future of the Black community (compare Kish, Chapter 15, on the ethical imaginaries of impact investing).

Speaking not to what she will study but of financial knowledge that *precedes* the university education that contributions to the UNCF enable, Sydni tells us that at 'only seventeen' she knows that to invest is to 'believe in something, buy shares in it, watch it grow'. Speaking the language of finance while humming the tune of the education gospel, Sydni embeds investment in belief and intellectual growth in speculative transactions, which extend into a financial proposition for her community's future: 'So, what if you could invest in the future, the future of kids, like a stock. Not the kind of stock that's about making money but a stock for social change.' Soon after, Sydni specifies that 'social change' in this context means philanthropy: 'When you invest it helps kids go to college. I could be one of the first college graduates from my family. The first philanthropist from my neighbourhood. And if I'm the first, then maybe there's a second and a third.' Here the line between 'making money' and 'social change' blurs as the entire cycle believe–invest–grow transforms Sydni into a figure for capitalism generally and finance capital in particular.

Karl Marx offers this formula for productive capitalism, Money →Commodity→Money^1 (M-C-M^1), which represents the movement from investment (M) in the production of the commodity (C) to value yielded as profit through exchange (M^1). This formula aims to capture the degree to which capitalist production is oriented towards the accumulation of ever more money, rather than the production of commodities for their 'use value'. In the terms of 'Sydni', funders invest in Sydni, who then earns a degree, which leads to the financial success that enables further philanthropy. On the one hand, the product is the college certification, especially since what Sydni will study is left unnamed, and once produced it is sold on the labour market for a handsome price; on the other hand, since the investment pitch focuses not on college but the would-be student, it is Sydni who is the commodity to be offered for sale on the future labour market. But the attempt to map belief→investment→grow onto Marx's M-C-M^1 ultimately breaks down because of this ambiguity around the commodity and the spot's embrace of financialization, which is better abbreviated as M-M^1. While the visual rhetoric of the spot clearly pictures Sydni, not higher education, as a worthy investment, her value is abstractly linked to the degree, without which there is no chance of becoming a philanthropist. Deserving of financial support, Sydni is translated into investment information; she is a young Black woman with purpose, a racialized entrepreneur of the self. Yet all this future labour is entirely abstract, lacking determinate content and with an undetermined value to be rendered at an unknown later date. Between hard-working high school Sydni and wealthy philanthropist Sydni is the generic university degree purchased through the UNCF, then sold on the labour market.

For Sydni the return on such an investment faces potential diminishment, since it is contingent on what she actually sells her labour for. But as an investment in financialized higher education it is a nearly immediate projection of value. After all, in the financialized university, where debt-financed loans pay tuition fees and enrolment is directly tied to the economic viability of institutions, every student increases the speculative value of the university. In this sense, casting Sydni as a 'dividend' unwittingly illustrates the two-fold financial logic the ad responds to. First, as promotion of the abstract, speculative value of higher education, 'Sydni' represents education as a sort of tradeable market position; second, as simultaneously embedding within that representation the speculative value of the similarly abstracted, future labours required of Sydni in college and after graduation for realization.

Expropriation and exploitation through inclusion: race, risk and student debt

Though the UNCF is not a creditor, it is important to see the ad as intimately bound up with student debt and the logic of financialization. The 'cost-sharing' model that justifies the student debt regime in US higher education is a form of securitization: distributing and privatizing the risk of educational investment by spreading it across students and institutions while also producing a tradeable (non) asset-backed financial product priced in terms of current market value and credit rating. In a system of securitization, the price of the security is based on the projected value of the underlying loan, that is, the potential value of the repayment of the interest-bearing loan, which relies on the borrower's future wages. Because this is speculative value it may never be realized and the student (or philanthropic investor) may never receive a dividend, but the projected increase in the value of the degree and the interest collected on the loan serve as derivative products that can be leveraged by financial institutions, hedge funds and boards of trustees through continued transactions.

Student debt comes to prominence as higher education expands to Black and other historically marginalized students. Inclusion into higher education follows a pattern of inclusion in liberal capitalism, leading not to, or not only to, opportunities for Black Americans, but to new forms of expropriation and exploitation through race. Student loans operate as what Keenaga-Yamahtta Taylor (2019) calls, in relation to race and the US housing market, 'predatory inclusion'. In that context, access to mortgage lending and the promise of homeownership exposed Black homebuyers to a realty industry structured by spatialized racial difference and unaccountable creditors backed by Federal policy. Black families became the owners of loans on substandard properties whose values were depressed by the history of redlining and white flight. Mortgage brokers, meanwhile, collected inflated interest payments until foreclosure came to pass. These practices culminated in the mortgage crisis of 2008, a collapse that precipitated a 40% drop in Black wealth. A different form of predatory lending in the contemporary US is discussed by Rossipal (Chapter 9), who examines the entanglement of immigration bonds and racialized border restrictions.

Scholar Jackie Wang points out a similar dynamic in the long-term effects of the 'racial debt gap' as 'Federal student loans – seemingly not designed to be predatory – facilitate predation' through for-profit colleges, and rising tuition fees at public universities leave 'black [sic] and Latinx students [to] graduate with greater debt loads than whites' (Wang 2018: 128). In fact, student debt is an especially noxious form of what Wang calls *'expropriation through financial inclusion'* [emphasis in original], since in the US it cannot be discharged through bankruptcy, affecting already racialized credit scores that are used to discriminate against Black job applicants. Here student debt's direct relationship to the labour market and the labour of the student is primary. This, in turn, suggests a revision of Wang's formulation insofar as student debt and the financialization of higher education combine *expropriation* – the direct extraction of profit or value through compounding interest on undischargeable debt – with *exploitation* – the compulsion to produce profit or surplus value for another through a wage. Because the 'asset' backing the student loan – the student's knowledge and labouring capacities – unlike a house, cannot be repossessed, the indebted student is yoked to their employment, unable to pursue job or career changes regardless of circumstance or desire. Thus, the Black student is hailed by an education gospel that promises a better spiritual and material life through increased earning potential, only to be permanently indentured to an ever-diminishing labour market.[1]

Conclusion

'Sydni' and the UNCF's 'I am your dividend' adoption of the language of finance must be understood in terms of the debt-driven financialization of US higher education and racialized risk. The spot, despite its insistence on the seemingly intrinsic value of education and hard work, elides both in what it says and shows us about Sydni. The only glimpse of schooling we see is Sydni carrying books, and a whiteboard with the word 'ECONOMICS' written on it; nowhere do we hear her speak passionately about what she will learn, or even the career she hopes to pursue. Instead we are given the figure of the philanthropist, someone that, by definition, has surplus capital they can gift to, or invest in, others (i.e., like those the ad targets as potential funders). Rhetorically disconnected from the labour market that Sydni is actually destined for, college is presented as a transaction leading to a future of riches. Indeed, if labour enters the picture at all, it is in the catch line 'I am your dividend', which might be understood as the continual production of profit through Sydni's future work in the economy where, the lower the wage, the higher return for the capitalist. Put in the context of the racialized distribution of risk, which would have to account for the dismal employment rate and wage data for Black Americans, combined with the extractive, predatory system of credit that targets Black communities, college becomes one long-shot bet among others in a system where, as in any other casino, the house always wins.

Further resources

Adamson, M. (2009) 'The Human Capital Strategy', *Ephemera: Theory & Politics in Organization* 9(4): 271–284.

Ferguson, R. (2017) *We Demand: The University and Student Protests.* Berkeley, CA: University of California Press.

Kish, Z. and Leroy, J. (2015) 'Bonded Life: Technologies of Racial Finance from Slave Insurance to Philanthrocapital', *Cultural Studies* 29(5–7): 630–651.

Martin, R. (2002) *Financialization of Daily Life.* Philadelphia, PA: Temple UP.

Moten, F. (2013) 'The Subprime and the Beautiful', *African Identities* 11(2): 237–245.

Works cited

Adamson, M. (2009) 'The Human Capital Strategy', *Ephemera: Theory & Politics in Organization* 9(4): 271–284.

Douglass, F. (2010 [1845]) *Narrative of the Life of Frederick Douglass.* San Francisco, CA: City Lights Books.

McMillan Cottom, T. (2017) *Lower Ed: The Troubling Rise of For-Profit Colleges in the New Economy.* New York: The New Press.

Taylor, K-Y. (2019) *Race for Profit: How Banks and the Real Estate Industry Undermined Black Homeownership.* Chapel Hill, NC: University of North Carolina Press.

Wang, J. (2018) *Carceral Capitalism.* Boston: Semiotext(e)/MIT Press.

Note

1 See the chapters by Medien (Chapter 7) and Dickson et al. (Chapter 8) on the new forms of unpayable debts imposed on migrants caught at the intersection of Britain's hostile border regime, and attempts to participate in social institutions supposedly designed to provide education and healthcare for all.

Part VII

Control

Control is another way of examining power. Power is not exclusively an overt, recognizable form of violence, although it can be. Control encompasses the subtleties of culture and social organization in the exercise of power. Economic understandings of control frame it as an obstacle to the free flow of money, goods or people within capitalism.

The radical French philosopher Gilles Deleuze introduced the notion of a 'society of control' that emerged under capitalism in the late twentieth century. While at first this may sound Orwellian, Deleuze was interested in how social power was increasingly operating not through centralized 'disciplinary' institutions (militaries, police, schools, factories) but through decentralized networks, creeping through society like a 'spirit or a gas'. Deleuze pointed specifically to the coercive power of debt and credit markets as a prime example: here power is exercised not through outright coercion but through the way it entraps its targets into exploitative and extractive relationships. Debt and credit are enforced not by some single bureaucracy or authority but by many different institutions at once (banks, retailers, credit bureaus, landlords etc.) and also by the indebted subject themselves as they endure shame, guilt and anxiety that shapes their actions. In a society of control, then, financial power operates from everywhere and nowhere at once.

The two chapters in this part challenge this established notion by expanding control to think about capitalism's built environment, which forms part of the techniques of control that modify the behaviour of society. Just think of the symbolic power of global financial centres as a specific built environment: clusters of high-rises that stand above those on the ground and dominate the skyline of the 'global city' (for further discussion see Aalbers 2009; Sassen 2002). Steel-and-glass towers are at once the illusion of frictionless transactions and as well an established landmark of permeance. Indeed, the building of the bourse, or exchange, was an important element of the history of building the global financial infrastructure (see Crosthwaite et al. 2014; Flandreau 2016).

Part VII examines more closely the obscure architecture that materially houses the abstract symbolic power of equity and credit. In economics or business studies, finance has no location of historical infrastructure; rather, finance is abstract capital or market of exchange. As Miranda Joseph (2014) examines in her excellent book *Debt to Society: Accounting for Life under Capitalism*, the abstract financial balance sheet acts as a moral register of social value. Thinking about the control that financial institutions have in the present day, much of it is derived from the balance sheet. For example, the balance sheet is the frame for justifying the monitoring and surveillance capacities of financial institutions to know the incomings and outgoings of all account holders. A historical example is the building of the stock exchange as a physical space for financial trading of ownership claims across a globalizing colonial empire. Starting with the location of finance allows the chapters in Part VII to follow the trail of social control via logics and iconic market representations.

Laura Kalba (Chapter 18), in 'The shape of the stock exchange is shapelessness', disrupts the presumed histories of spaces at the centre of financing colonial expansion as qualitatively different than the present day. Rather, this chapter offers a succinct account of how the London Stock Exchange, at its physical creation as a marketplace, forged a space permissive of violence and promoting extraction. Crucially, the chapter locates the London Stock Exchange at the heart of financing colonial extraction and redistributing the wealth gains. In sharp contrast to the popular view of British finance as being 'gentlemanly' – compared to the American 'wild West' – it demonstrates the violent colonial extraction that built the stock exchange in the first place. As Kalba notes: 'in the case of the stock exchange at least, violence was not simply a side-effect of financialization; it was inherent to how the marketplace operated'. By locating finance in the stock exchange Kalba makes clear that finance is not deterritorialized or disembodied, which means that we can find the Stock Exchange on Google Maps and there will be people there making it function. As Kalba says, 'The everyday, aggressively laddish behaviour of stock exchange members at once reflected and refracted, all the while officially disavowing, the violence associated with the forcible extraction of labour, land and resources overseas.' Importantly, the stock exchange is a powerful cultural symbol of economic self-interest and of wealth that writes the rules, one that resonates in everyday life to permit excessive extraction.

Jacquelene Drinkall (Chapter 19), in 'Data Centre Séance: telepathic surveillance capitalism, psychic debt and colonialism', examines the transactional symbolic violence of data surveillance and harvesting by the information and communication technology machinery of modern finance. High-speed imaginaries of complex and unknowable forces are juxtaposed with windowless buildings that materialized in urban spaces. Control exists as a series of techniques to modify human behaviour, the ways being watched, profiled and ranked, which mutates into a logic of security or insurance. As the chapter articulates, control is where 'tele-debt-and-risk-surveillance and a form of muscular mind/body turn into behavioural control'. Here, payment and debts are categories that carry the weight of human freedom, action and psychological well-being. In other words, control emerges from the telekinetic power of finance to monitor and discipline people – finance bestows power on others to act from a distance; finance is more than a ledger of money owed and money paid, it is an interwoven set of transactions that connect to everyday life. In turn, colonial framings of financial data are the reading and writing of culture and empires. In this chapter control is found in the 'psychic debt for humans' that animates the cognitive framing of capitalism.

Another way of thinking of the cognitive power of finance is to consider just how integrated financial markets are in everyday life. Just imagine how many would recognize the term 'London Stock Exchange' and associate it with money, wealth and power. Daily reports of the volume of shares traded and their market value are broadcast across multiple media channels, integrating concerns over 'how the stock market is doing' into the affairs of daily life. People tend to imagine that this concern is new, or more prevalent because of social media, but this is not true – speculative finance has a long history of widespread participation (Aitken 2005; De Goede 2005;

Harmes 2001). So, when we think of control in relation to the stock market, its power is historical and cultural, rather than the newest outcome of advanced financial technology.

Works cited

Aalbers, M. B. (2009) 'The globalization and Europeanization of mortgage markets'. *International Journal of Urban and Regional Research* 33(2): 389–410. DOI: 10.1111/j.1468-2427.2009.00877.x.

Aitken, R. (2005) '"A direct personal stake": Cultural economy, mass investment and the New York stock exchange'. *Review of International Political Economy* 12(2): 334–363.

Crosthwaite, P., Knight, P. and Marsh, N. (eds) (2014) *Show Me the Money: The Image of Finance, 1700 to the Present*. Manchester: Manchester University Press. https://eprints.soton.ac.uk/371812/ (accessed 7 October 2019).

De Goede, M. (2005) *Virtue, Fortune, and Faith: A Genealogy of Finance*. Minneapolis: University of Minnesota Press.

Flandreau, M. (2016) *Anthropologists in the Stock Exchange: A Financial History of Victorian Science*. Chicago: University of Chicago Press.

Harmes, A. (2001) 'Mass investment culture'. *New Left Review* 9 (May–June): 103–124.

Joseph, M. (2014) *Debt to Society: Accounting for Life under Capitalism*. Minneapolis: University of Minnesota Press.

Sassen, S. (2002) 'Locating cities on global circuits'. *Environment and Urbanization* 14(1): 13–30. DOI: 10.1177/095624780201400102.

18

'The shape of the Stock Exchange is shapeless'

Laura Anne Kalba

Writing in 1901, the financial journalist and author Charles Duguid mused that the physical expansion of the London Stock Exchange over the course of the nineteenth century – from James Peacock's original basilical building to Thomas Allason's mid-century glass-domed structure to the construction in the 1880s of John Jenkins Cole's massive eastern addition – provided a concrete, physical measure of the institution's growing economic importance. 'Even as the architecture of a nation is an index of its character,' he wrote, 'that of the Stock Exchange is intimately related to its history of never-ceasing growth. Structural extension has always been going on in all directions; it is going on now at its centenary and presumably always will be going on.' As a result of its piecemeal evolution, the building, he added, was more akin to 'some monument of the Middle Ages' than 'a modern building. The shape of the Stock Exchange is shapeless.' (Duguid 1901: 308–9)

Held in the London Metropolitan Archives (Guildhall Library), John Jenkins Cole's 1880 colour-coded floor plan of the soon-to-be expanded stock exchange (Figure 18.1) corroborates Duguid's assessment. The irregularly shaped trading floor of the stock exchange is divided into large, flat areas of contrasting colour, each representing a different market – or 'walk', to use local parlance. Coloured in a light yellow, the important consol market, where British government bonds were traded, is located right by the main entrance of the building. On the opposite side of the trading hall, in pink, is the large foreign market, where those dealing in foreign government bonds and shares of international joint-stock companies gathered. Other major players included the blue-coloured railway market,

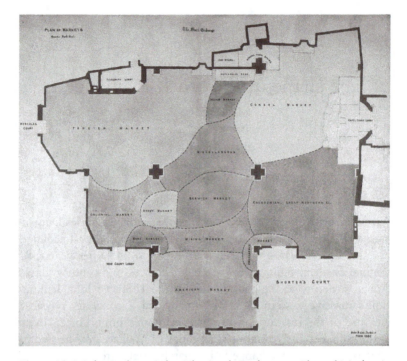

Figure 18.1 John Jenkins Cole, 'The Stock Exchange – Plan of Markets', February 1880.

labelled 'Caledonian, Great Northern Ec.', and the gold-coloured American market on the north side of the building. Synonymous with the modern financial industry and British global dominance, the exchange is oddly lopsided and, moreover, completely devoid of a proper façade.

The ownership of stocks, bonds and other financial assets remained highly concentrated during the latter half of the nineteenth century. More precisely, according to Ranald Michie's estimates, the percentage of Britons who owned securities rose from about 0.8% in 1870 to 2.2% in 1913 (Michie 1999: 72). Considering that most men and women had no savings whatsoever, these numbers are hardly surprising. Among the wealthy elite who *did* have savings, however, financial assets proved increasingly popular. By 1912–13, financial assets represented 64% of the total assets owned by British people, outpacing traditional investments in land and real estate (Michie 1999: 71).

Simultaneously, the nominal value of securities listed on the London Stock Exchange skyrocketed from £2.3 billion in 1873 to £11.3 billion in 1913 – more than the total value of securities listed on the Paris Bourse and New York Stock Exchange combined (Cassis 2006: 98). Movements of the London equity market had profound, often global, economic consequences. Britain was not only the 'workshop of the world', as the saying goes, but also its 'clearinghouse' (Ingham 1984: 40).

And, yet, for most Britons, including those who personally owned investments, the building where daily trading happened was a complete and utter mystery. Not only were ordinary members of the public strictly forbidden access but journalists were also excluded. Not surprisingly, visual representations of the building, interior views especially, are exceedingly rare. Owing partly to the rules and regulations that governed access to the marketplace and, partly, as we will see, to the design of the building itself, the London Stock Exchange played an astonishingly trivial role in how the public came to conceptualize the reality and promise of making money out of money. However well known or, depending on one's perspective, notorious, the stock exchange failed to conjure a mental image, apart, perhaps, from that of the Royal Exchange, the city's commodities exchange, with which the now no longer extant building is still routinely confused today.

Produced in preparation for the building of the stock exchange's large eastern addition, inaugurated roughly five years later, on 9 January 1885, Cole's floor plan is thus an exceedingly rare and atypical document. Compared to the handful of interior views produced for market outsiders, not to mention the more conventional ticker-tape ribbons and stock lists, the drawing provides an unusually clear sense of the concrete, physical premises where London's famed bulls and bears met to do business. It reminds us of how the buying and selling of credit took place in what was, after all, a real, bona fide marketplace. Indeed, as historical sociologist Alex Preda (2009) explains, the enclosure of the stock exchange in a specially designated, purposefully built space at the start of the century was key to the establishment of the financial market as something more than a series of disparate commercial exchanges. Combined with its formal reorganization as a members-only subscription room in 1801, the relocation of the stock exchange to Peacock's Capel Court building greatly enhanced the financial market's legitimacy in the public eye. In fact, as architectural historian Amy Thomas sees it, the London Stock Exchange was founded on a 'spatial contradiction': its existence as an ostensibly open, free and fair market was dependent upon the 'institutional confinement' of buying and selling activities (Thomas 2012: 1009).

This chapter draws attention to the various visual and material mechanisms by which this institutional confinement of the stock exchange was achieved. Foreshadowing the blinding reflection cast by the skyscrapers that house financial institutions today or, alternatively, the buildings' wilful inconspicuousness, these mechanisms worked not simply to confine but also to obscure and confound. Look closely at Cole's drawing and contemporaneous descriptions of the building and the daily events that took place there, and it soon becomes clear how the immateriality, unfathomableness and 'metaphysical extraterritoriality' of finance was achieved through the deployment of images and objects strategically designed, like the black boxes of today's computer-driven financial world, to create the illusion of an immaterial, geometric space of frictionless transactions. Drinkall (Chapter 19) engages directly with the opacity of contemporary financial architecture and its entanglement with new forms of predatory lending.

That the City's financiers were more attuned to events taking place in Mexico, New Zealand, Japan or Canada than the Midlands was already a well-worn cliché by the time Cole took on the role of architect to the London Stock Exchange in 1855. On the eve of the First World War, British investments abroad reached £4 billion – approximately 30% of the country's total wealth (Matthews et al. 1982: 128–9). 'Never before or since has one nation committed so much of its national income and savings to funding capital formation abroad or derived so much of its income from overseas assets' (Edelstein 1982: 3). Still, managers and members of the stock exchange resolve to *not* have a public presence in the City, and their general aniconism or opposition to visual representation was exceedingly singular. The shapeless unfathomableness of the stock exchange rested on a unique economy of visibility and violence, strategically devised to obfuscate both the marketplace's existence as a bona fide lived space and financiers' embeddedness within and responsibility toward the larger social order. As Styve (Chapter 21) shows, the lightness with which British finance found opportunities in South

Africa's emerging mining industry is inextricably entangled with the weighty scars borne by bodies and landscapes exposed to extractive operations.

A man goes behind a curtain

London's heyday as a global financial capital lasted for roughly a century, from the defeat of Napoleon in 1815 to the end of the First World War. The first brokers and jobbers who gathered in James Peacock's approximately 4,000 square-foot, basilical building off Capel Court dealt primarily in government bonds. With the development of railway, mining, steamship and colonial markets in the first half of the nineteenth century and attendant increase in the number of brokers and dealers frequenting the stock exchange, the building soon became uncomfortably crowded. Rather than relocate elsewhere, the owners of the stock exchange elected to demolish and rebuild. Inaugurated in March 1854, Allason's stock exchange building was roughly double the size of the original building. As the total number, variety and value of financial assets traded on the stock exchange continued to grow, however, so too did the number of members. The expansion of the foreign market, where securities issued by foreign governments and international joint-stock companies were traded, was the main culprit this time. Responding to the attendant increase in members, managers progressively added on to Allason's original building, further accentuating its asymmetrical, haphazard appearance.

Supervised by Cole, these extensions – a new entrance here, a new settlement room there, an eastward extension, a westward extension, followed by another – improved operations on the trading floor, but only for a time. Witnesses' testimonies to the Royal Commission on the London Stock Exchange held in 1877–78 paint an evocative picture of the overcrowded, noisy atmosphere: 'There is barely sufficient room now. If we had anything like another 100 members we should be obliged to add to the accommodation,' William Frederic Perowne, the secretary to the managers of the stock exchange, observed (London Stock Exchange Commission. Report of the Commissioners 1878: 18). Indeed, in the year before the opening of the new eastern addition, the square footage per person with right of admittance, including not only subscription-paying members but also over 1,400 clerks, was down to a meagre 2.08 – an area smaller than most aeroplane bathrooms (Michie 1999: 77). It's worth noting, however, that the entire membership of the stock exchange was seldom if ever present in the building at the same time. And, while space was unquestionably scarce, Perowne's and others' similar accounts, stressing the insufficiency of the exchange's accommodations, were not entirely unmotivated.

Prompted by a series of scandals involving foreign loans, the Commission made several recommendations to the British government – all of them ignored, whether out of fear of upsetting the City's powerful financial aristocracy or genuine commitment to self-regulation. Among the commissioners' ill-fated recommendations was, most notably, the proposal that the public be admitted to the Exchange. The final report didn't insist too much on this point, simply noting that 'if it were possible, it would be desirable that the Exchange should be opened to the public' (London Stock Exchange Commission. Report of the Commissioners 1878: 9). The commissioners leading the proceedings, however, made very little effort to hide their position on the matter. Wouldn't it be much better 'if the Stock Exchange were open like any other market is?' asked the chairman, for example (London Stock Exchange Commission. Report of the Commissioners 1878: 340). Was it not true that, as a result of its strict no-visitors rule, the average investor frequently wondered whether the whole thing was nothing but a sham – 'a man goes behind a curtain, as it were, pretends to do something, comes back, and announces what he has done?' asked another commissioner (London Stock Exchange Commission. Report of the Commissioners 1878: 346). In response to these and other similar suggestions, those questioned by the Commission invariably offered some version of the following as part of their answer: while perhaps desirable in theory, allowing members of the public into the stock exchange to see for themselves what went on there was impossible in practice. The building was simply too small. Investors would gain little to nothing from being there, while gawkers would simply get in the way.

Drafted in the interim period between the closure of the Royal Commission in 1878 and the start of construction on the stock exchange's eastern addition, Cole's plan lends credence to market insiders' descriptions of the trading floor. Demarcated with 'curved and perforated lines as if to highlight their flux and instability', the markets directly abut one another (Thomas 2012: 1027). Leaving no area uncoloured – every square foot, square inch of the trading floor is claimed – the design reinforces the idea that the existing building was simply too crowded to accommodate outsiders.

The size and spatial organization of the markets within the stock exchange was a matter of primary concern for members of the exchange. Developments in one market could easily affect prices in another; members needed to see and hear what was going on around them. 'Our markets move as it were by electricity,' as G. W. Medley, a dealer in American securities, put it (London Stock Exchange Commission. Report of the Commissioners 1878: 340). This was not, however, the type of information that normally appeared in architectural floor plans. The presentation is also highly unusual. For example, while colour per se was not uncommon, most architects used it to differentiate materials: carmine for brick walls, Prussian blue for stonework, Indian-yellow for wood floors and so on. In short, keeping his clients' needs and concerns foremost in mind, Cole produced a drawing that is a highly didactic, stylized diagram more reminiscent, in the end, of a map than a standard floor plan.

As diagrammatic representations of space, maps and architectural plans are closely related to one another. In fact, the two types of images share a common historical origin. Still, when compared to other floor plans, the extent to which the architect's diagram conveys an abstract, geometric and, moreover, cartographic understanding of markets at the expense of other, more social ones is striking. Take, for instance, the following eighteenth-century plan of the Royal Exchange (Figure 18.2). 'Shewing the Several Walks or Places of Resort Usually Frequented by the Different Merchants, Traders etc. Of this Great Metropolis', this early precedent reveals how, in the second half of the eighteenth century, trade at the commodities market continued to be organized geographically. Save for a few exceptions, walks are identified by traders' ethnicity (e.g. Italian) or country of origin (e.g. Portugal). Commodities, in other words, had not yet become independent of individuals who produced and transported them, as would later happen, according to Karl Marx,

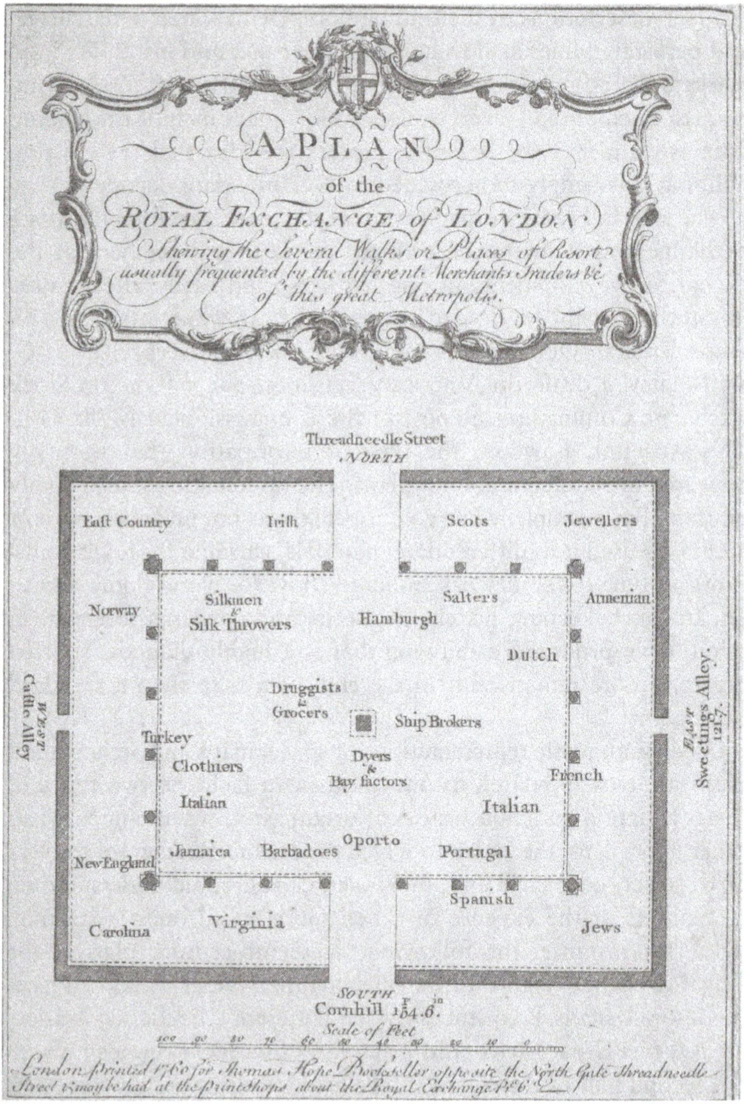

Figure 18.2 Thomas Hope (Publisher), 'A Plan of the Royal Exchange of London Shewing the several Walks, or Places of Resport, usually frequented by the different Merchants, Traders & c. of this great Metropolis', 1760.

once they became fetishized. At the stock exchange, conversely, the relationships between things – the idea of things, even – took clear precedence over relationships among people.

Naming conventions aren't the only difference worthy of note. Unlike the plan of the Royal Exchange, Cole's plan aims to convey a sense of markets' relative sizes. In fact, using the scale as reference, one could ostensibly calculate and compare the total area occupied by each walk. Contrary to brokers, whose presence at the stock exchange varied daily depending on their clients' orders, jobbers, who worked as independent dealers, typically spent the entire day at the stock exchange and were known to get quite territorial if someone tried to usurp their usual spot on the trading floor. Still, it's hard to imagine Cole surveying the trading floor in order to create a perfectly proportioned, measured drawing of the markets. Even on the busiest of trading days, it would have been impossible to determine the exact spot where one market began and another ended. More than simply suggest that there was no room left to spare on the trading floor, the flat, contiguous areas of colour separated by dotted lines give the impression that markets existed independently of the brokers and jobbers who congregated there. Conceived as taking place within an abstract, cartographic space, their behaviours and actions come across not as constitutive of the market but as passive expressions of naturalized, external market forces.

The map-like characteristics of Cole's floor plan, including the watercolour hues and dotted boundary lines, would have been immediately resonant to the trustees, managers, and regular members of the stock exchange. Besides the time-series plots that charted the ups and downs of share prices, maps were unquestionably the most ubiquitous visual tool of nineteenth-century finance capital. A constant fixture in the stock exchange's reading room and brokerage firm lobbies, they also appeared in prospectuses and illustrated press articles, chronicling the triumph of this or that overseas business venture. In the latter part of the nineteenth century, the London Stock Exchange was one of the places where Britain's formal and informal empires most explicitly intersected. And cartography was their shared visual idiom.

Maps not only represented but also facilitated and gave added legitimacy to the extension of Britain's political and economic control of new parts of Africa, Asia and the Pacific. By reducing complex topographical, not to mention political, social and economic, conditions to an organized system of symbols and place names, maps enhanced Britons' sense of control over the landscape and its inhabitants. What is more, maps' simplified design trained Britons to envision overseas territories as blank canvases awaiting European economic development. Indeed, while originally principally agricultural, industrial and commercial in nature, Britain's overseas economic interests were increasingly determined, during the latter part of the nineteenth century, by financial flows from the City. And, aside from more or less ornate share certificates, maps were frequently investors' sole means of visualizing the often yet-to-be realized enterprises in which they had invested their savings. Maps played an essential role, in other words, in cultivating Britons' ability to simultaneously see into the distance and into the future – that is, to literally *speculate*.

One might say, then, that it's especially fitting and not a little ironic that Cole's floor plan would resemble a map. Like the maps showing the progress of railway construction, telegraph lines, sea routes or the location of extant and future mines, the floor plan's design encouraged members of the stock exchange to think of space in temporal terms – as distances that needed to be breached, this time by sound, sight and human steps – and to *envision* the future. Indeed, as already noted, Cole's plan was likely drafted in anticipation of the construction of the massive eastern addition, known as the 'New House'. It would not be long before members would have to relocate to a new temporary building for the duration of the renovations and then redistribute themselves again across the New and Old houses. And, as we know from its reproduction in an 1884 pamphlet, Cole's floor plan was to serve a key role in members' parcelling up of the new, extended trading floor (Thomas 2012: 1027). Its purpose, in other words, was largely prospective.

The architect's map-like treatment of the trading floor, not to mention the drawing's uncanny resemblance to the African content, would likely have stimulated members to envision the marketplace as a *terra nullius*,[1] ripe for economic exploitation and colonization. Considering the timing of these decisions, the approach of members of the 'Sub-Committee formed to confer on the arrangements of the Market on the opening of the Eastern addition' would, in fact, have directly paralleled that of world leaders, who gathered a few months later at the Berlin Conference to parcel up the African continent.[2]

A building refuses to speak

Like the original 1801–2 building it replaced, the one Cole depicted in his floor plan was notoriously plain and inconspicuous. Sandwiched between two buildings owned by the Alliance Assurance Company, the court leading to the London Stock Exchange was no more than twenty feet wide – just enough space for a small entrance (Figure 18.3). In fact, as the *The Builder* explained to its readers, no proper elevation drawing of the building could be produced, for 'in no proper sense is there an exterior elevation, the suite being an area inclosed [*sic*] by other buildings' ("An Account of the London Stock Exchange" 1854: 49). In direct opposition to architectural ideals of the time, which dictated that a building's form and ornamentation should clearly communicate its function, the building was essentially façade-less; it categorically refused to speak.

At first glance, it would appear that the construction of the large, domed eastern addition and attendant alterations to the original building, including an extension of its street frontage, were designed to transform the London Stock Exchange from a shabby marketplace into a veritable 'monument' (Thomas 2012: 1010). In reality, however, these changes had very little impact on outsiders' experience of the stock exchange. Given the financial district's notoriously narrow streets, it's unlikely, for example, that anyone walking in the immediate vicinity would have been able to see Cole's dome. What is more, while technically part and parcel of the stock exchange, the sections of the building now lining Throgmorton and Old Broad streets were given over to offices. Their vaguely Italianate, trabeated façades made them indistinguishable from other buildings in the neighbour-hood. Compared, however, to the retreating plainness and anonymity that has become the hallmark of modern financial skyscrapers such as 200 West Street, the headquarters of Goldman Sachs, the London Stock Exchange's efforts to conceal itself were much more aggressive – violent, even.

Figure 18.3 Engraving of the London Stock Exchange, Capel Court, from George Walter Thornbury's *Old and New London, etc.* (1878)

Refusing the godly commonwealth

Looking at the global financial industry today, anthropologists Edward LiPuma and Benjamin Lee draw attention to how, 'lacking any sensible qualities', market phenomena such as interest and exchange rate volatility wreak a special kind of havoc on the lives of individuals living in the Global South (LiPuma and Lee 2004: 28). The way these market phenomena undermine individuals' freedom and material welfare is concrete and measurable, and yet appears to most ordinary observers to come out of nowhere. The 'abstract symbolic violence' of the contemporary global financial system differs fundamentally, they insist, 'from the economically motivated violence of the past, such as colonialism, in that it does not involve the inscription of new spatial relations, the subversion of local indigenous property arrangements, forcible resource extraction, or the conscription of labour. Space is no longer the raw material of international violence, in that the violence of finance is so far-removed and remote from the spaces of everyday life and the sovereignty of the states that it profoundly affects' (LiPuma and Lee 2004: 27–28). (See also Chapter 16 by Nir on the relationship between 'abstract' finance and violence.)

The history of the London Stock Exchange challenges LiPuma and Lee's distinctions between colonialism and the abstract, deterritorialized and symbolic violence of financial markets. Financial investments and other forms of gentlemanly capitalism were major drivers of imperial expansion. Moreover, in the case of the stock exchange at least, violence was not simply a side-effect of financialization; it was inherent to how the marketplace operated. Abstract symbolic violence, to borrow the anthropologists' phrase, was accompanied by acts of physical violence on the trading floor. Non-members who had the misfortune of entering the stock exchange were subjected to jeers and physical intimidation. Younger members, especially, were known to surround intruders and press themselves against them, smash in their hats and finally jostle them from one end of the room to the other until they were 'liberated' by one of the porters, who then expelled them from the premises. Members did not reserve violent, schoolboy pranks for intruders only. Rough play aimed at cultivating group cohesion was a central part of stock exchange culture. On at least one occasion, the 'injuries resulting from rough play in the House' sustained by a member were so severe that he was unable any longer to earn a living as a dealer (London Metropolitan Archives 1888). Taking advantage of the invisibility afforded by the stock exchange building, members knowingly engaged in behaviour deemed unbecoming of well-to-do British men. What bound them together was not only economic self-interest but also shame, social pressure and the unwavering sense that, within the confines of the stock exchange, members were free to write their own rules. The everyday, aggressively laddish behaviour of stock exchange members at once reflected and refracted, all the while officially disavowing, the violence associated with the forcible extraction of labour, land and resources overseas.

Being the most public form of art, architecture, not surprisingly, played an important role in British industrialists', merchants' and financiers' efforts to convince others of the well-foundedness of Adam Smith and other liberal thinkers' view that commercial activities contributed to the 'public good'. The fact that the public could walk into the Bank of England or Royal Exchange and see at first hand how credit and commerce were spatially ordered helped to legitimize these institutions' activities and their positions within the broader social order. Yet the leadership of the London Stock Exchange, as we've seen, took a radically different approach. Designed to enhance the illusion of open and free commercial exchange, the stock exchange was founded on traders' repeated, often violent, refusal to acknowledge their participation in the 'godly commonwealth'.[3] More than simply document its irregular, shapeless form, Cole's representation of the building spoke to financiers' uncharacteristically asocial – anti-social, even – understanding of the economy and their role within it.

Further resources

Handel, J. (2019) 'Incest and the stock exchange'. https://jhiblog.org/2019/04/22/incest-and-the-stock-exchange/ (accessed 20 September 2022).

Preda, A. (2005) 'Legitimacy and status groups in financial markets'. *British Journal of Sociology* 56(3): 451–474.

Preda, A. (2012) 'The social closure of the stock exchange'. In G. Poitras (ed.), *Handbook of Research on Stock Market Globalization*. Cheltenham: Edward Elgar, pp. 149–162.

Works cited

[Anon.] (1854) 'An account of the London Stock Exchange: Description of the new "House"'. *The Builder* (4 February): 49–50.

Duguid, C. (1901) *The Story of the Stock Exchange*. London: Grant Richards.

Cassis, Y. (2006) *Capitals of Capital: A History of International Financial Centres, 1780–2005*. Cambridge: Cambridge University Press.

Edelstein, M. (1982) *Overseas Investment in the Age of High Imperialism: The United Kingdom, 1850–1914*. New York: Columbia University Press.

Ingham, G. (1984) *Capitalism Divided? The City and Industry in British Social Development*. London: Red Globe Press.

LiPuma, E. and Lee, B. (2004) *Financial Derivatives and the Globalization of Risk*. Durham NC: Duke University Press.

London Metropolitan Archives (1888) CLC/B/004/C/04/MS14616/002, Stock Exchange, London, General Purpose Committee: Copies of notices posted in the House (vol. 2), notice dated 27 July.

London Stock Exchange Commission. Report of the Commissioners (1878). (C 2157).

Matthews, R. C. O., Feinstein, C. H. and Odling-Smee, J. C. (1982) *British Economic Growth, 1856–1973*. Oxford: Oxford University Press.

Michie, R. (1999) *The London Stock Exchange: A History*. Oxford: Oxford University Press.

Preda, A. (2009) *Framing Finance: The Boundaries of Markets and Modern Capitalism*. Chicago: University of Chicago Press.

Thomas, A. (2012) '"Mart of the world": An architectural and geographical history of the London Stock Exchange'. *The Journal of Architecture* 17(6): 1009–1048.

Notes

1 See the chapter by Randell-Moon (Chapter 14) for an account of how the British framing of Australia as a *'terra nullius'* was overturned by recognition of First Nations' relationships with land. Randell-Moon's chapter focuses on the ritual 'handover' of land from the Australian government to a Gurindji elder, an act of return captured by a First Nations photographer.

2 See the discussion of the Berlin conference in the chapter by Schubert (Chapter 11) on Portuguese colonization of Angola and its afterlives.

3 See also the chapter by Abdul Rahman (Chapter 6) on the entanglement of the London Metal Exchange – another, newer exchange in the City of London – with Malaysia's colonial and postcolonial economic fortunes. Abdul Rahman explores this entanglement via an examination of the role that tin – in particular Milo tins – plays in Malaysian economic and cultural circulations.

19

Data Centre Séance: telepathic surveillance capitalism, psychic debt and colonialism

Jacquelene Drinkall

The montage image in Figure 19.1 is a series of digital video stills of a collaborative art investigation of a data centre in Lower Manhattan, New York in 2017. The image is organized in a filmic sequence as event documentation. The austere data centre, built in the Brutalist style, is known as '33 Thomas Street', the 'AT&T Building', the 'Long Lines Building'. More recently, it was identified by Edward Snowden and then in Ryan Gallagher and Henrik Moltke's article published online in *The Intercept* as the National Security Agency's (NSA) centre in New York code named 'TITANPOINTE' (Gallagher and Moltke 2016). The twelve still video images all together represent key moments of the event. The video was filmed by Emanuel 'Manny' Migrano, who was sourced by my main New York proxy collaborators Vandana Jain and Mike Estabrook, both of the collaborative art and activist group Art Codex. My art practice has a long engagement with materials and performances of telecommunications and I wished to work with the invisible and immaterial presence of data centres in New York.

Through our work with the Occupy movement Jain, Estabrook and I were aware of the Occupy artist Mark Read and activists working with a New York data centre, and this work was a reference for our art collaboration years later. Jain and Estabrook and others are dressed to endure a mid-January snow blizzard without any outside public shelter provided by the data centre. The snow adds to the cold, alienating atmosphere and resembles the retro-futurist aura of *Bladerunner* in which radioactive 'kipple' rain provides a

Figure 19.1 Data Centre Séance

repetitive presence to the ambient possibility of future crimes generated by the science fiction telepathy of Phillip K. Dick's *Minority Report* (Dick 2002). Other participants included are a psychic called Neptune Sweet aka Electric Djinn aka OmniJenn aka Jennifer Berklich; a hacker called Ryan Holsopple; the Australian art critic for *ARTnews*, Peter Hill; as well as Glen Einbinder and others associated with Art Codex and ABC No Rio art and activism groups.

In this chapter I ask: how do data centres facilitate surveillance capitalism, psychic debt and colonialism in unseen ways? Why does 33 Thomas Street look haunted in this image? Why does 33 Thomas Street have no windows and only vents for the release of heat and a low humming generated by powerful computers, cables and switchboards? A number of chapters in this volume, including those by Medien (Chapter 7), Dickson et al. (Chapter 8), Rossipal (Chapter 9) and Stork (Chapter 17) investigate the relationship between predatory lending and new forms of indebtedness entangled with postcolonial border regimes and racial inequalities in social participation. This chapter asks, how can psychogeographic art and politics enable us to imagine 'psychic debt', or the mental trauma that accompanies unpayable debts? How does what Guy Debord called 'The Society of the Spectacle' (2005; written in 1967) intersect with financial speculation? How does debt manifest financially, ecologically and psychologically?

Data centres, digital colonialism and ecological debt

Data centres have become necessary for banking and finance services for many years and rely on maintaining a fortress of architectural, electronic surveillance and human resources security measures. The importance of data centres is growing with the demand for mobile, online and virtual colocation services in anticipation of future integration of artificial intelligence (AI), cryptocurrencies and blockchain. Most smartphone owners use a financial app, so stock trading by individuals is expected to increase into the future. High-frequency trading (HFT) is now normal practice within Wall Street trading firms. Data centres are crucial for HFT, ensuring the competitive data speeds required for algorithmic analysis and the fastest speeds for competitive trade actions. Data centres are also essential for facilitating risk compliance, especially in the wake of 9/11 and, increasingly, forecasts of the impact climate disasters on bank, finance and corporate infrastructure, capitalism and economies in general. Shoshana Zuboff notes that 'surveillance exceptionalism' blends technological opportunism and superpowers' transgression of usual social contracts: a desire for total information awareness trumps democratic norms. This is exemplified by the surveillance capitalism of Google and its flourishing under the protection of the so-called war on terror (Zuboff 2019: 82, 117–118, 194, 324). Zuboff explains further that it was by embracing Google and surveillance exceptionalism that the NSA internalized and repurposed Google's predictive algorithms, including Google's ability to 'predict future behaviour' (Zuboff 2019: 118).

Facebook has ten data centres on North America, four in Europe and one in Asia. India, Australia and other countries whose citizens use Facebook have recognized patterns such as this as a form of data colonialism and digital colonization. Countries are increasingly passing laws that require citizen data to be stored on domestic local servers. India's advanced digital culture and technical capability has contributed to its successful push for 'localisation' of citizen data. But for other countries such as Indonesia, as Michael Kwet says, 'Assimilation into the tech products, models, and ideologies of foreign powers – led by the United States – constitutes a twenty-first-century form of colonisation' (Kwet 2019: 4). Randell-Moon (Chapter 14) examined unpayable settler debts to First Nations and their Country in Australia. Automated debt recovery for Australian social security overpayments, known as Robodebt, has allowed the Australian state to use new techniques of digital colonialism. As Monique Mann and Simone Daly argue, Australia itself acted as Global North to deliver invasive welfare surveillance and traumatizing debt punishment to its own internal Global South (Mann and Daly 2019).

Data centres have a significant carbon footprint and are predicted to consume a fifth of global electricity by 2025. Forty per cent of total energy consumed by data centres goes to cooling information technology and data processors. Data centres in cold countries definitely have an advantage. In Switzerland, a data centre has adapted a former military bunker in the snow Alps, and in Norway the heat generated by data centres is being recycled to heat thousands of homes. With the reality of climate change, ecological debt increases with any increased use of data centres for economic or other purposes.

Psychogeographic debt and séance

Psychogeography is a term primarily associated with the writing of Guy Debord and the Situationist International. Psychogeography as a practice involves a revolutionary technique of the *dérive* described by Debord as 'a technique of rapid passage through varied ambiances' (Debord 1958: 2), drifting and walking about cities with observed attention to lost or hidden histories. The Situationists are known for their radical anti-capitalist political theory and influence on the

Paris student and worker riots of May 1968. They had a fierce and unforgiving integration of art and politics. The Situationist movement grew out of Surrealism and Lettrism, and, despite distancing itself from Surrealism's less strictly political work with artistic occultism, some aspects of engagement with telepathy and occultism are suggested by Alexander Trocchi's Sigma Group within Situationist International. For example, in Trocchi's text 'The invisible insurrection of a million minds' (Trocchi 1963) he advocates using 'mental ju-jitsu' and 'perpetual brainwave' in manifesting the 'spontaneous university'.

Professor of human geography Steve Pile (2005) has connected the work of the Situationist International to a psychoanalytic and psychic turn in contemporary geography. Pile investigates hauntings and telepathic communications in public space, drawing upon the work with telepathy by both Walter Benjamin and Sigmund Freud. Like Benjamin and Freud, Pile's theory engages with telepathy discourse to explore the magic and phantasmagoria of urban society and structures – spatial, temporal and semiotic. The Situationist psychogeographic *dérive* developed and further radicalized the technique of Benjamin's *flâneur* observations of bourgeois capitalism. For Benjamin, the *flâneur* was one who casually wandered through the city, at once entranced by its sensory riches and alienated by its overwhelming modernity. Pile's geographic work explores occult globalizations of urban modernity, and the dream-like, ghost-like experiences of city life. The intersection of the walking body and the city is a ripe area for exploring haunted subjectivity, haunted psychoanalysis and the haunted politics of urban space.

The artists and activists in Data Centre Séance engage in a psychogeographic *dérive* around 33 Thomas Street, witnessing and performing links between surveillance, séance and powers of capitalism. Data Centre Séance is indebted to Debord's 'Theory of the Dérive' (1958) and Benjamin's wandering *flâneur*, as a 'thought debt' that borrows cultural, social and psychological capital. Data storage and algorithms are now used in unseen yet muscular ways to enforce behaviour modification, mind control and invisible psychic/psychological labouring. One of the participants, Hill, knew the artist Ralph Rumney, one of the co-founders of the Situationist International and the London Psychogeographic Association. After participating in Data Centre Séance Hill founded the Sydney

Psychogeographical Association. The artwork actively nurtured and networked psychogeography as a global social practice.

Benjamin's telepathy, debt, gambling and surveillance

Almost one hundred years ago Benjamin worked with the intersection of telepathy, surveillance, gambling and debt across several texts. His short text '(Tele)pathy' proposes two options for experimental research: telepathy as media surveillance of criminals; and telepathy as gambling in which the 'losing gambler often attempts to only to [*sic*] increase his loss' (Benjamin 2016). For Benjamin, telepathy, surveillance and debt overlap within the realm of media, in gambling and fortune telling. Benjamin returns to these and related themes of magic and the occult in several papers including 'On mimetic faculty', 'Doctrine of the similar', 'Madame Ariane' from *One-Way Street* as well as '(Tele)pathy' (Benjamin 2016). It is in the interpenetration of self and the external world that Benjamin imagines unseen signs of debt interacting with visionary telepathetic spheres of clairvoyance.

Eric Downing explains further: 'Benjamin defines this interpenetrating connection as based on guilt or debt, as a Schudzusammenhang, although he also hedges on the implicit religious context and more straightforwardly calls it a natural life in man (ein naturliches Leben im Menschen). It is this well-nigh ontological connection to everything – to what he also calls bare life (das blosse Leben) – that allows the clairvoyant to connect the subject's fate to cards, hand-lines or planets, sign-things that, simply by making the connection, make it visible – connect it' (Downing 2011: 565) Through Benjamin's notion of bare life, visualizing debt as a force that moves between psychic interiority and the external world suggests a bio power connected to clairvoyant semiotics.

Benjamin's *flâneur* works with aesthetics of guilt, shame and debt, as a figure that laps the shop arcades of capitalism, feeding off the fog of its debt-producing economy. Benjamin associates fog and greyness with boredom, and rain with money. Inclement weather and its facilitation of boredom is an essential element in Benjamin's Arcades Project, through which he developed his writings on the *flâneur*.

Surveillance capitalism, psychic debt and action at a distance

Back in 2009, the Verizon data centre building and its network of telecommunications provided the fastest 'golden route' between Chicago and New York for capitalizing on price discrepancies via HFT. The windowless Verizon colocation data centre skyscraper in New York was the site for artist and activist Mark Read's projection of the Occupy movement's 'bat signal' and empowering memes such as 'We are the 99%' during the Occupy protests two days after the eviction of Zuccotti Park. Also located in Lower Manhattan is 33 Thomas Street – arguably an even more weird, formidable and mysterious windowless data centre. Gallagher and Moltke (2016) note that it is operated by the AT&T's New York Telephone Company, is the world's largest centre for processing long-distance telephone calls and thus is arguably the US's most important data centre, and can access the information of other AT&T data centres.

Capitalism relies on muscular techniques of surveillance such as mind control, and centralized towers have long been used to enforce debt. In the eighteenth-century London docklands, the government was unable to pay dock workers, which understandably led dockyard workers to appropriate resources of value. David Graeber explains that eventually wage labour was introduced and punishment meted out for 'workplace pilfering' (Graeber 2011: 353). Samuel Bentham built a giant tower in the docklands and introduced constant surveillance, and this centralized surveillance tower idea was adapted into the Panopticon of Samuel's brother Jeremy Bentham (Graeber 2011: 353). Surveillance and accounting enforce payments, debts and psychic control. Without a financial payback, a debt can become a psychic wound geared towards revenge. If a debt cannot be paid with money, it can become a psychic debt. Something that can't be paid back can result in a psychic debt, a mental trauma. Gifts are a force of sort that expect or create some kind of payback even when expressly forbidden. Max Haiven notes that spirituality is often used in society to transform vengeance into debt (Haiven 2020: 49–50).

Zuboff also looks at how debt is managed via telematics to telecommunicate information primarily for vehicles known as 'economies of actions' and argues that these techniques of control are used to modify behaviour; for example, drivers are motivated to wear seatbelts for insurance purposes, and when drivers fall behind in payments vehicles can be disabled via telematics (Zuboff 2019: 215). According to Zuboff, telematics are a form of tele-debt-and-risk-surveillance and a form of muscular mind/body and behavioural control. Zuboff shows how the latest tele-tech innovations facilitate debt and surveillance techniques used to predict and control human psyche and action via new telekinetic techniques of action-at-distance.

Five thousand years of telepathic psychic debt and beyond

David Porush's work on the simultaneous development of writing and telepathic alphabetic consciousness is firmly located at the start of the timeframe of the first agrarian empires (3500–800 BC). Porush and Graeber are both very concerned with this timeframe and this same mushrooming of similar social developments within Mesopotamia, India and Egypt that were dominated by virtual credit money, before the shift to metal coinage and bullion in the Axial Age (Graeber 2011: 214). Organized religion arose at this time too, forever altering structures of spiritual experience and psychical cognition. Porush's exemplary attention to telepathy resonates with both anthropological thought and cybernetic research. Significantly, Porush also focuses attention to imperialism, slavery, trade and taxes in his text 'Telepathy: Alphabetic consciousness and the age of cyborg illiteracy':

> In fact, everywhere pictographic writing makes its advent, we find the sudden emergence of what I call tech-writing empires. These civilizations were akin to the rationalized hive structures of ants or bees. In China, among the Aztecs of Mexico or Incas in Peru, in Babylon, Sumeria, and Egypt, we see the same pattern of social, epistemological, and metaphysical organization arise when writing is discovered. Along with these scripts come other inventions so predictably similar that they seem to derive directly from imperatives in the nervous system itself, amplified or newly grown by use of the new cyborg device: centralized authority in god/kings; a monumental ziggurat-like or pyramidal architecture; hierarchies of priest-scribes; complex, self-perpetuating bureaucracies; fluid but clearly demarcated social/economic classes; trade or craft guilds; imperialism; slavery; canalizing educational systems; confederations of tribes into nations; standardized monetary

systems and trade; taxes; and so on. Almost every conceivable aspect
of empire, in its gross forms, was entailed in pictographic writing.
(Porush 1998: 63)

For Porush, the advent of accounting and the alphabet is the
invention of a new form of mind reading and telepathy, and it is
accompanied by transformation of the earth into rectilinear clay
tablets, rectilinear school tables and buildings, and he refers to this
as a process of city-building 'canalization'. The transformation of
the brain through reading and writing also lead to a geological and
architectural transformation of agrarian culture into city culture
and empires. A psychic debt for humans is also an ecological debt
because of human's ability to transform their environment with
their brains. The problem of telepathy is one of evolution, debt
culture and its acceleration for Porush, something that some other
theorists of telepathy and cognitive capitalism also explore, such as
Warren Neidich and myself (Drinkall 2016; Neidich 2019). Human
powers of economy and the invention of coinage accelerated cultures
of capitalism, indebtedness and metabolism of natural resources.
Ecological debt has clearly emerged after a period of time when
for several centuries debt was held in check via religious ethics,
values and beliefs. For a while, Christianity considered loaning and
charging interest repayment as morally wrong and usury was a high
crime, but ecological debts operate beyond financial logic and are
grounded in material telluric reality. As Andrew Simms notes, the
Renaissance brought increased trade and need for financial borrowing.
This softened religious ideals and the West began running up not
only financial debt but also ecological debts (Simms 2005: 55).
Ecological debt works with energetic feedback loops and has an
automatized revenge upon the human psyche, body and architecture
with global warming and novel viruses and as animal worlds collide
through mass farming, deforestation and mass migration of animals
south to seek cooler climates. Szeman (Chapter 1) reminds us of
the persistence of fossil fuel economies in spite of tech booms, and
Ly (Chapter 12) reminds us that 'green capitalism' relies on the
continued sacrifice of extractive zones in the ghostly landscapes of
Inner Mongolia. In this chapter I have traced out the entanglements
between surveillance capitalism, unpayable psychic debts and the
energetic costs of the ghostly data centres which haunt the cityscapes

of global financial centres: big data eco-energy debts create big weather.

Further resources

Benjamin, W. (2016) '(Tele)pathy', trans. M. Kolke, 18 May. http:// lived.ink/2016/05/18/walter-benjamin-telepathy/ (accessed 13 September 2022).

Gallagher, R. (2016) 'Titanpointe: The NSA's spy hub in New York, hidden in plain sight', *The Intercept*. https://theintercept.com/2016/11/16/the-nsas-spy-hub-in-new-york-hidden-in-plain-sight/ (accessed 18 August 2022).

Graeber, D. (2011) *Debt: The First 5,000 Years*. New York: Melville House Publishing.

Porush, D. (1998) 'Telepathy: Alphabetic consciousness and the age of cyborg illiteracy'. In J. Broadhurst Dixon and E. Cassedy (eds), *Virtual Futures: Cyberotics, Technology and Posthuman Pragmatism*. New York and London: Routledge, pp. 57–84.

Zuboff, S. (2019) *The Age of Surveillance Capitalism: The Fight for a Human Future at the New Frontier of Power*. London: Profile Books.

Works cited

Benjamin, W. (2016) '(Tele)pathy', trans. M. Kolke, 18 May. http:// lived.ink/2016/05/18/walter-benjamin-telepathy/

Debord, G. (1958) 'Theory of the Dérive'. Bureau of Public Secrets. www.bopsecrets.org/SI/2.derive.htm (accessed 14 September 2022).

Debord, G. (2005) *The Society of the Spectacle*. Translated by Ken Knabb. London: Rebel Press.

Dick, P. K. (2002) *Selected Stories of Philip K. Dick*. New York: Pantheon.

Downing, E. (2011) 'Divining Benjamin: Reading fate, graphology, gambling'. *MLN* 126: 561–580.

Drinkall, J. (2016) 'Neuromodulations of extro-scientific telepathy'. In W. Neidich (ed.), *Psychopathologies of Cognitive Capitalism Volume Three*, Berlin: Archive Books, pp. 315–365.

Gallagher, R. and Moltke, H. (2016) 'Titanpointe: The NSA's spy hub in New York, hidden in plain sight', *The Intercept*. https:// theintercept.com/2016/11/16/the-nsas-spy-hub-in-new-york-hidden-in-plain-sight/ (accessed 18 August 2022).

Graeber, D. (2011) *Debt: The First 5,000 Years*. New York: Melville House Publishing.

Haiven, M. (2020) *Revenge Capitalism: The Ghosts of Empire, the Demons of Capital, and the Settling of Unpayable Debts.* London: Pluto Press.

Kwet, M. (2019) 'Digital colonialism: US empire and the new imperialism in the Global South'. *Race & Class* 60(4): 1–24.

Mann, M. and Daly, A. (2019) '(Big) data and the North-in-South: Australia's informational imperialism and digital colonialism'. *Television & New Media* 20(4): 379–395.

Neidich, W. (2019) '2050, for what will we use our brains? Telepathy and materialism'. Saas Fee Summer Institute of Arts, New York, 8 June. https://vimeo.com/370063798

Pile, S. (2005) *Real Cities: Modernity, Space and the Phantasmagorias of City Life.* London: Sage Publications.

Porush, D. (1998) 'Telepathy: Alphabetic consciousness and the age of cyborg illiteracy'. In J. Broadhurst Dixon and E. Cassedy (eds), *Virtual Futures: Cyberotics, Technology and Posthuman Pragmatism.* New York and London: Routledge, pp. 57–84.

Simms, A. (2005) *Ecological Debt: The Health of the Planet and the Wealth of Nations.* London: Pluto Press.

Trocchi, A. (1963) 'The Invisible Insurrection of a Million Minds'. *International Situationist* 8 (January). Situationist International Online. www.cddc.vt.edu/sionline/si/invisible.html (accessed 30 November 2020)

Zuboff, S. (2019) *The Age of Surveillance Capitalism: The Fight for a Human Future at the New Frontier of Power.* London: Profile Books.

Part VIII

Imaginaries

It's common to hear that 'globalization' is marked by a profound change in the nature of space and time, compared to the past. Today, information races around the world nearly instantly, connecting us as never before. Global markets pulsate day and night, with money rushing around the globe, for better and for worse. For many living in London, global cities like Berlin, Shanghai or New York feel 'closer' than towns and villages geographically nearby. Many of us have friends and family spread around the world but only a click away, whereas we hardly know the person living across the hall or the street. Meanwhile, as many people learned the hard way in the 2020–21 COVID-19 pandemic, time feels and is experienced very differently, depending on what one is (or is not) doing and how one is living one's life. There are, of course, objective measurements of space and time that exist outside human perceptions, relative, for instance, to the circumference, orbit and rotation of the Earth. But there are many different *experiences* of space and time, shaped by culture, experience, society and economy. And, importantly, there are many ways of *imagining* space and time and what connects us across them or keeps us separate.

One of the consistent elements of European colonialism and the birth of capitalism was the sometimes intentional, sometimes incidental effort to transform the way people imagine space, time and connection. Consider the bird's-eye view map, drawn from a perspective no human would achieve until the advent of flight but extremely useful for Europe's oceanic navigators, who used it to advance imperialism, for whom maps were jealously guarded secrets. By contrast, Polynesian navigators, whose lives also revolved around transit across vast fathoms of dangerous oceans, communicated and came to imagine space with extreme accuracy and reliability not with bird's-eye maps but a combination of songs, stories and techniques for interpreting the 'feel' of waves on the hull of their boats.

Capitalism developed in part through the imposition of a rigid 'clock time' on workers who, until that time, had been – like most humans – accustomed to calibrating their time to the rise and fall of the sun and the cycle of seasons as they affected agricultural production. In this view, time is an arrow travelling from past through present to future, onward, upward.

This capitalist 'chronotope' (a way of imagining time) also helped to establish a narrative of historical 'progress' where 'advanced civilizations' were on a path to ever greater achievements. In contrast, most Indigenous cosmologies on Turtle Island (North America) or the lands now known as Australia framed time as an array of complex, intertwined cycles where past, present and future were all entangled.

Bird's-eye maps and clock time were not only crucial to European navigation of the oceans that enabled colonialism and capitalism; they were also essential to the management of colonies and workforces. And as these ways of imagining space and time became dominant, they erased other traditions for imagining space and time as well. The dominant European model became the dominant global model. Nineteenth-century with efforts to regularize space through latitudes and longitudes were mirrored in the standardization, of time. Today these frames for space and time are 'baked in' to the computer systems that are the infrastructure of our digitally connected 'globalized' world.

Yet what do these dominant forms of imagining space and time hide? Part VIII focuses on the way activists, scholars and artists today are challenging the way we have learned to imagine space and time, thanks to the forces of financialization and neoliberalism. In all three chapters we are introduced experimental techniques for seeing the relation between things in space and time.

Gargi Bhattacharyya (Chapter 22) introduces her attempt to 'map' s by noting the influence of imperial world maps on her imagination of the elemental relationships of the form of global racial capitalism. The chapter elaborates further on how this imaginary map shapes our world in the wake of colonialism. Those maps, of course, located

Western Europe at the centre and were often skewed to make us imagine that these nations were proportionately larger, befitting their status as global hegemons. This model of centre and periphery was accompanied by a notion of time that placed Europeans at the vanguard of cultural and civilizational progress, with all other 'races of man' stranded in some backwards state. Bhattacharyya's diagram begins from an attempt to create an image, and so help us to *imagine*, how the world system might appear if we 'mapped' it from the perspective of how dominant systems are related. If the imperial maps of old told a story of space and time that glorified and normalized the power of empires, Bhattacharyya's map helps us to tell the story of the world those empires created, with an eye to changing it.

Samaniego and Mantz (Chapter 20) show us how the Beehive Design Collective of artists, educators and activists has drawn on interviews and research with activists to create a different image of time. Specifically, against the celebratory culture of corporate-led globalization that promises that it will bring peace and prosperity to Latin America. Like an 'ant's eye' map, the poster they analyse visualizes how the forces of neoliberal financialization are entangled together in a process that immiserates the majority, continues colonial legacies and deepens ecological injustice. Meanwhile, this poster also shows the underground spirit and practices of resistance. Indeed, as the authors point out, the poster also 'maps' out the connections between resistance in the present and in the past, connecting today's struggles against extraction and state violence to those of Indigenous people and campesinos over the past 500 years of colonial history.

Likewise, Styve (Chapter 21) interprets Otobong Nkanga's mixed media piece *The Weight of Scars* (2015) (featured on this book's cover), which features printed photographs of Namibian landscapes fractured by extractive mining within a broader tapestry of traditional fibres. Here, Styve argues, Nkanga is seeking to encourage us to tell a different story about the relationship of finance, colonialism and ecological destruction. In this sense, the artwork is almost like an alternative map of the interconnected earth: whereas some maps teach us to focus on the largely arbitrary lines between nation-states (most of them drawn by imperialism, especially in Africa, which was carved up by European powers in Berlin in 1885), this map asks us to seek new connections that otherwise are made invisible.

At stake in all three of these pieces is the question: how does the global system of financialization and neoliberalism shape our sense of space and time? How have we come to be accustomed to certain ways of seeing our interconnected planet? What other ways might there be for imagining what connects us and what drives us apart?

20

Mesoamérica Resiste: staging the battle over Mesoamerica – capitalist fantasies vs grassroots liberation

Debbie Samaniego and Felix Mantz

This chapter introduces the reader to the *Mesoamérica Resiste* poster by the Beehive Design Collective, a self-described all-volunteer, artist-activist and grassroots collective producing art whose imagery is not only resistant to hegemonic structures that maintain the global order but also radical in its process of creation, cooperation and dissemination. This poster was produced in response to the 2001 Plan Puebla Panama or 2008 Mesoamerican project to record the ongoing battle over Mesoamerica between neoliberal and financial agendas, on the one hand, and Indigenous, poor and grassroots liberation mobilizations, on the other. The former agendas depend on colonial legacies, imperial violence, extractivism, commodification and the destruction of both human and non-human life; the latter, however, is rooted in Indigenous cosmologies and worldviews, grassroots modes of communalism and democracy, and the land, including its spirits and ancestors. In this chapter we introduce the Beehive Design Collective and the poster in order to ask how it helps us to understand colonial violence as ongoing. How can *Mesoamérica Resiste* help us to understand colonialism as a structure of power, rather than a historical event confined to the past? How do the two sides of the poster – the folded developmentalist map, and the unfolded Indigenous vision – help us to make sense of struggles over Mesoamerica's future?

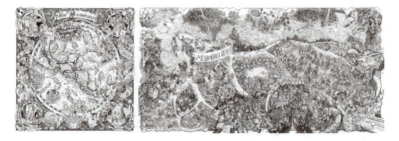

Figure 20.1 *Mesoamérica Resiste*, by Beehive Design Collective, 2013.

Contextualizing the Beehive Design Collective and *Mesoamérica Resiste*

The work produced by the Beehive Design Collective is not credited to one single individual and the Collective is openly anti-copyright, allowing communities and individuals around the world to use their work freely as learning and teaching tools. The Beehive Design Collective is committed to art as a political act of resistance as well as a tool for dismantling and reconstructing the narratives of developmentalism which continue to obscure processes of appropriation, genocide and dispossession experienced by peoples of the Global South. Specifically, the *Mesoamérica Resiste* graphic constitutes a response to the Plan Puebla Panama (PPP), which was adopted by nine Mesoamerican countries and put forth a neoliberal and developmentalist vision for the region. In 2004, the artists and activists of the Collective conducted a five-month tour of Mesoamerica to listen and learn from various communities organizing against PPP in different places between Mexico and Panama. The creation of this artwork took nine years. Once it was completed, the Collective continued their work by holding presentations on the poster's images and symbols, which depict the larger structures of capitalism, industrialization, consumerism, developmentalism and colonialism while simultaneously highlighting the bottom-up perspectives of resistance and resilience from the communities which were negatively impacted by them. The *Mesoamérica Resiste* poster bridges social and ecological struggles – often discussed as separate issues in mainstream discourses – by using over 400 species of insects, plants and animals native to Mesoamerica as characters representing the communities which are resisting capitalist/colonial encroachment.

The Collective's focus on art as narrative bears close similarities to other community-based art forms, such as the Chicanx Muralism that emerged in the 1960s. These murals often require the active movement of the viewer to follow the narratives along neighbourhood walls. However, this movement is not always linear as the images in murals, similar to the *Mesoamérica Resiste* poster, spill over and connect to other images. If anything, this required movement is decolonial, as the conceptual interaction between the art piece and the viewer is about a relationality which transcends Eurocentric conceptions of time and space. What does this mean? Similar to various Chicanx murals, the *Mesoamérica Resiste* poster portrays various struggles across different timelines and lands rather than one place at one particular point in time. This non-linearity opposes the hierarchies of recency and individuality by visually denying an end or beginning, and instead forcing the viewer to recognize the interconnectedness of collective struggles against various imperial designs. Such a non-linear depiction of the passage of time avoids creating the impression that colonialism or coloniality is confined to the past and instead emphasizes that violent processes of colonial extraction repeat themselves and reoccur across time periods and at different scales. This concern with non-linear time, and the representation of ongoing colonialism in the present, is also taken up in the chapters by Ly (Chapter 12) and Styve (Chapter 21). Moreover, the poster's narrative does not delineate an ending to the storyline, as there is yet to be an end to colonial/imperial/developmentalist encroachments for all Mesoamerican communities.

Introducing the poster: insurgent aesthetics and Indigenous remembrance

The poster's juxtaposition of Indigenous symbolism and imagery against mainstream consumerist logos and icons serves as a backdrop to demonstrate the not-so-benign impact of transnational corporations. This juxtaposition can be found in the poster's portrayal of the 'Osito Bimbo', the bear mascot for Grupo Bimbo bakeries, trying to ram a train through a blockade to bring in mass-produced, nutritionally empty food products that would destroy the traditional local market (found on the inner bottom right side of the poster).[1] The carriages of the train are made up of a bottle labelled 'Capitalismo' in Coca-Cola font, a Nescafé box and a loaf of Bimbo bread. Other artists have used this type of juxtaposition to demonstrate the cultural and spiritual violence which Western consumer products impose on Global South communities. For instance, *Codex Espangliensis: From Columbus to Border Patrol*, by Enrique Chagoya, Guillermo Gómez-Peña and Felicia Rice, uses Western cultural figures such as Superman and Mickey Mouse within an artefact that resembles a pre-Hispanic codex to demonstrate the 'collision between Western and indigenous worlds' (Austin and Montiel 2012: 88) and puts forth the overall 'political vision – resistance to the power of the American mainstream' (Austin and Montiel 2012: 94). Imbued with political meaning, the Collective's work follows a line of art for social justice which forcefully invokes the knowledges of Indigenous communities and sacred symbols, such as the Quetzal or, in the case of Chagoya, Gómez-Peña and Rice's work, the codex itself, to demonstrate that Indigenous knowledges and peoples have not been erased or defeated.

Collaborative, community-based art such as the pieces created by the Beehive Collective or the Chicanx murals found in the streets of Los Angeles, San Diego or Chicago, to name a few, are crucial for the ongoing dismantling of Western narratives of benevolent developmentalism, to unveil the darker side of consumer/mainstream culture and to combat the collective amnesia of colonial/imperial violence which continues to this day. According to Martineau and Ritskes (2014: 5), '[s]ettler discourses of appropriation and inclusion are disrupted by Indigenous remembrance and re-presencing on the land'. This disruption is evident in the art pieces discussed, and specifically in the Collective's vibrant representation of human and more-than-human resistance in Mesoamerica to the colonial plans of developmentalism, neoliberal capitalism and high finance. Historically, the act of remembering stands as an act of resistance to the collective amnesia of the West (Smith 2012). Hence, the *Mesoamérica Resiste* poster is radical in its invocation of narrative and remembrance of Mesoamerican struggles, as well as its appeal to the viewer to decipher the images in relation to their own participation in the institutions which attempt to implement the developmentalist and colonial plans for Mesoamerica.

Mesoamérica Resiste brings together two oppositional agendas regarding financialization, commodification and neoliberalism in Mesoamerica. It connects the capitalist plans as proposed and executed by the major financial institutions – the International Monetary Fund, World Bank, World Trade Organization and Inter-American Development Bank – on the one hand, and the resistance against these plans by grassroots struggles in the region which propose alternative worldviews and visions, on the other. Those who engage with the poster are able to explore the different dimensions, aspects and real examples of this struggle of worldviews. When folded together, the poster shows the agenda and vision for Mesoamerica as implemented by financial institutions and neoliberal 'free' trade agreements. Through incredible detail, the poster highlights several elements of this agenda, which we want to briefly outline here to incentivize the reader to explore the complex themes and detailed examples on their own.

Capitalist fantasies for Mesoamerica

Colonial legacies

The very aesthetics of *Mesoamérica Resiste* make it clear that the global financial and neoliberal governance systems are the current colonial institutions which seek to subjugate and dominate the Global South. The map itself mirrors the style of colonial maps which were generated to (mis)represent the lands, territories, resources and populations of the Americas and to plan their subjugation. The limitations placed on photographs and maps as one-dimensional 'evidence' of colonial encounters is discussed throughout Part V, 'Gestures', in chapters by Ferrini (Chapter 13), Randell-Moon (Chapter 14) and Kish (Chapter 15). This mapping style also emulates the top-down view of the policies of global financial institutions, which are represented in each corner as conquistadors, judges, bankers and surgeons plotting the invasion into Mesoamerica. These institutions even have their own pawns on the map, represented by feudal

European ships manned by corporations, banks and Western pop-culture symbols heading towards Mesoamerica. This aesthetic depiction of global financial institutions and their agendas charges that they operate on the same logics and ideals which drove the initial European conquest of the Americas in 1492. The poster's aesthetics invites the audience to discover these legacies of colonization by suggesting that colonialism is not something of the past, but anchored in the present – that colonialism is better understood as a *structure of power* which unleashes violence in the present rather than as a *historical event* which took place in the past.

Violence

The poster challenges the dominant representation of financialization and the policies of neoliberal and financial institutions as straightforward, clean, rational and abstract processes that take place in banking offices or legislative chambers. While this view is often promoted in mainstream media outlets and taught in schools around the globe, the poster offers a different perspective. Specifically, it demonstrates the need for vast and grotesque forms of violence to implement capitalist financial policies and protocols which have a direct material impact on people, communities and landscapes. The depiction of monumental weapons, police forces and life-sucking machinery unleashed on Mesoamerica suggests that such policies are not sterile and abstract, but messy, violent and material. More so, the poster conveys the impression that this violence is by no means a question of one 'bad apple' or an exception to the rule. Instead, large-scale and systematic violence is a central and fundamental element of implementing and realizing the vision of financial and neoliberal institutions.

Extractivism and commodification

The poster suggests that the top-down plan for Mesoamerica is based on the commodification and extraction of life. All of Mesoamerica on this colonial map is covered by walls, dams and electric grids, while pipelines penetrate the Earth's crust and access roads transport Mesoamerican life into the pockets and purses of international financial institutions. The poster shows that, in the process, life (in the form of forests, streams, mountains and human and non-human bodies, among others) is transformed first into 'resources' and then into money, which is funnelled into the global circuits of capital and finance.[2] While this transformation from life to resources to money comes through different avenues and projects, which are described by the poster, it always constitutes a basic premise for the colonial vision of Mesoamerica. We leave it to the reader to explore these different avenues and projects for themselves.

Worldview

The poster reveals some central characteristics of the dominant plan for Mesoamerica. This plan is an undemocratic one. It is decided by four powerful financial entities who are all headquartered in the metropoles of the Global North. From this colonial perspective, it is these institutions which seem to know best and which decide the future of and for Mesoamerica. The confidence in their plan and their faith in capitalism is so inflated that the use of direct and indirect violence to implement their vision is legitimized. In their eyes, financialization, neoliberalism, commodification and privatization are inevitable processes of history which do not need to be debated but only to be executed in order to reach the equally uncontested ideals of progress and development. Together these elements (and we are confident the reader will identify additional ones), which arise from the cumulative impressions on this side of the poster, testify to the dark side of capitalism, financialization and commodification, which is often sanitized and disconnected from its inherent colonialism and violent techniques.

Resisting the colonial visions and financialized futures for Mesoamerica

When unfolded, the poster shows an alternative perspective of and vision for Mesoamerica. This alternative vision is articulated by Indigenous peoples and peasant communities in Mesoamerica who have been impacted upon in one way or another by the top-down agenda of the global financial institutions. It not only testifies to the violence of financialization and neoliberalism, but also proposes alternative worldviews and ways of living together which are part of their anti-capitalist struggle.

Worldviews in struggles

The Indigenous and peasant struggles against neoliberal globalization and financial capitalism include the revitalization and defence of the grassroots vision for Mesoamerica. What that means is that the projects envisioned and implemented by global financial governance institutions target not only Mesoamerican people, communities and ecosystems, but also Indigenous knowledges, alternative visions and communal ways of living together which are in contrast to the individualism and greed at the heart of neoliberalism. In other words, the struggle for Indigenous peoples and rights for local communities is also a struggle against a 'monoculture' of knowledge and future. It is a struggle for multiple and alternative futures and worlds, which are under threat from capitalist and extractive projects and which are harnessed, mobilized and put into practice throughout the resistance itself. Examples of this are numerous in the poster, from democratic circle meetings to communal child-rearing practices and Indigenous spiritual caretaking.

Spirits and ancestors

A central aspect of Indigenous worldviews that distinguish the grassroots vision from the capitalist agenda is the central role of ancestors and spirits, which are depicted in multiple forms and shapes throughout the poster. Based on regional indigenous world-views, ancestors are not erased from existence after death but reinhabit parts of the spirit and socio-natural worlds of Indigenous nations. They are not relegated to the past, but are anchored in the present and in the land where they contribute to the shaping of futures, including the influencing of current resistance against neoliberal projects. This understanding of time, spirits and ancestors within the grassroots vision challenges the top-down ideas of progress as an inevitable phenomenon which develops linearly and universally through history. Instead, the poster's many scenes and examples suggest that building futures and alternatives does not have one universal and predetermined road to follow, but that there are many possibilities, shapes, modes and ways – there is room to dream (Subcomandante Marcos 2001). The ancestors and spirits which run through the ecosystems, people, communities and their relationships demonstrate that these are sacred and meaningful in ways that go far beyond the ideas of value and meaning propagated by the capitalist visions. For the capitalist vision, neither people, communities nor ecosystems have value beyond their immediate utility for a capitalist system that is geared towards endless growth and expansion. Here spirits and ancestors do not exist.

Communalism and democracy

The Indigenous worldviews which constitute the bottom-up alternatives for Mesoamerica include a way of decision making as well as working and living together which fundamentally contrasts the top-down agenda for the region. The poster shows multiple scenes of various animal and plant species engaging in mutual aid, work sharing, consensus-based decision making and communal organizing. These scenes cover all aspects of the resistance, from front-line confrontation to food preparation and childbirthing. This stands in stark contrast to the approach of the global financial and development institutions, which enforce their vision from afar, non-democratically and through authoritarian and fascist violence. Instead of an organic process with energy, aid and work flowing circularly and in multiple directions as depicted in the grassroots perspective, the top-down agenda is a one-way extractive process.

The very set-up of the grassroots vision reinforces this impression. Contrasting the top-down view which relies on a colonial map to know, engage and enforce its vision, all the scenes of the grassroots perspective take place literally at the roots of a *ceiba* tree. In Mayan cosmology, the ceiba is the mother tree who protects the world and holds it in place after it was set on her head by the first gods (Subcomandante Marcos 2001). Hence, whereas the neoliberal and financial fantasy for Mesoamerica is a colonial implant from elsewhere, the grassroots perspective is a grounded view, anchored in the land, its cosmology and knowledges, and concerned with the defence of worlds.

The notorious and charismatic Subcomandante Marcos, spokesperson for the Indigenous Zapatista uprising that emerged in the south Mexican state of Chiapas in 1994, teaches us (Subcomandante Marcos 2001: 330) that, sitting above the head of mother *ceiba*, the world is at risk of being pushed over by the 'winds from above', the winds of Power, including the global neoliberal and financial fantasies which try to make the world fall into oblivion – that is, so it would die and be forgotten. Fortunately, however, the world has not fallen yet, thanks to the 'true men and women from all the worlds that make up the world [who] have become the trunk and branches and leaves and roots next to mother *ceiba* so the world will not fall.' *Mesoamérica Resiste* is a testimony to this battle between the 'winds from above', from the powerful, and the 'winds from below', the dispossessed, which takes place not only in Mesoamerica but all across the world. We invite the reader to explore and listen to the battle recorded in *Mesoamérica Resiste* so that they might learn from its testimonies in their own battles against empire.

Further resources

Beehive Design Collective (2013) 'Mesoamerica Resiste – a large col-laboratively drawn illustration on global struggles'. www.youtube.com/watch?v=JqUsKLKCBSM (accessed 4 September 2022).

Galeano, E. (2009) *Open Veins of Latin America: Five Centuries of the Pillage of a Continent*. London: Serpent's Tail.

Walsh, C. E. (2018) 'Part I: Decoloniality in/as praxis', in W. Mignolo and C. E. Walsh, *On Decoloniality: Concepts, Analytics, Praxis*. Durham: Duke University Press, pp. 15–102.

Works cited

Austin, K. and Montiel, C.-U. (2012) '*Codex Espangliensis:* Neo-Baroque art of resistance'. *Latin American Perspectives* 39(3): 88–105.

Chagoya, E., Gómez-Peña, G. and Rice, F. (2000) *Codex Espangliensis: From Columbus to the Border Patrol*. San Francisco: City Lights Books.

Martineau, J. and Ritskes, E. (2014) 'Fugitive indigeneity: Reclaiming the terrain of decolonial struggle through Indigenous art', *Decolonization: Indigeneity, Education & Society* 3(1): i–xii.

Smith, L. T. (2012) *Decolonizing Methodologies: Research and Indigenous Peoples*. London: Zed Books Ltd.

Subcomandante Marcos (2001) *Our Word Is Our Weapon: Selected Writings*. London: Seven Stories Press.

Notes

1 On cheap food, see Szeman (Chapter 1).
2 On resource making see also Ly (Chapter 12).

21

Extractive scars and the lightness of finance

Maria Dyveke Styve

The Weight of Scars forms part of a larger exhibition of Otobong Nkanga's work that was held at the Tate St Ives in Cornwall in the UK from September 2019 to January 2020. I had studied images of the tapestry before, but I could never have imagined how delicately the threads shine when you stand in front of it. Gold, silver, orange hues sparkling from the depths of the woven fabrics. What intuitively looks like it could be a map of the world, with shapes and colours evocative of land and seas, bears no resemblance to more familiar mappings of the continents. In entirely new shapes, the all-encompassing oceans and interspersed lands are nowhere and everywhere at the same time. The darker shades of blue might be reminiscent of the little screen on the seat in front of you when you fly long-distance, that indicates the areas of the globe where it is night-time, but the shades here do not follow the same strict pattern created by the earth's rotation in relation to the sun. If the distinction between night and day is blurred, then time zones, and perhaps time itself, become uncertain, invalid and inoperable. Nkanga's tapestry lets us break with linear and simplistic understandings of the movement of time and the relationship between land, extraction and human activities. If the past is no longer simply a past left behind, but one that leaves traces and scars in the present, how does that let us think differently about extractive industries, their colonial histories and the indelible marks they leave? These questions are also posed by Ly (Chapter 12) and by Samaniego and Mantz (Chapter 20). This chapter asks: in what ways can a work of art guide us towards new understandings of extraction, colonialism and financialization? How might Nkanga's work help us to understand the logics of mining

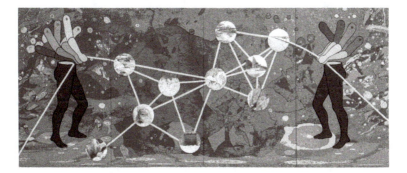

Figure 21.1 Otobong Nkanga, 'The Weight of Scars' (2015). Tapestry: woven textile/viscose bast, mohair, polyester, bio cotton, linen, acrylic and ten inkjet photographs on Forex plates. Four tapestries 253 × 153 cm each (together 253 × 612 cm).

finance in places like the financial district of the City of London, and their relationship with the violence of mineral extraction?

On either side of Nkanga's tapestry, a collection of arms that look both bolted down and mobile hover over lower bodies cut off in the middle. The mechanical yet also organic-looking arms hold on to a set of lines vaguely suggestive of ropes, and look like they can pull, move and drive processes of extraction. The lines, one seamlessly becoming a pipeline itself, connect black-and-white photographs of different scenes of mining, holes in the ground, cracked soil and brick walls. These photographs placed on top of the tapestry suggest snapshots of specific places and moments in time, that in their photographic form makes a break with the tapestry, while at the same time being tied into it through the lines of connections drawn out between them. The multilayered and montage form itself invites a reading that is not necessarily linear, and that opens up for complex webs of intertwined connections across time and space. In this chapter, I will attempt to move along these lines of connections to show some of the ways in which the relationship between the City of London as a centre of mining finance and the South African mining industry is still infused with the colonial and violent histories of mineral extraction. The main argument that I will make is that if we look at these complex patterns we can see how mining finance continues to rely on a system of extraction that is premised on racial violence and that leaves indelible scars that Nkanga's art works point us towards.

The lightness of finance

The weight of the scars inflicted by mining stands in sharp contrast to the ease and lightness of the world of mining finance professionals in the UK and South Africa. During large international conferences where investors come to meet with mining companies, to a large extent white and male spaces, everything is set up to increase convenience and ease of contact, floating on a sense of lightness far from the impacts of mining where it actually takes place (Styve 2019). Nkanga's tapestry was also exhibited in an earlier exhibition in Chicago in 2018, called 'To Dig a Hole that Collapses Again'. The title of that exhibition bears a resemblance to one of the expressions I often heard when doing fieldwork within mining finance circles – in London, Cape Town and Johannesburg – of 'the hole in the ground that cannot be moved', although with quite different connotations. Within mining finance, the expression refers to the fact that once a mining project has been started, the mine cannot be moved if the circumstances change, and in this sense the investments into a project are quite literally sunk in the ground. The title 'To Dig a Hole that Collapses Again' might imply a sense of endless repetitions and perhaps a feeling of futility, as the riches that are carried out of the mines rarely remain with the diggers.

This is quite a different frustration from the one expressed within mining finance, where the problem with the hole in the ground was, rather, that it made investors vulnerable to the changing winds of politics, as the hole, once it has been dug, simply cannot be moved. The tension here is between the desire for global mobility in mining finance, where the drive is towards investing in the most profitable metals and minerals across the world, and the fact that the actual mines are tied down to a particular location where they are subject to changing national politics. The ever-present possibility that national policies might be changed, and new demands for higher taxation or greater local ownership might be instituted, is seen as an important 'political risk' factor within mining finance (Gilbert 2020). The spatial rootedness of the mine contrasts with the ambitions of global mobility for mining financiers and the desire to be able to move investments to wherever the next big boom can be found. The sense of repetition in Nkanga's title also reverberates with the concerns about boom and bust cycles in mining finance circles. While much of the focus in mining finance is on how to minimize risks and maximize profits, and in that sense is very future oriented, the temporalities of mining finance also contain contradictory relations to both past and future. The desire for policy certainty, for instance, can be understood as a desire for the future to look as much as possible like the past in the political domain. The historical legacies of mining in the places where extraction actually takes place are, however, rarely given attention by mining financiers, nor do they figure in their risk assessments and valuations. As Kalba (Chapter 18) shows, financiers in London have a long history of denying their entanglements with the patterns of earthly and bodily scarring that follow their allocations of capital.

The echoes of history

The ease and lightness of the world of mining finance stands in sharp contrast to the historical reverberations of the mining industry in South Africa. The long historical trajectory of mining in South Africa can be traced back to the establishment of the industry in the three last decades of the nineteenth century. While diamonds were the first to be discovered in Kimberley in 1867, it was after gold was discovered on the Rand (in what would later become Johannesburg) that investments from abroad started to play a key role (Cain and Hopkins 1980: 487). The expansion of finance capital that came via London into the South African mining industry should be seen in the context of the increasing financialization of the British national economy in the late nineteenth century (Cain and Hopkins 1987: 19). The period from the 1870s, at least until the First World War, was characterized by the fluidity and global expansion of financial capital.

The establishment of the mining industry in South Africa had devastating consequences and created severe ruptures of social relations within the entire southern African region. After imperial conquest and wars over the whole of the nineteenth century, the vast dispossession of land culminated with the 1913 Land Act that dispossessed Africans of over 90% of the land in South Africa. The nascent mining industry was in severe need of labourers, and the dispossession of land, as well as the imposition of taxes, contributed to the proletarianization of Black mineworkers through forcing African men to start work on the mines (Magubane 2007: 203; Marks and Trapido 1979: 64; Terreblanche 2002: 259, 396–397). A migrant labour system was put in place that recruited mineworkers from the entire region, in particular from Mozambique and Lesotho, and from within South Africa many came from the Eastern Cape (First 1983: 30; Wolpe 1972). The lives of the workers on the mines were strictly controlled, through the establishment of mine compounds where they had to live, and 'pass laws' that meant they could not move around freely. Combined with entrenched imperial racism, the way that the mines were organized contributed to an extremely racialized pattern of capital accumulation on the mines, where profits were dependent on the super-exploitation of Black workers (Ncube 1985: 17–18; Feinstein 2005: 67; Turrell 1986: 48). This also then means that the financial gains that were made in London on investments in the South African mining industry relied precisely on the anti-Black nature of how the industry operated.

From the early days of mining, the access to cheap Black labour had been the basis of the South African economy, with dispossession and proletarianization used to ensure a labour force for the industry. However, by the time these processes had been completed by the 1970s, labour became more expensive and a shift took place to replace labour with more capital-intensive production. The result has been rising unemployment and ensuing increases in poverty (Terreblanche 2002: 378–380). While the shift to more capital-intensive production happened throughout the economy, the mining industry, and in particular gold and platinum production, has not been able to mechanize on a large scale and is still reliant on having a large number of mineworkers, as it was in the late nineteenth century (Stewart 2013, 51).

When the first free elections were held in 1994 and the brutal apartheid system finally came to an end, the optimism in South Africa was effervescent. More than twenty-five years later, however, there has been increasing anger and frustration at the continued glaring inequalities. Despite the growth of a new Black elite, capital accumulation and wealth distribution remain highly racialized. In 2012, a particular event sent shockwaves throughout the country. During a strike against the London-listed company Lonmin, thirty-four black mineworkers were killed by police forces, and another seventy-eight were wounded, on 16 August 2012 in Marikana in the north-west of South Africa. The Marikana massacre was reminiscent of a past where Black resistance was met with the violent response of the state, and showed how the mining industry, and the world of mining finance that underwrites it, continues to operate on anti-Black foundations that rely on racial violence in moments of crisis (Styve 2019). The way in which Marikana entered the imaginary of global business and current affairs media is examined in more detail by Alami (Chapter 10).

While the contemporary political economy of South Africa of course differs from the time when the industry was established, some of the core contradictions and problems with the extroversion of the economy could be argued to have structural roots in the mineral discoveries in the late nineteenth century. The global reach and intensified growth of financial capital since the late 1970s also have a clear historical precedent in the period of financial expansion in the late nineteenth century. Increasing financialization and large-scale illegal capital flight, especially connected to mining, has been a key feature of the post-apartheid political economy of South Africa (Ashman, Fine and Newman 2011). Today we see large transnational corporations, instead of the iconic mining magnates and family dynasties in the late nineteenth and early twentieth centuries, of which Anglo-American is a prime example. Alongside its corporate modernization, Anglo-American has reinvented itself as a putative agent of apartheid's demise, rather than a linchpin in South Africa's racist policy of 'separate development' which served to provide mines with cheap labour (Rajak 2014). Capital from the mining industry has now expanded globally from South Africa through London, instead of finance capital being channelled to South Africa as in the early period. While it may no longer move only *from* the City of London *to* South Africa's mining belts, much of this money still moves *through* the City of London, which has been able to maintain its position as a key international financial centre after the demise of the formal British empire (Palan 2015; Palan and Stern-Weiner 2012). After the Marikana massacre in 2012, the Alternative Information and Development Centre demonstrated that terminating a Bermuda-based profit-shifting arrangement could have freed up funds required to meet the wage-increase demands of the strikers (Forslund 2015). Like the levers that operate sites of extraction across time zones in Nkanga's tapestry, the lightness of finance as it moves through Britain's 'second empire' of offshore jurisdictions is inextricably linked to the violent weight of extraction.

In one of the performances shown on video at her 2019 installation, we see Nkanga facing the closed-down Tsumeb mine in Namibia, which is also the mine where the photographs on the tapestry are from. Balancing on her left foot, her right arm holding her other leg pulled up behind her while her left arm is stretched out towards the horizon, she balances what looks to be mineral rocks on her head and sings to the mine. In yet another video, Nkanga explains how the performance was created spontaneously when she visited the mine and saw the hole and dent in the space. She explains how she began singing to the mine to appease it, to call out the names of the minerals and ask for the original names. The Tsumeb mine is one of the most mineral-rich places in the world, and was originally mined by the Ovambo before German colonization began at the end of the nineteenth century. Nkanga speaks of the weight of scars – mental scars, emotional scars, lasting scars on the landscape from extraction and our endless addiction to resources. In another performance (also shown on video), her voice can be heard saying: 'Our future is to live with bruises, uneven, hapless, splintery, earthly, sometimes brittle [...], malleable, flexible, elastic.'

The bruises and scars left from extraction and colonization leave indelible marks that persist over time. Otobong Nkanga's tapestry likewise points us towards how beneath the ease and lightness of the world of mining finance lies the weight of scars that reflect how the past still reverberates in the present, even if mining financiers disavow these legacies, concerned only with 'policy certainty'. However, Nkanga's work might also tell us something about potential openings, ways of creating connections and seeing the world anew that might defy the profit-hunting ways of finance capital, or at least make visible the bruises that repetitive cycles of extraction leave behind.

Further resources

Alexander, P., Lekgowa, T., Mmope, B., Sinwell, L. and Xezwi, B. (2012) *Marikana: A View from the Mountain and a Case to Answer*. Johannesburg: Jacana.

Forslund, D. (2015) 'The Bermuda connection: Profit shifting, inequality and unaffordability at Lonmin 1999–2012. Johannesburg: AIDC Alternative Information and Development Centre.

Nkanga, O. (2017) 'Imagining the Scars of a Landscape'. www.youtube.com/watch?v=qZZruEToDCI (accessed 25 January 2022).

Oswald, M. (2017) *The Spider's Web: Britain's Second Empire* [Documentary]. http://spiderswebfilm.com/ (accessed 22 December 2020).

SAHO (2013a) 'Timeline of land dispossession and segregation in South Africa 1800–1899'. South African History Online. www.sahistory.org.za/topic/timeline-land-dispossession-and-segregation-south-africa-1800-1899 (accessed 21 December 2020).

SAHO (2013b) 'Land: Dispossession, resistance and restitution'. South African History Online. www.sahistory.org.za/article/land-dispossession-resistance-and-restitution (accessed 21 December 2020).

SAHO (2015) 'The mineral revolution in South Africa'. South African History Online. www.sahistory.org.za/article/grade-8-term-2-mineral-revolution-south-africa (accessed 21 December 2020).

Works cited

Ashman, S., Fine, B. and Newman, S. (2011) 'Amnesty International? The Nature, Scale and Impact of Capital Flight from South Africa.' *Journal of Southern African Studies* 37(1): 7–25.

Cain, P. J. and Hopkins, A. G. (1980) 'The political economy of British expansion overseas'. *The Economic History Review* 33(4): 463–490.

Cain, P. J. and Hopkins, A. G. (1987) 'Gentlemanly capitalism and British expansion overseas II: The new imperialism, 1850–1945'. *The Economic History Review* 40(1): 1–26.

Feinstein, C. H. (2005) *An Economic History of South Africa: Conquest, Discrimination and Development*. Cambridge: Cambridge University Press.

First, R. (1983) *Black Gold: The Mozambican Miner, Proletarian and Peasant*. Sussex: The Harvester Press.

Forslund, D. (2015) 'The Bermuda connection: Profit shifting, inequality and unaffordability at Lonmin 1999–2012. Johannesburg: AIDC Alternative Information and Development Centre.

Gilbert, P. R. (2020) 'Expropriating the future: Turning ore deposits and legitimate expectations into assets'. In K. Birch and F. Muniesa (eds), *Assetization: Turning Things into Assets in Technoscientific Capitalism*. Cambridge MA: MIT Press, pp. 173–201.

Magubane, B. M. (2007) *Race and the Construction of the Dispensable Other*. Pretoria: Unisa Press.

Marks, S. and Trapido, S. (1979) 'Lord Milner and the South African state'. *History Workshop* 8: 50–80.

Ncube, D. (1985) *Black Trade Unions in South Africa*. Johannesburg: Skotaville Publishers.

Palan, R. (2015) 'The second British empire and the re-emergence of global finance'. In S. Halperin and R. Palan (eds), *Legacies of Empire: The Imperial Roots of the Contemporary Global Order*. Cambridge: Cambridge University Press, pp. 50–68.

Palan, P. and Stern-Weiner, J. (2012) 'Britain's second empire'. www. newleftproject.org/index.php/site/article_comments/britains_second_empire (accessed 5 March 2018; URL no longer active 14 September 2022).

Rajak, D. (2014) 'Corporate memory: Historical revisionism, legitimation and the invention of tradition in a multinational mining company'. *PoLAR: Political and Legal Anthropology Review* 37(2): 259–280.

Stewart, P. (2013) '"Kings of the mine": Rock drill operators and the 2012 strike wave on South African mines'. *South African Review of Sociology* 44(3): 42–63.

Styve, M. D. (2019) 'From Marikana to London: The anti-blackness of mining finance'. PhD thesis, Social Anthropology, University of Bergen.

Terreblanche, S. (2002) *A History of Inequality in South Africa 1652–2002*. Scottsville: University of KwaZulu-Natal Press.

Turrell, Rob. 1986. 'Diamonds and mining labour in South Africa 1869–1910'. *History Today* 35(5): 45–49.

Wolpe, H. (1972) 'Capitalism and cheap labour-power in South Africa: From segregation to apartheid'. *Economy and Society* 1(4): 425–456.

22

Imagined maps of racial capitalism

Gargi Bhattacharyya

When I was young, I was transfixed by maps of empire presented as menageries of diverse life and tributaries of commodified abundance. These spectacularized maps served to affirm Britain as the centre of the world, and perhaps the universe. At the same time, this was mapping as display, as catalogue (both in the sense of categorization and also in the later manner of Argos, the UK's ubiquitous catalogue retailer), as we learned to view empire as the infrastructure for a delectable consumer experience. The imperial map with the world bringing its bounty to lay at the feet of Britannia is a melding together of the geographical and the imaginative. We are supposed to understand that it is only the commodity routes of a globe reordered to Britannia's will that can offer up its fruits and pleasures to our ravenous eyes. Although the imagined map that I offer here (Figure 22.1) is less celebratory, there is something of the catalogue of possibilities in this depiction. So, if the imagined map of empire transforms violence into imagined plenty, then perhaps the imagined map of racial capitalism reveals the infrastructure of violence enabling the supposed victories of global capitalism.

Why imagine, why a map?

My imagined map of racial capitalism learns something from these earlier imperial maps, in particular the blurring of spatial depictions and storytelling. Somewhere between treasure map and hieroglyph, the map of racial capitalism reveals something about the interconnected overlappingness of racial capitalism that seems to get lost in narratives

Figure 22.1 Imagined maps of racial capitalism

about race and class. The imaginary map tries to circumvent this non-debate, revealing the interdependence of differing modes of value extraction. Instead of pitting wagedness against non- or lesser wagedness, or race against class, we 'see' the interpenetration and balancing between modes of capitalist violence.

So this is not a map for navigation. Not a shortcut to avoiding the ugly bottlenecks of dehumanization that, awkwardly, clutter up the landscape of consumerist promise. This is another kind of mapping, one designed to help us orient ourselves and to register our relations to each other.

Some points about racial capitalism

The racial capitalism of the map is one where something called 'race' (although sometimes also 'migration', 'religion' or 'caste') serves as an arbitrary marker positioning us all differentially in the landscape of economic life. These differential statuses lead to: varieties of exclusion or partial exclusion from or inclusion in the formal economy or the more protected/regulated forms of waged work; greater and lesser vulnerability to non-waged forms of economic exploitation; more and less likelihood of finding value scraped or squeezed or outright stolen from the realm of social reproduction. The analytic framework of racial capitalism – which I prefer to think of as a question rather than an assertion – helps us to understand the manner in which capitalism has both inhabited and mobilized racialized differentiations in the process allocating populations to realms of economic activity that operate in parallel or in segmented ways that disrupt the possibility of class unity. The point of this critique is not to say, oh look, abracadabra, let us see beyond the false divisions of racial logics to the truth of our essential unity. Instead, this is a question which asks, if we are divided not merely by poor ideas but also through the materiality of racialized divisions embodied in an economic landscape where our differential status is not an aside but is core to the functioning of the exploitative whole, what then? How should we seek to understand our world of injustice and the possibilities of change then? The map is one small contribution to how we might begin to think about this challenge.

Everything is social reproduction

A significant lesson of the imaginary map is the extent of the realm of social reproduction. In fact, the two-dimensional image cannot do justice to the depth and volume of this segment. You, the viewer, see a large amorphous shape in which the majority of the slice is taken up with the highly varied business and resources of social (and other) reproduction. What you cannot see is the three-dimensional bulk in which social reproduction becomes almost the whole object, a lumpy and shifting ball of interdependence with the greatest weight in the segments where human and non-human life meet.

Another clue in the image, for those attentive enough to see it, is the small but important element of the productive economy that bulges out from the larger activities of social reproduction. Except for some parts of the productive economy – which deplete, but return nothing – everything is contained within the virtuous body of social reproduction.

The components of the map

The secret map of racial capitalism tries to indicate what is the larger whole and what is the smaller activity. So one key lesson of the map is to expand our sense of where and what social reproduction might be. Social reproduction in this account is the whole thing. Far, far more than the small but necessary activities undertaken to remake the worker before the next day of grinding toil, or just dull bureaucracy. More than the mundane bodycare of feeding and cleaning. More, even, than the too-often heteronormative accounts of remaking the species.

Instead, the map reminds us that social reproduction is far more than what happens in households; and, of course, as we have increasingly learned to say to each other, social reproduction is far, far more than the merely human. Largely, we have been trained to think of social reproduction as something that happens within species, or at least this has been our habit until recently. However, our world on fire forces us to think about social reproduction as a far greater complex, intertwining species and modes of being and forms of life, and also as the infrastructure that enables life in a way that is so far beyond the capacity of any one species that I blush to think of our former foolishness. The map tries to nudge towards this larger understanding, imaging our awkward attempts to live and order the world as always taking place alongside modes of being where our human endeavours make sense only as modes of coexistence.

I hope that the map reveals that there is something joyous about seeing the image of social reproduction dwarfing our small human ambitions. And also to see some of our most pernicious and damaging human ambitions as the sphere that breaks out of a much longer history of social reproduction through mutuality. The map encourages us to think of this, the so-called 'real economy' as the anomaly, an aberration that leeches energy out of a symbiotic system that preceded it and may well come to outlive it.

Of course there are some parts of that productive economy that rest within the sphere of social reproduction; the things that we do to build and make, sustain and invent, rest in this space. The productive economy continues to overlap with what we must do to stay alive. It melds together, still now in places, the business of care and the business of manufacture. However, other parts of the supposedly productive economy seem to increasingly ebb away from what can remake life.

Of course that's an old, old story.

But perhaps we forget it too often, that there is the business of life and there is the business of profit, and although they can and do overlap, they are not at all the same thing. And when we divert too many of the Earth's resources to the carbuncle that has been added to social reproduction, the realm of the productive economy that is increasingly distanced from the remaking of life, perhaps everyone then suffers. Perhaps that cannot be sustained. And perhaps we all need to think of some way of adjusting things a little so that our collective endeavour regains a focus on the remaking of life.

What about the natural world?

I was uncertain when drawing the picture about whether the realm of so-called nature should fall within or outside the realm of social reproduction. Are we within a realm of nature as humans have thought before, in a constant battle to master resources and forces that go far beyond us?

In the end I decided to put the markers of the natural world within the realm of social reproduction. And, in particular, to point out the realms of the natural world which are in symbiosis with other living things, including us human beings. If this was a larger project, I would zoom into the three realms of water, air and land to image and narrate the histories of appropriation and of interdependence that can be understood by thinking of these arenas without which there is no life. For now, the viewer must imagine these unseen worlds.

I realized that the scale here is a little bit confusing and I could not quite get that right. But the clue is to understand how our occasional ability to achieve coexistence with other living things, and with the landscape that the world gives us, has been and will continue to be a major element of what social reproduction can be. These are human and non-human practices that are right at the heart of what sustaining life can be. And they have never gone away.

It is true, we may have got more embarrassed about these habits. Perhaps they are not what is valued. Most of the time, they are seen to be in contradistinction to the productive economy, not something that can be planned for. Not the business of development, and certainly not how life is remade. But the world shakes us, and reminds us that in fact, far more than the world of productivity, these are the activities that might keep us all alive.

The necropolis

One part of the map to note, a part that is smaller and less detailed but nevertheless highly significant, is the location of the necropolis in the metropolis. When I started this drawing it was before COVID, before we understood that the landscape of death could remake every sense of the economy that we ever had.

Now, of course, we understand, all too clearly, that being made additionally vulnerable to avoidable death is precisely the logic that distributes us differentially across the economic landscape. The necropolis is more literally that than we may have realized before.

And equally, it continues to embed itself within the most shiny and forward-looking of urban landscapes. In this emergent map I include the small nod to the double location of the necropolis to remind us all that the excessive dehumanizing and bloodthirsty exploitation at the heart of racial capitalism is not elsewhere, nor far away. Quite the contrary. This violence resides within the heartland of capitalist progress. And also ripples across the globe, within every commodity chain, and also within every extractive process. The death is all around and the necropolis, also, is one of the hidden truths of racial capitalism. The manner in which the business of staying alive is enmeshed in the too-early and avoidable death of others.

The pleasures of staying alive

Some other parts of the map are more cheerful, or try to be. I try to point to some of the activity, which seems less registered in accounts that remain over-focused on the production. If the more established account of social reproduction is the work that surrounds and sup-plements the productive economy, but which is still recognizable as something like work, albeit work that does not merit a wage, social reproduction as depicted on the map extends far further into all manner of activity and coexistence.

Social reproduction as it appears in this map contains those elements of the natural world where we have practised forms of life where we are able to cohabit, utilize and sustain but not corrupt and destroy. But it also includes all of that other stuff that could never really be characterized as work of any kind, waged or unwaged. The work of social reproduction which is not work at all. The myriad of things that we do that are the business of life, and which also sustain life. This is the section of the map that reminds us of the pleasure and necessity of sleep. And the very many varied forms in which sleep can happen. A section that tries to indicate the importance of play, not play as an educative function or play as a training for adult life, but play as the thing in itself that makes it possible for us all to live the lives that we were supposed to have.

Perhaps most importantly, the quite open section, which was so hard to draw in any way that made sense, that points to the excess that belongs to us and to us alone. The eight hours for what we will, not the eight hours in which we labour. Or the eight hours in which we rest, which is a recuperation for some other force when we rest our bodies not for ourselves, but to prepare us for the production of work to come. Not those two sections of eight, but the third, unmarked section where our will and our desire and our imagination and the excess of what we wish from our lives, whether or not we ever reach it, can take place.

Racial capitalism, sadly, also describes the processes by which that other segment of our lives can be recuperated into productive circles. Racial capitalism describes the manner in which, beyond the wage relation, other aspects of the remaking of life can be squeezed for value, where the activity that we undertake for no other master somehow can be used against us.

The imagined map reminds us, so sadly, that all of that stuff – the stuff we choose, the stuff we find, the stuff we do together, and the stuff we choose to do when we're most alone – all of it might in the end be squeezed back into a world which sees most human endeavours as no more than a source of wealth for someone else. Most of the map reminds us of this unhappy possibility. More than possibility, an unhappy reality for far too many. But it also reminds us that this utopian wish for the time and the space and the resources to do as we will ripples along, despite the violence that we all suffer today. And that ripple of a utopian undercurrent is also part of what links us in the unhappy present of racial capitalism.

Instead of trying to teach us how to navigate around the obstacles of a world scarred and broken by racial capitalism, the map is a way of appreciating our role in an interdependent complex. Of course, as with all these snapshots, the attempt to visualize something that is always in movement – of people moving in and out of different components, different segments, different modes of activity – doesn't quite work. The lived map of racial capitalism is nothing like as clean and tidy as the picture before you. However, I do hope there's something in its strange, amoeba-like interconnection that reveals some of the secrets of racial capitalism.

And, more than that, reveals them in a way that lets us relearn our connections to each other. Because at heart that is the real promise and contribution of accounts of racial capitalism, not only how we are divided but how, despite the violence, the exploitation, the arbitrary allocation of differential status, despite all of that, we are in this ugly, ugly thing together. Which means that we are each other's best hope.

Index